# A Fresh Word for Today

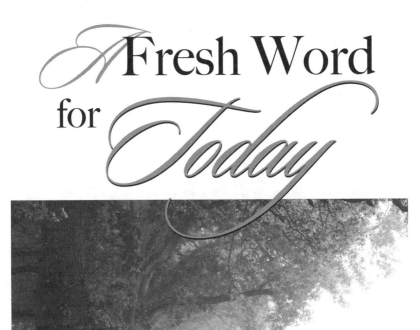

365 INSIGHTS FOR DAILY LIVING

# BOB GASS

**Bridge-Logos**
Alachua, FL 32615

**Bridge-Logos**

Alachua, FL 32615 USA

*A Fresh Word for Today*
by Bob Gass

Printed in the United States of America.

Library of Congress Catalog Card Number: 98-74414
International Standard Book Number 978-0-88270-770-9

G616.316.N.m807.35230

# Dedication

To Pastor Sarah Utterbach, whose insights have enriched
the pages of this book more times than I could count.

To my sister, Ruth, whose love for poetry showed me
the eternal value of a verse well chosen.

# Preface

B ob Gass is my friend and mentor. He's not afraid to admit to his mistakes, but the test of the mettle in this man is his singular desire to put the Word of God into practice.

*The Word for Today* has proved to be so popular that we are now printing over one million of these devotionals each quarter. This book contains 365 of the very best of those daily Bible readings.

You'll discover much that has been learned during a lifetime's work serving the Lord. I trust that what Bob has written here will strengthen your relationsip with Jesus and provoke you to go "scurrying" to your Bible to check out what God is saying to you today!

Gareth Littler

Managing Director

United Christian Broadcasters

Europe

*Happy New Year*

**The LORD himself goes before you ... he will never leave you nor forsake you. Do not be afraid; do not be discouraged. (Deuteronomy 31:8, NIV)**

This year you're going to walk a prepared path! God has your next twelve months planned out. Ask Him, and He'll reveal it to you a day at a time (sometimes hourly). David said, "You chart the path ahead of me ... every moment You know where I am. You know what I am going to say before I even say it. You both precede me and follow me and place Your hand of blessing on my head" (Psalms 139:2-5, TLB).

Take some time today to get alone with God. You'll be glad you did! As you face this year, you need to know that the one who fed and clothed His children in the wilderness for forty years and never missed a day will watch over you every night as you sleep and meet you every morning when you awake. Nothing will come up this year that He can't handle. For you "Happy New Year" isn't a wish—it's a guarantee! Do what David said, "Commit thy way unto the LORD; trust also in him; and he shall bring it to pass" (Psalms 37:5). You'll be able to sing:

Great is Thy faithfulness; Great is Thy faithfulness;
Morning by morning new mercies I see.
All I have needed thy hand hath provided,
Great is Thy faithfulness, Lord, unto me!

**HE'LL BE WITH YOU EVERY DAY OF THIS YEAR!**

**So also is My Word. I send it out and it always produces fruit.
(Isaiah 55:11, TLB)**

Are you worried today? If you are, begin to pray these words until they take root in your heart, awaken your faith, and become your fixed attitude towards God! This prayer will bring results!

"Father, You told me not to fear, for You are with me. You will strengthen me, You will help me, and You will uphold me with the right hand of Your righteousness. You said those who rise up against me will be confounded (see Isaiah 41:10-11). You also said that no evil would befall me, neither would any plague come near my dwelling, for You have given Your angels charge over me to keep me in all my ways (see Psalms 91:10-11). You declared that when I walk through the rivers of difficulty, You won't let me drown. When I walk through the fires of oppression, I will not be burned, for You are the Lord my God (see Isaiah 43:2-3).

"You said that no weapon that is formed against me will prosper and that You will silence every tongue that rises against me in judgement because I am Your servant (see Isaiah 54:17). You promised that if I ask anything according to Your will, You would hear me and that I could have it (see 1 John 5:14-15). You said I am blessed when I go out and blessed when I come in (see Deuteronomy 28:6). You told me to cast all my cares on You, and You would take care of me (see 1 Peter 5:7)."

—◊—

"THESE ARE YOUR WORDS AND I THANK YOU FOR
BRINGING THEM TO PASS IN MY LIFE. YOU SAID IT!
I BELIEVE IT! AND THAT SETTLES IT! AMEN"

# Wearing Out

**And he shall speak great words against the most High, and shall wear out the saints. (Daniel 7:25)**

Satan is out to get you. There are two strategies he'll always use. First, he'll attack you at your weakest spot, so keep it well protected. Temptation not resisted leads to compromise, and compromise to indulgence, and indulgence to defeat. Paul says, "Make no provision for the flesh" (see Romans 13:13). Don't give Satan an inch or he'll take a mile.

His next strategy is the one Daniel speaks about: "He'll wear out the saints." Is that what he's been doing to you lately? When you're exhausted and worn out, you're vulnerable. The Bible warns us to be careful "lest we become weary and faint in our minds" (see Hebrews 12:3). Your mind is where the real attacks come. You're never defeated until you're defeated on the inside!

Learn the signals! If he can wear you out, he can wipe you out. Take time to restore your soul and replenish your strength in God's presence. It is too easy to get caught up in the vision and not spend time with the One who gave you the vision. Listen: "Are you tired? Are you worn out? Burned out on religion? Come to Me; get away with Me, and you will recover your life. I will show you how to take a real rest. Walk with Me and work with Me—and watch how I do it. I will not lay anything heavy or ill-fitting on you. Keep company with Me and you will learn to live" (Matthew 11:28-29, TM). There is no burnout in the will of God!

HE'S INVITING YOU TO COME UNTO HIM, SPEND TIME IN HIS PRESENCE, AND LEARN HOW TO LIVE ABOVE THE STRESS AND ANXIETY OF THIS AGE.

# Burnt Ground

**But Christ gave himself to God for our sins . . .
one sacrifice for all time. (Hebrews 10:12)**

I once gave a questionnaire to my former congregation in Bangor, Maine, asking, "If you were to suddenly die and stand before God and He should ask, 'Why should I let you into Heaven?' What would you tell Him?" You wouldn't believe the answers I got. The best came form a teenager who wrote, "I'd say I'm standing on the finished work of Christ. No less will avail and no more is needed!" She got it right!

In the Old Testament the priests were commanded to take the ashes of the burnt sin offering, sprinkle them on the ground, and then stand on them. They were standing on the finished work! In the early days of the American West one of the greatest fears the wagon trains had was prairie fires. The hot sun could start them, and before you knew it you were engulfed in flames. But a wise wagon master would immediately give the order to back up the horses and the wagons onto the ground that had already been burnt. The fire could not come where the fire had already been!

At Calvary, Jesus "took the heat" for every one of us. Peter says, "He bore our sins in his own body on the tree" (1 Peter 2:24). Charles Wesley wrote, "Payment God will not twice demand, first at my bleeding Surety's hand, and then again at mine."

—m—

IF THE DEVIL IS BEATING YOU UP BECAUSE OF YOUR
FAULTS AND FAILURES TODAY, JUST LOOK AT HIM
AND SAY, "I'M NOT PERFECT—JUST FORGIVEN!"

# God Reveals Our Hearts

**Woe is me! for I am undone; because I am a man of unclean lips, . . . for mine eyes have seen the King. (Isaiah 6:5)**

There were some things about himself Isaiah didn't know—until he got into God's presence. One moment in the presence of God can lead to a place of repentance and renewal that you'll never find on your own. Peter said God "gave repentance to the people" (Acts 5:31, NIV). Repentance is God's gift to the struggling heart. Without it, you'll never change. That's why the enemy will do everything he can to keep you from it!

In God's presence, Isaiah became convicted over things he'd been saying. They hadn't bothered him before. Now he's aware of his words. How about you? Angry words, bitter words, judgmental words, careless words. Listen: "Let no corrupt communication proceed out of your mouth, but that which is good to the use of edifying, that it may minister grace unto the hearers. And grieve not the Holy Spirit of God" (Ephesians 2:29-30). Your words can grieve God!

David Robinson told me of a prayer group in Ireland with people from "both sides." Suddenly a lady began to weep and say, "God forgive me for the things I've said this day about others!" A lady from "the other side" cried, "O, God forgive me for judging them, for my judgment is so imperfect." Before it was over God brought healing to both of them.

―∿―

**TODAY, ASK GOD TO REVEAL YOUR HEART AND TOUCH YOUR LIPS. HE'LL DO IT!**

# Get Up and Get Going

**My grace is sufficient for thee: for my strength is made perfect in weakness. (2 Corinthians 12:9)**

The theme of Christianity is rising again! Regardless of what tripped you, allow God's power to lift you today and put you back on your feet again. People who never experience failure are often people who don't do anything. There's a certain safety in being dormant. Nothing's won, but nothing's lost. Personally, I'd rather walk on water with Jesus. I'd rather nearly drown and have to be saved, than to play it safe and never know His power.

If you intend to accomplish anything for God, then learn to react to adversity like yeast. When the heat is on, it rises! The hotter it gets, the more it rises. God will set you in uncomfortable places so you can rise. Look at the children of Israel in Egypt. The more the enemy afflicted them, the more they grew. The bad times often do more to strengthen us than all our mountaintop experiences put together.

So you fell again! Get up again! If a baby had to learn to walk without falling, he'd never walk. He learns as much from falling as he does from his first wobbly steps. If things don't work one way, try another. You'd be surprised how many people never focus on a goal. They do several things haphazardly, but they never discover how forceful they could really be if they ever decided to commit themselves totally to a cause. The difference between the masterful and the mediocre is a focused effort.

—ɱ—

LISTEN: "REACHING FORWARD TO THOSE THINGS WHICH ARE AHEAD, I PRESS TOWARDS THE GOAL" (PHILIPPIANS 3:13,14). SO GET UP AND GET GOING!

# The Peace Test

**Many are saying ... "God will not deliver him."**
**But ... to the LORD I cry aloud, and he answers me.**
**(Psalms 3:2-4, NIV)**

It's hard when you realize that some people don't want you to succeed. However, many saying it doesn't make it so! The safest place in the world to be is in the will of God. If you align your plan with His purpose, ultimately you'll win. And there's nothing they can do to stop you!

The question you must answer today is, have you heard clearly from God? Are you doing what He told you? Or are you trying to convince Him that He should bless what you are trying to accomplish. What you really need to do is spend time in prayer asking God to reveal His purpose. When you do what God has commanded, you'll be blessed because God's plan is already blessed. All of us go through times of frustration. We struggle with ideas that are born of our own will instead of God's. But we soon learn that God won't be manipulated. If He said it, that settles it! No amount of praying will cause Him to change His mind. He knows what's best for you.

Have you tried the "peace test"? The will of God is seldom easy and never cheap, but it will always bring one thing—peace. Paul said, "And let the peace of God rule in your hearts ... and be thankful" (Colossians 3:15). Get into His presence and talk it over with Him.

WHEN YOU EXPERIENCE HIS PEACE AND A SENSE OF
GRATITUDE, THEN YOU'LL KNOW YOU'RE
ON THE RIGHT TRACK.

**Our light affliction, which is but for a moment, worketh for us.**
**(2 Corinthians 4:17)**

There are times when everything you attempt to do will seem to go wrong. Regardless of your faith and your consecration, adversity will come. You can't pray away God's seasons. The Lord has a purpose for not allowing you to be fruitful all the time. You need seasons of struggle as well as seasons of success. These times destroy pride in our own ability and increase our dependency upon God.

Paul says these light afflictions are only for a moment. Because you can't change it, doesn't mean you can't survive it. If you can't alter it—outlive it! Be like a tree. In winter it silently refurbishes its strength, preparing for the next season of fruitfulness.

If you look back on your accomplishments, you'll notice that they are seasonal. There are seasons of sunshine as well as rain. Each season has its own purpose. Never make permanent decisions based on temporary circumstances. Again Paul says, "The things which are seen are temporary; but the things which are not seen are eternal" (2 Corinthians 4:18). The word "temporary" means "subject to change." Rejoice; it's not always going to be this way. Just hold steady.

Temporary circumstances don't always require action. I've found that prayer brings patience, and patience results in trust. You can't trust a God you don't talk to! Paul says, "Light affliction works for us."

—m—

IN WAYS THAT YOU CANNOT SEE OR UNDERSTAND,
GOD IS MAKING THE CIRCUMSTANCES YOU'RE IN TODAY
WORK FOR YOU.

# Learn to Wait

**The vision is yet for an appointed time, … though it tarry, wait for it; because it will surely come. (Habakkuk 2:3)**

God is a God of order. Everything He does is by appointment. An appointment is simply a meeting that has already been set up. God has scheduled an appointment to bring to pass His promises and His purpose in your life. You can count on that. Whatever you're going through today, there's great peace in knowing that nothing the enemy does will preempt the plan of God for your life.

The problems arise when you try to rush God's timing. When the Lord speaks a word into your life, it is like a seed. It needs time to germinate and then sprout. Every mother knows the order: First the seed, then the pregnancy and development within the womb, and finally the day of delivery. David says, "Don't be impatient for the Lord to act. Keep traveling steadily along His pathway, and in due season He will honour you with every blessing" (Psalm 37:34, TLB). You must learn the difference between what you can do and what God can do! If you don't want to risk derailing God's plan for your life, learn to wait. If you want to live without anxiety, trust God and learn to wait. The prophet said, "Though it tarry, wait for it; because it will surely come."

TELL THE DEVIL AND ALL THE DOUBTERS, "MY LIFE CANNOT END WITHOUT CERTAIN THINGS HAPPENING. GOD HAS PROMISED IT AND IT WILL SURELY COME!"

# God's Blessings

**Well done, good and faithful servant; thou hast been faithful over a few things, I will make thee ruler over many things.**
**(Matthew 25:23)**

Before you reach for more of God's blessing, remember that He's watching you with what you already have! It's in the day of small beginnings that He teaches you patience and consistency. Here you develop the ability to stand up to the pressures that accompany blessing. Those pressures are real. The things I've been through have equipped me to handle what I enjoy today. Had He given them to me sooner, they'd have destroyed me, but He loves me too much to let that happen. For example, if you were having difficulty handling criticism from a few people, how would you do if God made you a pastor or a company president?

The more you have, the more you're responsible for. People who have no car need no gas. Everything God gives you requires maintenance. God gave Adam the garden, but he had to dress it. Jesus said, "No man builds without counting the cost" (Luke 14:28). Are you willing to pay the price?

We want things because they look good in someone else's life. You want a husband, but are you really ready to start living sacrificially? You need a wife, but are you ready to love her and "give yourself for her" (Ephesians 5:25)? Think about the price of possessing the blessings.

—m—

ASK GOD TO HELP YOU GROW SO YOU CAN HANDLE ALL
HE HAS PREPARED FOR YOU.

# What is Success?

**It is God who works in you to will and to act according to his good purpose. (Philippians 2:13, NIV)**

God is the only one who can really define what success means in your life! Success is determined by God's purpose for you! You'd be surprised how many gifted people are tormented by the need to evaluate themselves in the light of somebody else's calling. Are you doing that? Success is walking and working in your own vineyard Listen: "My own vineyard is before me" (Song of Solomon 8:12).

Only the God who called you knows whether you're successful or not. In short, there's no way to define success without understanding the purpose! In the Kingdom of God there are two questions that matter. First, what's your job? Next, how's your job going? If you're doing what God told you to do, and seeking to excel in it, then you're a success. If you're not, it doesn't matter how smart or rich or famous you are—you're not a success! Look out! When people other than God define your success, it can become idolatry.

Suppose your heart said to your kidneys, "Unless you pump blood you're not successful!" If the kidneys believed that, they'd shut down the whole body. Hearts pump blood, kidneys purify it! Each has a different function in the body, and until you find your place and function in it you can't be successful.

YOU DON'T HAVE A MORE IMPORTANT ASSIGNMENT THAN TO SEEK GOD UNTIL HE REVEALS CLEARLY TO YOU WHAT HE HAS CALLED YOU TO. THEN ASK HIM TO EMPOWER YOU TO DO IT!

## Reach Higher

**He that walketh with wise men shall be wise.**
**(Proverbs 13:20)**

There are certain people who stir up the fire within you to be all you can be to God. Find them, and feed off them. When you have little or no water in your own well, you draw it from theirs! Some things can be taught. Other things must be caught!

At thirteen I knew I was called of God. The problem was, I didn't know how to pursue or develop my calling. Then God put some wonderful people into my life. My heart burned as I listened to them preach; I longed to be just like them. I did whatever it took to spend time with them. They moulded the early years of my life and ministry. You must have a foundation—and you can't build it yourself!

Seeing God bless someone else can increase your desire to reach higher. I don't mean envy, just a strong provocation to receive more. Look at Hannah, Elkanah's wife. She wanted a child. In order to stir her up, God used Peninnah, who was married to the same man but able to bear children. The more Hannah saw Peninnah have children, the more she desired her own. Peninnah provoked her! She even made Hannah pray. It wasn't that Hannah was jealous and didn't want to see Peninnah blessed—it was just that she wanted her own blessing! If seeing others blessed makes you want to sabotage their success, then you'll never be fruitful!

LEARN HOW TO REJOICE OVER THE BLESSINGS OF
OTHERS. REALIZE THAT THE SAME GOD WHO BLESSED
THEM CAN BLESS YOU. LET THEIR BLESSINGS
CHALLENGE YOU TO REACH HIGHER TODAY.

# God's Best

**What does the LORD your God ask of you?
(Deuteronomy 10:12, NIV)**

Do you want God's best in your life? If you do, get ready for some major adjustments. It's not easy to get up early while others sleep and prepare for the challenge. Like Jesus in Gethsemane, you'll discover it's difficult to find people who'll stand with you while you're in preparation. But there can be no celebration without preparation. You've got to pay the price!

Not everybody can handle success; some would rather have tranquillity. They don't like criticism, and they can't take pressure. But if you're the kind of person who desperately wants to attain the hope of His calling—then go for it! You'll never be satisfied sitting on the bench while others play the game. If you have the passion, the price doesn't matter! You're compelled, drawn, and driven towards the goal. Paul said, "The love of Christ compels us" (2 Corinthians 5:14).

Sometimes you'll have tears in your eyes and dirt under your fingernails. But in spite of the bruises and scrapes there's a joy that will help you to sing at midnight and a sense of mission that will cause you to cry, "Here am I; send me" (Isaiah 6:8). Nobody said it was going to be easy! Some days all you can do is stand! When you cannot seem to put one foot in front of the other—stand! Just realize that there's never been a day that lasted forever.

DON'T GIVE UP AND DON'T GIVE IN! BITE YOUR LIP, TASTE YOUR TEARS, AND STAND ON WHAT GOD HAS PROMISED YOU, FOR IT WILL SURELY COME TO PASS.

**But one thing I do. (Philippians 3:13)**

How strong is your desire to win? If you don't have sufficient passion, you'll never overcome your own limitations or Satan's obstacles. Real power comes from desire kindled in the furnace of need—unfulfilled need! A need that refuses to concede defeat or remain silent.

I'm told that long distance runners make steady strides and focus on endurance, not speed. They take their laps and stretch their limits and give themselves to one thing only—reaching the finish line. Perspiration pours out of them. The taste of exhaustion is in their mouths. As they near the finish line, a final burst of energy kicks in. It's the last lap. No excuses—it's now or never! At least once before they lay you in your casket, you owe it to God and yourself to experience that last-lap feeling of giving it your all!

Paul says, "Be prepared. You're up against more than you can handle on your own. Take all the help you can get—every weapon God has issued—so that when it's all over but the shouting, you will still be on your feet. Truth, righteousness, peace, faith, and salvation are more than words. Learn how to apply them. You'll need them throughout your life. God's Word is an indispensable weapon ... prayer is essential in this ongoing warfare. Pray hard and long. Pray for your brothers and sisters. Keep your eyes open. Keep each other's spirits up so that no one falls behind or drops out" (Ephesians 6:12-18, TM).

—m—

TODAY YOU CAN MAKE IT, BUT YOU HAVE TO WANT IT
WITH ALL YOUR HEART!

**Pharaoh's chariots and his army He has cast into the sea ...
The deeps cover them. (Exodus 15:4-5)**

That's all you can do with the past, regardless of what it was, or who was at fault. The key is *are you ready to move on yet*? To forget doesn't mean you lose awareness of the event; you don't have to be senile to be delivered! No, it means you release the resentment and the pain from your memory.

You say, "How do I do that?" First, forgive what you cannot forget, and keep on forgiving until it loses its power to hold you. That breaks your first link with the past. Next, declare that in Jesus' name the power these unsettled issues have over you are now broken by the power of God. Go ahead—do it! You'll have whatever you say (see Mark 11:23). It'll happen for you because God's Word on the issue has now become *your* word—and that makes it the final word! Look out! Old memories will try to negotiate another deal with you to see if you are serious about "moving on." Tell the devil, "Enough is enough!"

Paul said, "Reckon yourselves to be dead" (Romans 6:11). But death doesn't bring "closure"—you need burial! You need a time and a place and an epitaph that reads, "It is finished; the past ends right here!" Pharaoh belongs to the past; tell his hosts and his ghosts they've lost their power to hurt you any longer.

TODAY STAND UP AND DECLARE, "I'M FREE INDEED!"

# Seeing God

**Blessed are the pure in heart: for they shall see God.**
**(Matthew 5:8)**

What do you say when you worship? Jesus taught that a pure heart would "see God." The problem is not God's inability to be seen; it's our inability to behold Him. To the blind all things are invisible. No wonder David cried out, "Create in me a pure heart" (Psalms 51:10). Our word "pure" is from the Greek word *katharos*, which means "to clean out," much like a laxative. That may seem funny, but it's true. Jesus is saying, "If you've heard too much and seen too much," give your heart a laxative. Don't carry around what God wants discarded. Get rid of "every weight and the sin which so easily ensnares us" (Hebrews 12:1). What God wants to show you is worth cleaning up to see!

Jesus said, "You are already clean because of the Word I have spoken to you" (John 15:3). The Word will cleanse you! It takes clarity to flow in divine authority. Only a pure heart can know what God is doing and see how He is moving. Unidentified, unconfessed, unforgiven sin will block your spiritual arteries like cholesterol.

A heart that's not pure will keep you seeking the wisdom of men rather than the ways of God. It will keep you needing prayer instead of offering prayer for others.

—◊—

YOU NEED TO CLEAN OUT YOUR HEART SO THAT YOU CAN
HEAR, WORSHIP, AND EXPERIENCE GOD IN A
NEW DIMENSION. THAT'S HIS WORD TO YOU TODAY!

# A Strong Foundation

**As a wise master builder I laid a foundation,...**
**But let each man be careful how he builds upon it.**
**(1 Corinthians 3:10, NASB)**

If a thing's worth doing, it's worth doing well! That's why God takes time developing us. Look at Moses! He was trained in leadership while shoveling sheep dung in the desert for forty years. Some of his skills may have been learned in the courts of Pharaoh, but his character was shaped here. Who would have thought, looking at him, that he would lead the greatest movement in the history of the Old Testament? Just because God promises to anoint you for a particular purpose doesn't mean it will happen quickly. After David was called to lead Israel, he was sent back into the field to feed sheep. These are the things you need to know if you plan to be used of God.

In my early ministry I fasted, prayed, and pleaded with God to make me successful in His service. First, I began to realize that you can't hurry the plan of God. Next, I discovered God's more interested in building the man than building the ministry. When your ministry becomes bigger than you, you're in trouble! If the house outgrows the foundation, great will be the fall of it. All growth takes time! Some of the strongest Christians you know today were once in desperate need of prayer because of their own struggles.

You'll be amazed at what you become when you put your life daily into His hands. Every day you'll see a little more of your immaturity, and you'll understand why He needs to keep working on you (see 2 Corinthians 3:18).

CHILD OF GOD, HE'S CHANGING YOU DAY BY DAY,
SO STAY IN HIS PRESENCE AND LET HIM
COMPLETE THE WORK.

# Time to Go to Work

**Then I heard the voice of the Lord saying, "Whom shall I send? And who will go for us?" And I said, "Here am I. Send me!" (Isaiah 6:8, NIV)**

The priest went into the Holy of Holies to see the glory of the Lord, but the work of the Lord was done outside amongst the people! Imagine being in God's presence to such an extent that the building shakes around you. Isaiah was. (See Isaiah 6:1-4.) But then he had to leave the glory of God to go out and perform the purpose of God. There's a balance! We must spend time in His presence, building our relationship, but then we must carry from His presence the answers that are desperately needed by hurting people all around us.

Why do we always want to build booths on the mountain? One day Jesus took His disciples to a high place and was transfigured before them. Peter was so caught up in the experience that He wanted to stay there. Listen to him: "Lord, it is good for us to be here … I will put up three shelters" (Matthew 17:4, NIV). But Jesus simply told them not to talk about their experience, and He promptly led them down the mountain to begin ministering to others. Are you getting the message? It's hard to leave something that wonderful—but you must! Paul said, "I will not … speak of anything except what Christ has accomplished through me" (Romans 15:18, NIV). He didn't glory in what Christ had done for him, but in what Christ had done through him! It's time to come down from the mountain and go to work.

---

GOD HAS ONLY ONE REASON FOR FILLING YOU AND THAT'S FOR POURING YOU OUT!

## Annointed Purpose

**The Spirit of the Lord is on me, because he has anointed me.**
**(Luke 4:18, NIV)**

The greatest testimony is a life you can't explain without God! Jesus said He was anointed for others! (See Luke 4:18.) If you are a temple of the Holy Spirit, that means you should take God's presence with you wherever you go. Do you? The anointing goes with the assignment. *You're always anointed to do something.* Have you discovered yet what that is? Until you can answer that question, you'll never get anywhere with God. He doesn't bless hard work. He blesses commanded work! What's your vision? What has God told you to do? Until you can see it, you can't move towards it!

Ghandi, Mother Teresa, Albert Schweitzer, Billy Graham, Paul the Apostle, and a lot of lesser-known people who've made a difference in the world had one thing in common—they knew their assignment, and they refused to be sidetracked by lesser things.

Walt Disney died before the official opening of Disney World in Florida. At the opening ceremonies the speaker said, "I wish Walt could have seen this!" Behind him, Walt Disney's wife whispered, "He did!" The visionary sees "those things which are not, as though they are." He speaks into being the plan and purpose of God long before it ever happens. Listen, "These all died in faith, not having received the promises, but having seen them afar off" (Hebrews 11:13).

WHAT YOU SEE WILL SUSTAIN YOU AND WHAT YOU
PERCEIVE WILL GIVE YOU THE ABILITY TO PERSEVERE
THROUGH THE ROUGH TIMES. AND REMEMBER,
IF GOD'S IN IT, IT CAN'T FAIL!

# You've Got to Have Vision

**Where there is no vision, the people perish.**
**(Proverbs 29:18)**

We're not called to be relevant, we're called to be prophetic! We're supposed to meet today's needs and be ahead of tomorrow's. Jesus said, "You are the light of the world; a city that is set on a hill cannot be hidden" (Matthew 5:14). The original word for "hidden" is "ignored." If the world is ignoring us, something's wrong! Pastor Ray Bevin said that in a recent survey, 70% of the pastors in his part of the country said they were not interested in growing. How can that be? Look at the New Testament church: "They went out and preached everywhere … And the Lord added *daily* to the church those who were being saved" (Mark 16:20). (See also Acts 2:47.)

God is not against small churches, but He does have trouble with *small-minded* churches! He condemned the Church of Laodicea because they boasted, "We have need of nothing" (Revelation 3:16-18). Without direction we die! Without vision we decay on the inside. Instead of praying for a move of God, start praying for a move of the Church! God's already moving; it's time to get in step with Him. Head for the nearest school or hospital or old folks home and begin to minister, and you'll see a move of God. When God gives you a vision, you'll be able to look beyond the hardness and see the harvest.

YOU WON'T JUST SEE THE RUINS, YOU'LL SEE THE
REBUILDING, AND HE WILL DO SOMETHING ELSE TOO—
HE'LL MAKE YOU PART OF IT!

# It's Their Backyard

**"Lord, and what about this man?" "... what is that to you? You follow Me!" (John 21:21-22, NASB)**

Learn to identify who owns what. That's what Jesus was trying to teach Peter and us! It's their backyard—let them mow it, or live with the weeds. If they play the martyr or get what they want by guilt-tripping or manipulating others, that's their issue; don't make it yours! If they're living with consequences, it's their consequence—not yours!

If they deny their problems or can't think clearly on a particular issue, the confusion is theirs! It's *not* your job to change them. If they don't seem to be capable of loving, or showing appreciation, or even apologizing when they're wrong—that's their property. When you can admit you're wrong, it means you're wiser today than you were yesterday. Maybe tomorrow they'll be wiser, too, but for today—it's their backyard—stop trying to mow it!

If your hopes, your peace, and your joy are dependent on them, then you need to learn how to "detach." You're not a joint tenant with them, you are a joint-heir with Christ! (See Romans 8:17.) Has it occurred to you that God could be waiting for you to get out of the way so that He can go to work in their situation? The truth is, you are powerless over them—but God's not!

—⚍—

HE MAY LET THEM FALL BEFORE HE LIFTS THEM, BUT HE'LL DO WHAT'S RIGHT AND WHAT'S BEST. SO JUST FOLLOW HIM AND LEARN TO MOW YOUR OWN BACKYARD.

# Bearing Fruit

**And he shall be like a tree planted by the rivers of water, that bringeth forth his fruit in his season; his leaf also shall not wither; and whatsoever he doeth shall prosper. (Psalm 1:3)**

If you are not growing and bearing fruit, it doesn't matter how long your life is. David said the blessed man doesn't just grow; he's planted! God plants him at a definite time in a definite place to accomplish a definite purpose. You may ask, "How can I know I am planted?" Because you'll grow *down* before you grow *up,* and you'll grow fruit. God's not concerned about how high your trunk grows, He's concerned about how deep your roots go, for that determines what you produce!

God will take every struggle and every experience you've been through and use them to cultivate the soil needed to make you fruitful. He'll even remove those who "stand in the way" of what He wants to do in your life. Jesus said, "Every branch in me that beareth not fruit he taketh away" (John 15:2). Did you hear that? He took them away, so don't go running after them! He knows what's best for you both.

Listen to Paul, "Live in vital union with Him. Let your roots go down into Him and draw up nourishment from Him. See that you go on growing in the Lord, and become strong and vigorous in the truth you were taught" (Colossians 2:6-7, TLB). Remember, the richest soil, uncultivated, can only produce weeds. There are no shortcuts to any place that's worth going.

ASK GOD TODAY TO STRENGTHEN YOUR ROOTS, AND CAUSE YOU TO GROW UP IN HIM, AND BEAR "MUCH FRUIT" (JOHN 15:8).

# Out of Season

**Be ready in season and out of season; reprove, rebuke, exhort, with great patience and instruction. (2 Timothy 4:2)**

When Paul tells Timothy, "Be ready in season and out of season," he is telling him to diversify. Sometimes you have to convince and rebuke; at other times you must be longsuffering and encourage people. A wise farmer rotates his crops. In one season he'll plant corn in a certain field. Eventually the corn will go "out of season. (He always thinks in terms of tomorrow.) Then he'll allow that field to rest from growing corn. In the spring he'll plant it with alfalfa. If you look, you'll also notice that the field which produced alfalfa last season is now producing corn this season. This man understands the seasons. He'll always be productive because he understands the importance of diversity!

Too many of us lose our sense of self-worth and direction because we don't understand when we're leaving one season and entering another. We're unprepared for it. But this does not have to be, for if you listen carefully to the voice of God, you can be productive at every stage of life. God will never put you in a place too small to grow. But growing involves risk—you can't steal second base and still keep your foot on first. Let me ask you a question: Do you expect to get any better than you are right now? Are you going to go any further, or is this it? Are you going to grow anymore, or just stay as you are?

**TAKE A LITTLE TIME OUT TODAY, GET INTO GOD'S PRESENCE, AND PRAYERFULLY THINK ABOUT THESE THINGS. YOUR FUTURE DEPENDS ON IT!**

# His Handiwork

**We are the clay, you are the potter; we are all the work of your hand. (Isaiah 64:8, NIV)**

Many people drown needlessly because they struggle. If only they'd relax and trust, the same water that took them under would bear them up. It's not the circumstances that are so damaging to us—it's our reaction to them! Our struggling and our anxiety cause us to go under when the same current would actually carry us over, if only we would trust in God and keep our wits about us. Listen: "When you pass through the waters, I will be with you; and through the rivers, they shall not overflow you" (Isaiah 43:2).

When you find God, you won't need many of the things you've been desperately struggling to get. After all, what's a problem if He's there? He doesn't have to do anything but be there—and it's over! The three Hebrews who were cast into the fiery furnace (see Daniel 3:8-25) discovered that He shows up when you need Him most! When David was being hunted by King Saul, his answer was the presence of God. Listen: "In your presence is fullness of joy" (Psalm 16:11). He wrote those words from a cave, not a palace. Get into His presence today!

Don't make the mistake of thinking that God's only at work when the blessings come! When the blessings are delayed, He's working on your faith, your patience, and you're character!

BLESSING IS THE REWARD THAT COMES AFTER YOU
LEARN OBEDIENCE THROUGH THE THINGS YOU SUFFER
WHILE YOU'RE WAITING. (SEE HEBREWS 5:8.)

# Stay in Balance

**To every thing there is a season, and a time to every purpose under the heaven. (Colossians 3:16, NIV)**

When you lose your sense of balance, you fall in one direction or another. I know, for it's happened to me. How about you?

Martha worked for Jesus, but Mary spent time with Him. There's a place in your life for both. Don't let this little daily devotional be all the time you have for God. Make it your entry point into His Word and your door into His presence. Water the ground with His Word. Till the soil of your heart with repentance and submission to Him or the ground will become hard and barren, and before you know it nothing will grow; nothing's new; there's no fruit! Jesus said, "Abide in Me and I in you. As the branch cannot bear fruit of itself, unless it abides in the vine; neither can you, unless you abide in Me" (John 15:4).

Workaholic, you may be admired for your "get up and go," but is your soul barren? Are you thirsty and dry? What does it all mean anyway if you gain the whole world but fail to please God? Christian worker, if you give out more than you take in, you'll get "out of balance," and before you know it, you'll be in trouble. You know what to do! Go back to the source. The medicine didn't fail—you just stopped taking it. The fulfillment you think is waiting for you when you reach some lofty goal can only be found in His presence. And it just might be sitting around your dinner table in the faces of your family and loved ones—if you'd only take time to discover how wonderful they are and build a relationship with them, too.

**THE WORD FOR YOU TODAY IS, "LEARN BALANCE!"**

# Seeds of Bitterness

**See to it that … no bitter root grows up to cause trouble and defile many. (Hebrews 12:15, NIV)**

When you "move on" what will you leave behind? Be careful what you say, especially when it shapes the opinions and infects the spirit of others. Your views are only based on what you know at the moment. James says, "Let every man be swift to hear and slow to speak" (James 1:19).

You know that person's actions, but you don't know their heart or their struggles. It's wonderful when you move from resentment to forgiveness; but what about the people you have left behind who only know what you said? Have you left them feeling bitter? One word of bitterness can defile so many. That should concern us greatly! Did you make a permanent decision based on a temporary circumstance? Did you hand down a verdict when you only had a few of the facts? Now you know better, but has your pride pushed you into a corner?

Make amends to those you've hurt. Clear the record with those you've left feeling resentful toward someone you now see differently. This is hard to do, but we all need to do it.

IT TAKES HUMILITY TO GO BACK AND STRAIGHTEN THINGS OUT, BUT UNTIL YOU DO, YOU WILL NEVER BE RIGHT BEFORE GOD.

# New Wineskins

**Who would use old wineskins to store new wine?
For the old skins would burst with the pressure, and the
new wine would be spilled. (Matthew 9:17, TLB)**

Chris Dimetriou told me recently that the original Greek word used here for *new* is "that which never existed before; not part of the old regime or the old mind set." What insight! I believe that God is pouring out His Spirit today, but He can't pour it into old wineskins. Jesus said they'd burst. No, God is creating new wineskins that can carry the new wine of His Spirit (a new structure and a new breed). If that means dying to the old and the familiar and the comfortable, then so be it! God's time always comes for the prepared heart. Listen: "I will give you a new heart and put a new spirit within you" (Ezekiel 36:26). Before you can receive the new spirit, you must receive the new heart.

This is an exciting time for those who have "a renewed heart." People whom God had waiting their turn are suddenly going to burst into the forefront. Trained by patience and humbled by personal challenges, they'll usher in a new season in the Kingdom of God. The question is, are you part of what God is doing, or are you still looking back at what He has done?

**TODAY, GET INTO HIS PRESENCE AND ASK HIM TO
PREPARE YOU FOR WHAT HE'S GOING TO DO. AFTER ALL,
WHAT COULD BE MORE IMPORTANT IN YOUR LIFE?**

# In Your Season

**He is like a tree planted by streams of water, which yields its fruit in season. (Psalm 1:3, NIV)**

Your opportunities to advance are regulated by God's purposes. Think about that. Usually, obscurity precedes notoriety. God told Elijah to go and hide himself by the brook called Kerith. (See 1 Kings 17:3.) There are some lessons you can only learn when you are "hidden away" with God. Before Elijah could call down fire at Mt. Carmel he had to spend time "hidden away" with God at Kerith. So how much time have you been spending with Him lately?

The first Psalm teaches that the blessed man meditates on the Word while he waits (see Psalms 1:2-3). It says that he yields fruit in his own season. It's good to recognize your season and prepare for it before it comes! Fruit won't grow prior to its season. All the praying, pleading, and confessing in the world won't change that. Even restaurant menus note that certain items can be served only "in season."

Those seasons are "the green light" times. You feel as though you have been waiting *forever* without seeing any results—like a car waiting at an intersection. Then God changes the light from red to green and you're free to move. Suddenly you start accomplishing things you had tried to at other times but failed. Stop pushing and straining!

WHEN YOUR SEASON COMES, YOU'LL KNOW IT—FOR
WHATEVER YOU DO WILL PROSPER. (PSALM 1:3)

## A Life Observed

**In due season we shall reap, if we faint not.
(Galatians 6:9)**

Your struggles and your efforts are being noted! Your integrity and your endurance are being evaluated at this moment. Just because you don't know who's watching you, doesn't change that one bit. Someone is always observing you who is capable of blessing you. That's how the favor of God works—through people. Listen: "Do you see a man who excels in his work? He will stand before kings" (Proverbs 22:29).

It happened to Ruth. Boaz, the boss, noticed her hard work and her unselfish care for Naomi, her mother-in-law, as she labored day after day in his fields. Ruth didn't know whose field she was working in. Maybe you don't either. All it took was the favour of Boaz and her life turned around. Listen to what he told her: "It has been fully reported to me, all that you have done" (Ruth 2:11). You have no idea who's observing your life today. Every hour you have spent restoring, healing, and blessing others will produce a harvest. Paul said, "In due season we shall reap if we do not lose heart" (Galatians 6:9). Your harvest is coming! Boaz married Ruth and gave her a son. From that child came King David and Jesus Christ. What incredible favor!

Picture this: You are running your race, and the grandstand is packed with spectators. Do you have any idea who's in that grandstand? Listen: "Since we are surrounded by so great a cloud of witnesses … let us run" (Hebrews 12:1).

**DON'T WAIT FOR SOME GLORIOUS FUTURE TO ARRIVE. PUT EXCELLENCE INTO YOUR PRESENT. YOUR EFFORTS ARE BEING OBSERVED AND YOUR REWARDS ARE ABSOLUTELY GUARANTEED.**

# Prayer Not Answered

**Ask, and ye shall receive, that your joy may be full.**
**(John 16:24)**

Have you prayed but God doesn't seem to be answering? (At least not the way you want Him to.) If so, check the following things carefully. How's your relationship with the Lord? David said, "If I regard iniquity in my heart, the Lord will not hear" (Psalm 66:18). Anything that affects your relationship with Him will also affect your prayers. God won't overlook your sin—He'll forgive it, but only if you turn to Him.

How's your faith? Listen: "Without faith it is impossible to please Him, for he who comes to God must believe that He is, and that He is a rewarder of those who diligently seek Him" (Hebrews 13:6). God longs for people who'll believe Him and expect Him to do what He says. Build up your faith. Get into the Word, and get the Word into you. (See Romans 10:17.) Multiply your faith by the faith of others and offer up a "faith offering" to God. Jesus said, "If two of you agree," the answer will be given. (See Matthew 18:19.)

How's your patience? Patience is just faith taking its time! Listen again: "For you have need of endurance, so that after you have done the will of God, you may receive the promise" (Hebrews 10:36). Until the answer comes, He'll give you grace to stand.

—◆◆◆—

REMEMBER ALSO, YOU'RE IN A WAR.
LEARN HOW TO FIGHT AND HOW TO PERSEVERE—
UNTIL THE ANSWER COMES.

# Timing Is Everything

**Until God's time finally came, how God tested his patience.
(Psalm 105:19, TLB)**

It is hard to see God bless others while you are forced to wait. This is not injustice. It's order! There's always a price to be paid for anything worthwhile. No matter how many people hold your hand, you've got to shed your own tears. Others can cry *with* you, but they can't cry *for* you. But there's good news: "If you go out in tears, you will come back rejoicing, bringing the fruits of your harvest with you" (Psalms 126:6). You are going to rejoice again. Tears are for the sower, but joy is for the reaper. When you come into your harvest, don't let the devil keep you weeping any longer. You've paid your dues; you've shed your tears; now get ready for your benefits! Your tears have a purpose. What good are seeds without water? Before anything can be born there must be travail.

Look at Joseph. He is being "tested" by the very promises God gave Him. Can't you hear Satan whisper, "I thought the dream said you were going to be in charge? What are you doing here in prison?" But Satan miscalculated. He always "overplays" his hand. It only *looks* like a dungeon. In reality it's the birthplace of promise and the day of small beginnings. God has not changed His mind, so don't you! When He's going to build something great, He takes extra time to lay a great foundation. Listen: "Jesus grew in favour with God and man" (Luke 2:52).

PLEASE ALLOW YOURSELF TIME TO GROW
FOR GOD HAS GREAT THINGS IN STORE FOR YOU.
REJOICE, YOUR BEST DAYS ARE JUST AHEAD!

# A New Identity

**She called his name Benoni: but his father
called him Benjamin. (Genesis 35:18)**

Are you still battling the old names they gave you and the old images you have of yourself? Nothing will change in your life until it first changes in your mind. Let me tell you a story. Jacob's wife Rachel died in the desert in childbirth. Just before she died, she gave birth and named her son Ben-Oni, which means "son of my sorrow." When the midwife handed him to his father, Jacob, he said, "He shall not be called Ben-Oni, the son of my sorrow; he shall be called Benjamin, the son of my right hand. He is my strength, not my sorrow!" Guess whose name prevailed? Benjamin! You are who your Father says you are!

If your heavenly Father didn't give you that name—it's not yours! Only accept the identity He places on you. No one knew better than Jacob/Israel the power of a name change! It was in God's presence that he discovered he was not a trickster, but a prince! When Christ lives in you, He breaks the strength of every other name that would attach itself to you. You're a saint not a sinner! Not a loser but a winner! When people try to label you, tell them you don't answer to that name anymore. The person they're talking about died and was buried two thousand years ago.

YOU HAVE A NEW IDENTITY! YOU'RE A NEW CREATURE.
(SEE 2 CORINTHIANS 5:17.) SO START ACTING LIKE ONE!

# Enabling Grace

**My grace is sufficient for thee.**
**(2 Corinthians 12:9)**

The word "grace" here simply means "all of God you need for all you're going through." When you believe God for something, it may take time for it to become a reality. As a result, the spirit of "discouragement" will try to latch onto you and drag you down. The enemy will whisper, "You're not going to get it." Child of God, don't buy it! Satan is a liar and the father of lies (see John 8:44). He wants you to think there is no help in God and no balm in Gilead. God may not come when you want Him to, but He'll always be right on time—if you wait on Him. Listen: "No good thing will He withhold from those who walk uprightly" (Psalms 84:11). His delays are not His denials.

God has never said anything to you that He couldn't back up. He's never promised you anything He couldn't deliver, so disregard your circumstances, stand on the promise that He has given to you, and declare, "If God is for us, who can be against us?" (Romans 8:31). Never be in a position where you're too good or too busy to ask God for help, or think that you can make it on your own. That's pride! Before a fall there is pride; after pride there's always destruction. Check your attitude today. You can't do anything without God! (See John 15:5.) You can't breathe without Him; you can't think without Him; you can't even get out of bed in the morning without Him. Don't even try it!

—⧢—

REACH FOR HIS ENABLING GRACE, AND YOU'LL
DISCOVER IT'S SUFFICIENT FOR YOU TODAY.

# Be a Finisher

**"My food," said Jesus, "is to do the will of him who sent me and to finish his work." (John 4:34, NIV)**

Jesus was a "finisher," and He wants you to be one, too. (See Hebrews 12:2.) His obsession was to complete His assignment. He thought it, He talked it, He lived it. He even said, "No man, having put his hand to the plow and looking back, is fit for the Kingdom of God" (Luke 9:62). Look out! Satan will always attack when something important is about to be birthed in your life. It may be the birth of a ministry, a revelation, or even a child that God will use. Your difficult child may be a child of destiny; that's why they come under attack more often than your other children. They have an assignment which the enemy has discerned.

Satan has tried to destroy me many times because he discerned my future. I just heard that the first Spanish edition of *The Word for Today* has been published. Again I'm reminded of his strategy—destroy the author, and the book will never be born. The battle is always over your future. Discern what the struggle in your life is about, and you'll take a giant step towards victory.

Sometimes you'll be tempted to give up. Listen: "From that time many of His disciples went back and walked with Him no more" (John 6:66). You may have lost a few battles but the war is not over! You may have been wounded, but He'll restore you and give you the grace to get back on your feet again. This time you'll win. If you quit, God can do nothing more for you.

—◊—

STAND AND FIGHT, AND HE'LL COME TO YOUR AID.
HE'LL GIVE YOU STRENGTH AND BRING YOU THROUGH IN
TRIUMPH. HIS WORD TO YOU TODAY IS "BE A FINISHER!"

# Replaying Your Past

**Behold I will do a new thing. (Isaiah 43:19)**

Realize it's not God who's bringing up your past! He says, "I, even I, am He who blots out your transgressions ... and I will not remember your sins" (Isaiah 43:25). If Satan's been replaying your past, it's because he's running low on material! He has nothing fresh to hit you with. All he can do is rearrange the old pictures and try to defeat you. Don't let him!

Focusing on tomorrow will help you to move away from yesterday! God said, "Behold I will do a new thing; now it shall spring forth ... will make a way" (Isaiah 43:19). He's going to make a way for you. As surely as Pharaoh and Herod wiped out every baby boy to get at Moses and Jesus, so Satan will do whatever it takes to keep you from reaching your destiny. No matter what your past is like, your future is worth fighting for, and he knows that!

If you seek God, He'll show you a ministry that can come from the mess you are presently in. God can bring healing to the brokenness in others through the very things you've experienced. Examine the attacks you've gone through and then ask the Holy Spirit what you are being qualified for. Mike Murdock says, "The pain you can feel is the pain you can heal!"

—m—

START LOOKING AT "THE JOY THAT IS BEFORE YOU" (SEE Hebrews 2:2), AND YOU'LL BE ABLE TO ENDURE THE PRESENT CIRCUMSTANCES!

# *Under Attack?*

**"Lest Satan should take advantage of us.
(2 Corinthians 2:11)**

Do you feel like Satan has singled you out for special attack? Perhaps you're wondering, "Why would he even bother with me?" The answer is influence! Job's influence was a constant irritant to the devil. Listen to what God said about Job: "Have you considered my servant Job, that there is none like him?" (Job 1:8). That's why Satan attacked his health, his children, his finances, his marriage and his career! Daniel's influence was touching a whole nation—so Satan hindered the answer to his prayers for twenty-one days (see Daniel 10:11-15).

You can't get God's attention without getting Satan's, too! Whatever glorifies God enrages him. Have you noticed that there are seasons when you feel no adversity or opposition whatsoever? And other seasons when everything you have is under attack. Here's something you need to know: Humans multiply—demons don't. Satan doesn't have enough demons to assign them all to your case, so he picks his times and places carefully.

In Daniel's story we learn that the moment demons attack us, angels are dispatched to minister to us and protect us. Where do banks position security guards? Wherever the treasure is! Satan's after the deposit of God in your life. He has seen the shipping invoice with your name on it, and he's out to intercept it.

—m—

YOU ARE AT A MAJOR TURNING POINT, AND
SOMETHING GOOD IS GOING TO HAPPEN TO YOU.

# Learning From Crisis

**Think it not strange concerning the fiery trial which is to try you, as though some strange thing happened unto you ... But rejoice. (1 Peter 4:12-13)**

Crisis never surprises God! Anyone He ever uses seems to move from one crisis to another. Listen to Paul: "People are watching us as we stay at our post ... when we are praised and when we are blamed; slandered and honoured; true to our word though distrusted; ignored by the world but recognised by God; terrifically alive though rumoured to be dead; beaten within an inch of our lives but refusing to die; immersed in tears yet always filled with deep joy; living on handouts yet enriching many; having nothing yet having it all!" (2 Corinthians 6:4-10, TM). God never promised you a rose garden, but He'll stand with you on the battlefield, meet with you in the storm, and turn your prison into a place of praise and thanksgiving.

Your crisis will attract his power and bring His strength into your situation. Listen again: "For My strength is made perfect in weakness. Therefore most gladly I will rather boast in my infirmities that the power of Christ may rest upon me" (2 Corinthians 12:9). One of my mother's favorite songs was "Standing Somewhere in the Shadows You'll Find Jesus!" The disciples experienced Him in the storm in a way they never knew Him before. Even Jesus learned obedience by the things which He suffered (see Hebrews 5:8). You're not losing—you're learning! Child of God, let the crisis you are going through today drive you into "the secret place."

—m—

**THERE YOU'LL DISCOVER GOD'S POWER, GOD'S PROTECTION, AND GOD'S PURPOSES.**

# Being Qualified

**You have been faithful with a few things; I will put you in charge of many things. (Matthew 25:23, NIV)**

Before you decide to reach for more, remember, God's watching you with what you already have! It's in the day of small beginnings that He teaches you patience and consistency; He teaches you to handle the pressures that accompany His blessing and caring. You must be qualified before you're promoted. Listen: "If anyone does not know how to manage his own family, how can he take care of God's?" (1 Timothy 3:5, NIV). If you can't handle a small area—don't ask God to enlarge your territory.

If you want to know who God will use, look at Philip. He began as a deacon, waiting on tables and doing whatever had to be done. When he had proven himself faithful, he was made an evangelist, and he took Samaria for God. Listen to the test he had to pass: "Choose several men from among you who are known to be full of the Spirit and wisdom" (Acts 6:3, NIV). Are you known to be "full" of the Spirit? David said, "I have been anointed with fresh oil" (Psalms 92:10). Your anointing must be fresh every day. That means time out and time alone with Jesus. It is God's job to baptize you, but it is your job to stay filled. (See Ephesians 5:18.)

And what about wisdom? You can have lots of knowledge—but no wisdom! Knowledge can be gained from a book, but wisdom comes from walking with God. Jesus said, "Come to Me … learn of Me" (Matthew 11:28, 29).

---

**YOU MUST DO BOTH! YOUR FUTURE DEPENDS ON IT! TAKE SOME TIME TODAY AND GET ALONE WITH GOD.**

# Bury It, Move On

**Pulling down of strongholds ... casting down imaginations ... bringing into captivity every thought. (2 Corinthians 10:4-5)**

Today God's giving you the power to pull down those old strongholds that have ruled your life; He's giving you authority to cast down those imaginations that have had such influence over you and to bring into captivity every thought that doesn't line up with His Word. If you don't, they'll refuse to relinquish their hold over you. God will not do this without you, but He will do it through you! Old thought patterns and unhealed wounds will always try to re-establish control over you. Be careful who your friends are! If they can barely stay afloat themselves, how can they lift you? What you need is release, not reinforcement.

As long as these old issues reign in your life, Christ's seat is taken. If they are on the throne, then Christ is still on the cross. Put Christ on the throne and your *past* on the cross.

In the Old Testament a priest could not come into God's presence if he had touched anything dead. (See Numbers 19:11.) What a picture. If you are going to walk with God, you must bury the past. Forgive those who've hurt you—including yourself; then move on with God. Don't even "touch" those old dead issues anymore. The issue is not *whether* you remember, but *how* you remember. God is able to take the sting out of the memory and still leave the sweet taste of victory intact.

No longer will you be limited by what you have been through. Instead you'll be enriched! (See Romans 8:28.)

# First and Last Laugh

**The LORD said to Abraham, "Why did Sarah laugh?"
Sarah ... bore a son to Abraham ... at the very time God had
promised. And Sarah said, God has brought me laughter.
(Genesis 18: 13; 21:2-6, NIV)**

The first time Sarah laughed in unbelief; the next time she laughed in victory. But between the first and the last laugh she went through the worst time of her life. Twice Abraham betrayed her to save himself. A heathen king took her to his harem and would have raped her had God not stepped in to rescue her. Only a woman who has idolized her husband could begin to understand what she experienced that night. Between the first laugh and the last you'll do a lot of growing. You'll rejoice when one arrives, and mourn when another departs. Sometimes you'll feel like you can't go a step further, but through it all you'll learn to trust Him more than you ever dreamed.

Child of God, when you share your testimony, don't just tell how you started or where you are today; tell them what God has brought you through, for those are the very things they are struggling with, too. Go ahead, tell them about the awful "trying of your faith" that preceded your coming forth as gold. Don't leave them feeling defeated because they named it and claimed it and still didn't get it. King Abimelech's tent was in Gerar, which means "the halting place." There will be times when you'll feel like your life has come to a screeching halt; you're getting nowhere. Maybe that's where you are today. If it is, please know this: God will be faithful to you!

—⟋⟍—

NOT ONLY WILL HE BRING YOU THROUGH, BUT LIKE
SARAH, YOU'LL LAUGH AGAIN AS YOU WATCH HIM
FULFILL HIS PROMISES IN YOUR LIFE.

# *Father Knows Best*

**No man, having put his hand to the plow, and looking back, is fit for the kingdom of God. (Luke 9:62)**

The prodigal asked for it all and got it; but it turned out to be the worst thing that ever happened to him. I thank God for the times He's said "no" to me. How about you? The Bible says, "There is a way that seems right to a man, but the end thereof are the ways of death!" (Proverbs 14:12). Trust Him when He says "no" and thank Him when He pulls back on the reins. It's better to be alone with Jesus than surrounded by people or things that will ruin you.

Are you a prodigal somewhere between the blessing you used to have and the famine that's just about to hit your life? Things will keep getting worse until you stop walking in your will and start walking in God's. Jesus said the shepherd went looking for his lost sheep, the woman went looking for her lost coin, but nobody went looking for the prodigal son. He took himself away, he let himself down, he picked himself up, and he brought himself back. Nobody's going to do this for you. You know the way back, and you have to take the first step. When he left home he said, "Give me," but when he came back, he was saying, "Forgive me." That's still the way it works!

Listen: "When he was a great way off, his father saw him, and had compassion, and ran, and fell on his neck and kissed him ... and said, 'For this my son was dead and is alive again; he was lost and is found'" (Luke 15:20-23).

**TODAY YOUR FATHER IS WAITING FOR YOU TO COME HOME. DON'T PUT IT OFF—COME NOW!**

# Valley of Dry Bones

**Prophesy upon these bones, and say unto them, O ye dry bones, hear the word of the LORD.... I will cause breath to enter into you, and ye shall live. (Ezekiel 37:4-5)**

Child of God, the answer to the dryness and the disorder in your life is to "hear the Word of the Lord!" Read Ezekiel 37. First, there was a "shaking" and then there was a "coming together" ( vs.7). Is God shaking you up? Rejoice, that means He's "putting things together" for you. That's the way He works! Ezekiel saw dry bones, but God saw a great army. Ezekiel saw the present chaos, but God saw the final victory. You may feel like you're in a "dry place" at the moment, but God's about to send a wind into your valley! He's going to speak life into those circumstances you're standing in!

God can put life back into your dead business, your dead marriage, your dead ministry, and even your dying body. If you believe His Word, then stand up and declare it over your circumstances. (See Mark 11:23.) In Old Testament times "restoration" sometimes meant getting back seven times as much as you'd lost. (See Proverbs 6:31.) It doesn't matter what you were before the enemy attacked you, he miscalculated! He attacked a Sunday school teacher and gave birth to a prophet! He attacked your little savings account and started a harvest "seven times greater"! The trials and tribulations you're going through right now are just stepping stones to greater blessing! What God did in Ezekiel's valley, He can do in your life today.

---

WHY DON'T YOU TAKE A LITTLE TIME OUT AND BEGIN TO PRAISE HIM FOR WHAT HE IS ABOUT TO DO FOR YOU!

# Pray for Boldness

**Lord, behold their threatenings:
and grant unto thy servants … boldness. (Acts 4:29)**

Recently I was reduced to tears as I listened to a pastor from Pakistan tell of a Muslim family who had given their lives to Christ and joined his church. One day Islamic soldiers came to their home and took their baby. They held it upside down by its feet with a sword to its head and told the family to "renounce their faith in Christ." When they refused, the soldier cut off the baby's head and hung it by its feet from a tree as a warning to the villagers not to attend that church.

The pastor who told us the story said, "This family is not asking for your sympathy, they're asking for prayer so that they'll be strong." What a challenge! We sit surrounded by God's blessings and benefits, yet most of us haven't even told the people we work with or live with about Jesus. Have you? Forty years ago, Hudson Taylor cried, "I cannot go on living unless I tell the people of China about Jesus!" He personally trained one thousand missionaries and an army of native workers and planted the church in that nation. Today it's a hundred million strong—and growing! Boldness is the child of compassion!

These disciples were not praying for lighter burdens—they were praying for stronger backs! Here is a prayer we all need to pray today: "Lord, grant to your servants that with all boldness they may speak your Word!"

**IF WE DON'T TELL A LOST WORLD ABOUT JESUS,
WHO WILL?**

# Use the Power

**I saw Satan fall like lightning from heaven.
I have given you authority … to overcome all the power of the
enemy; nothing will harm you. (Luke 10:18-19)**

You have not been called to defeat Satan; Jesus did that two thousand years ago. You've been called to enforce his defeat! Paul says that Jesus disarmed Satan and made a public spectacle of him at the cross. (See Colossians 2:15, NIV.)

When General MacArthur met with the supreme commander of the Japanese forces at the end of World War II, he walked over to him, ripped the glittering metals from his chest and stood on them. He took out his sword, broke it in two, and as the world watched, he declared total victory for all the allies and enforced the terms of surrender on the enemy. That's what Jesus did for you at the cross! When He died and rose again, He stripped the devil of his power, took the sword out of his hand, and declared, "All power in heaven and earth is given to Me. Go therefore" (Matthew 28:18-19).

Go in His power!

Go in His authority!

Go in His Name!

—∽∾—

**USE THAT AUTHORITY TODAY!**

# God's Gifts

**He gives them to each one, just as he determines.
(1 Corinthians 12:11, NIV)**

You've been given something God can use; find it and make it available to Him today! List what you've received. Check the people with whom God has given you favor and access. Raise everything you possess at this moment to its highest level of excellence, then watch God move on your behalf!

Don't copy anybody else—be yourself. You're unique! Everything you need you already possess in "seed" form. Water it, protect it, and develop it. Don't just spend your life trying to correct your weaknesses; begin defining and developing your strengths. Those strengths are the weapons God has given you for warfare. He's not interested in what you can't do, He just wants to know what you're willing to do. Your limitations won't stop God from using you if your heart's right.

Jeremiah said, "Behold I cannot speak, for I am a youth." But God said, "Do not say 'I am a youth;' for you shall go to all to whom I send you, and whatever I command you, you shall speak" (Jeremiah 1:7). The "supernatural" is simply God adding His super to your natural. Start acknowledging the strengths and the good things God has placed within you. Paul said your faith will become strong "by the acknowledgment of every good thing which is in you" (Philemon 1:6).

EXPECT YOUR STRENGTHS AND YOUR GIFTS TO
CONTINUE GROWING BECAUSE, "HE WHO BEGAN A
GOOD WORK IN YOU WILL COMPLETE IT UNTIL THE DAY OF
JESUS CHRIST" (PHILIPPIANS 1:6).

# It's in God's Hands

**You intended to harm me, but God intended it for good.
(Genesis 50:20, NIV)**

When God wants you in a palace, nobody else can keep you in a pit! Your future is not in the hands of others, it's in the hands of God! Your assignment doesn't always require the cooperation of everyone else, but it does require the cooperation of one person—you!

Are others saying and doing things that affect your life negatively? Joseph's brothers made the wrong decision in hating him. Potiphar's wife made the wrong decision in accusing him. The butler made the wrong decision in forgetting him. But God never forgot him! He arranged every step Joseph took, all the way to the throne.

The purposes of God will always overcome the plans of men. No one else can prevent God from using you, blessing you or giving you success—except you. God has a reason for everything. When you cannot understand it, stand on His Word, remember His faithfulness, and trust Him. He'll even make the wrong decisions of those around you work for your good. Don't look for someone to blame; look for the hand of God at work.

PAUL SAYS, "AND WE KNOW THAT ALL THAT HAPPENS TO US IS WORKING FOR OUR GOOD IF WE LOVE GOD AND ARE FITTING INTO HIS PLANS" (ROMANS 8:28, TLB). JUST MAKE SURE YOU ARE!

# Be of Good Cheer

**Therefore, keep up your courage, men, for I believe God, that it will turn out exactly as I have been told. (Acts 27:25)**

You'll never reach your destiny without going through some storms! Paul wrote, "For many days ... the storm continued raging ... and we finally gave up all hope of being saved" (Acts 27:20). But look how he handled it. First, he kept his joy while all around him others were falling apart and making mistakes. You say "How did he do it?" Listen: "For there stood by me this night the angel of God, to whom I belong and whom I serve, saying, 'Do not be afraid ... God has granted all those who sail with you'" (Acts 27:23-25). God protects what He owns; that means you! He keeps what you commit to Him. It is the uncommitted areas of your life that Satan can attack and the storms can destroy. Have you committed it all to Him yet? Don't go a step further until you do!

Next, Paul kept before him a picture of future victory, while others were worrying about present circumstances. God has already arranged your future; let that sink in! God used that shipwreck to reach an entire population with the Gospel. Listen to what happened before they left that island: "They honoured us in many ways, and when we were ready to sail, they furnished us with the supplies we needed" (Acts 28:10, NIV). Child of God, stop worrying; God has everything under control! If you're a child of God, then you're not a victim of circumstances!

---

YOUR FUTURE IS NOT IN THE HANDS OF PEOPLE—
IT'S IN THE HANDS OF GOD. IF HE'S ON YOUR SIDE,
SUCCESS IS INEVITABLE. JUST SUBMIT TO HIM,
TRUST HIM, AND BE OF GOOD CHEER.

# His Hand at Work

**The steps of the good men are directed by the Lord ... if they fall, it is not fatal, for the Lord holds them with His hand.**
**(Psalm 37: 23-24, TLB)**

God has children like Jacob who walk with a limp. Are you one of them? Has something so painful happened that it's affected every area of your life? Do you find it difficult to trust people? Have you become your own worst critic? Maybe you think your ministry or your career is over, or worse, it never got off the ground—you've been crippled! If that's where you are, then read the following verses: Psalm 84:7; Proverbs 4:18; 1 Timothy 4:15.

God loves to use people just like you, for when they're successful, they're not arrogant like some who think they deserve it. They're a little warmer, a little more willing to reach out and embrace others without fear of rejection. They understand that without God they would never have survived. They have a "Joseph spirit."

Look how he treated his once-hateful brothers. Not only did he forgive them but he fed them. You ask how can someone do that? Because Joseph saw the hand of God at work in all his circumstances. Have you seen His hand in yours yet? Listen: "God sent me before you to preserve you ... and save your lives by a great deliverance" (Genesis 45:4-7). God has a way of bringing us out of bondage and then making us remember where we came from.

WHEN WE BEGIN TO EXPERIENCE SUCCESS, HE REMINDS US THAT HE OPENED THE DOOR OF OUR PRISON. HE GAVE US FAVOR IN THE EYES OF MEN. NOW IT IS OUR TURN TO BLESS OTHERS.

# You've Been Loved

**Be ye kind one to another, tenderhearted, forgiving one another, even as God for Christ's sake hath forgiven you. (Ephesians 4:32)**

God's looking for people with enough compassion to stop and ask, "How are you today?" And then stay around long enough to hear the answer! When people have been hurt, they need special care, extra attention, and unconditional love. They have to be held a little closer and prayed over a little longer. Instead of always expecting someone to bless you, why don't you reach out to help a brother or sister who's in need today. After all, it was God's grace that brought *you* through. Now it is your turn to help and encourage someone else who's experiencing a similar problem.

I know pastors who trusted their associates only to be betrayed. Now they're unable to minister. I know people who've been "used" by leaders and then discarded like an old coat. Today, they're crippled by unforgiveness and distrust. If you feel this way, then come spend some time with Jesus. He'll heal your wounds and tear down your walls of unforgiveness. If not, bitterness will stop you dead in your tracks! (See Mark 11:25,26.)

Today He's saying to you, "I know you're hurting, but I'm going to heal you. I know your weaknesses, but I'm going to strengthen you. I know you need a lot of help, but I'm going to be your support. I know you've been abandoned, but I'm going to stand by you!" (Hebrews 13:5).

THAT KIND OF LOVE WILL SET YOU FREE TO LOVE OTHERS, AND ENJOY GOD'S BEST IN YOUR LIFE. WHY SETTLE FOR LESS?

## Start Testifying

**Has the Lord redeemed you? Then speak out!**
**(Psalm 107:2, TLB)**

You have more potential than you think! You can achieve more than most people expect of you. You can go as far as your faith will take you! People may have said you won't make it, but there's another opinion—God's! God sees potential in you that not even *you* know is there. You may be saying to yourself today, "I've gone too far; I can't come back."

Don't you believe it for one minute! It doesn't matter where you have been. God is the God of second chances. Listen: "Now the Word of the Lord came to Jonah the second time" (Jonah 3:1). When God decides to restore you, it doesn't matter what they say about you. When God raises you up, no demon in hell can keep you down!

If God has been good to you, shout it from the rooftops! Nobody else really knows what God has done for you. Nobody else knows how far you've come. Nobody else knows what you've been through. But you know. It may have taken you a little longer than everyone else, but God has given you the victory, so don't let the devil steal your testimony. He'd love to silence you because he knows if you tell what God has done for you, someone else is going to be set free!

---

**SO HAS THE LORD REDEEMED YOU?**
**THEN SPEAK OUT!**

# Where Would You Be?

**O give thanks unto the LORD, for he is good:
for his mercy endureth for ever. (Psalm 107:1)**

There's not one of us today who has not needed and benefited from God's mercy. When Adam and Eve sinned God could have scrapped everything and started all over again. But He was merciful. He gave them the promise that their seed would redeem back what they had lost. When Jonah refused to go to Nineveh, God could have killed him and found someone else to go in his place. But God knew what was in Jonah just as He knows what's in you and me, and He gave him another chance.

Sometimes God allows us to fall, for it's then that we realize that without Him we are nothing. Quit acting as if you've made it by yourself! Don't let the devil deceive you into thinking that your deliverance was at least in part some act or power of your own. Listen: "Not by works of righteousness which we have done, but according to His mercy He saved us" (Titus 3:5). Did you hear that? His mercy saved you and brought you to this point.

Ray McCauley, who pastors a great church of 20,000 in Johannesburg, tells of a night in a hotel when he saw a man who was stone drunk. Ray looked at him in disgust. Suddenly God said to Ray, "The only difference between him and you—is Me!" Before God saved John Newton he was a slave trader, a drunk, and a violent man. After God saved him, he wrote the words, "Twas grace that brought me safe thus far, and grace will lead me home!"

WHY DON'T YOU LIFT UP YOUR HEART TODAY AND
BEGIN TO THANK HIM FOR HIS MERCY AND HIS GRACE.
WITHOUT IT, WHERE WOULD YOU BE?

# *Be a Witness*

**I have appeared unto thee ... to make thee a witness ...
Delivering thee from the people. (Acts 26:16,17)**

You're not called to be a judge, and you're not called to be a lawyer; you're called to be a witness to God's saving and keeping power in your life. Only talk about the God you've experienced! Tell people what He's done for you. Their God may be a distant deity who doesn't get involved. Or He may be angry with them because He's an auditor, and their books don't balance. When nine out of ten people don't go to church, there's got to be a reason. We've been called to be "salt and light," but if the light is not shining and the salt is not doing its job, how will they ever be reached and won? (See Matthew 5:13-14.)

Please notice what God said to Paul, for it's a key for you. He promised to "deliver him from the people" (Acts 26:17). Some of us need to be delivered from the people! Love them; lead them; lay down your life for them—but don't be afraid of them. If you're anointed, then your authority comes from God, not them. When you've heard clearly from Him, you can face anybody! When God fills you with His Spirit, you'll receive a new boldness. Look at Peter; a few days ago he was denying Jesus and running from a mere girl; now he's preaching to multitudes and winning them to Christ. What happened? He was empowered by the Holy Spirit!

TODAY GOD WANTS TO FILL YOU WITH HIS SPIRIT,
TO SET YOU FREE FROM THE PEOPLE, AND
MAKE YOU A WITNESS. WILL YOU LET HIM?

# God Isn't an Infidel

**But if any provide not for his own ... he hath denied the faith, and is worse than an infidel. (1 Timothy 5:8)**

After reading this verse, Sarah Utterbach said to me, "Bob, if God is our father and we are His children, wouldn't He be worse than an infidel if He didn't provide for us, too?" What a great question! Jesus said, "People who don't know God and the way He works fuss over these things, but you know both God and how He works. Steep your life in God-reality, God-initiative, God-provision. Don't worry about missing out. You'll find all your everyday human concerns will be met" (Matthew 6:32-33, TM). God has promised to take care of us! So how come we keep doubting Him?

Sure, you'll go through times of difficulty and testing. When God called Abraham to leave everything and follow Him, he suddenly found himself in the middle of a famine. You say, "How could that happen?" Because God will put you in situations that stretch your faith; you may be in one right now! The question from God's angle is always, "Will you trust Me?" God didn't leave Abraham there—and He won't leave you there either. Listen: "So Abram went up from Egypt ... and ... had become very wealthy in livestock and in silver and gold" (Genesis 13:1-22, NIV). Before it was over, Abraham received more than he gave up and more then he had asked for. God even introduced himself by a new name—*El Shaddai*, which means, "The God who is more than enough."

—✺—

REJOICE—ABRAHAM'S GOD IS YOUR GOD!

# Paying the Price

**Compared to the high privilege of knowing Christ … everything
I once thought I had going for me is insignificant.
(Philippians 3:7, TM)**

When Jesus cast the demons out of one man, they entered into a herd of pigs, which rushed down a hillside into the sea and drowned. Immediately, the people asked Him to leave and not come back again. (See Matthew 8:34.) The message was clear, "Solve our problems—but save our pigs." It's called success without sacrifice. But it doesn't work!

Why does the average church in America have only seventy people? Because that's the approximate number required to maintain a building and pay a pastor. So we stop growing! But Jesus said, "Go out into the highways and hedges and compel them to come in" (Luke 14:23). But we say, "That won't work here." People who say that are only testifying to their own experiences. It'll work, if you pay the price!

E. Stanley Jones, the great missionary to India, wrote in the twilight of his life, "When I get to Heaven, I will ask for 24 hours to see my friends. Then I'll go up to my Master and say, 'Haven't you a world somewhere with fallen people, who need an evangelist like me? Please send me there, for I know of no heaven beyond preaching the Gospel to people. That is Heaven to me. It has been and it ever shall be.'"

**HE WAS WILLING TO PAY THE PRICE. SO WAS PAUL.
THE QUESTION IS—ARE YOU?**

# You've Got to See It!

**By faith Moses ... persevered because he saw Him who is invisible. (Hebrews 11:24-27, NIV)**

Why would Moses give up life in a palace to live like a slave? Because he saw what others didn't see! And when you begin to see who you really are and what God's called you to do, you'll give up anything that stands in your way. Without a vision, even the smallest problem will trip you up and keep you from reaching your goal. God said to Abraham, "Lift up your eyes from where you are and look ... All the land that you see I will give to you" (Genesis 13:14-15, NIV). Did you hear that? If you can "see it," God will give it to you. He didn't say it would be easy or cheap, but if you're willing to pay the price, it can be yours!

Notice, God also said, "Lift up your eyes from where you are." You can see it from where you are! There's gold under your feet, if you're willing to dig for it. James says, "Ye have not, because ye ask not" (James 4:2). We don't ask, because we don't see, so we live far short of our potential. Refuse to live that way another day. Ask Him to give you a vision of who you are. Then ask Him to show you who He is, for His Word says that He's "... able to do exceeding abundantly beyond all that we ask or think, according to the power that works within us" (Ephesians 3:20, NASB).

—m—

HOW WONDERFUL!
HIS POWER IS ALREADY AT WORK IN YOU TODAY!

# Have Problems?

**But none of these things move me.
(Acts 20:24)**

Why do some people with huge problems whistle through life, while others with smaller problems are constantly in despair? Because your problem is not your problem—your attitude is! What you cannot change, God will give you the grace to overcome. That's why Paul could say, "None of these things move me."

Did you hear about the man whose lawn was besieged with dandelions? He tried everything and still couldn't get rid of them. Finally, in frustration he wrote to the Department of Agriculture, explaining all the different dandelion deterrents he'd tried and asked what he should do next. The answer came back from the Department of Agriculture: "Try getting used to them!" Now that may not be what you want to hear, but it's the truth.

Life is not television—you can't switch to another channel! Just because you have dandelions in your yard, doesn't mean you have to let them mess up your whole life. If you're looking for a problem-free world, forget it. It's the battles that produce the victories and the victors! Listen to these words: "We are hard pressed on every side, but not crushed; perplexed, but not in despair; persecuted, but not abandoned; struck down, but not destroyed" (2 Corinthians 4:8, NIV).

---

GOD WILL CHANGE EITHER YOUR CIRCUMSTANCES
OR HE'LL CHANGE YOU. EITHER WAY,
HE'LL BRING YOU OUT ON TOP!

# Defensive Praise

**And immediately she was made straight, and glorified God.
And the ruler of the synagogue answered with indignation,
because that Jesus had healed on the sabbath day. (Luke 13:13-14)**

What a scene! They were angry, and they were arguing because Jesus had healed this woman on the Sabbath day. But she stood apart from it all and just praised God. Can you imagine what would have happened if she had stopped glorifying God and started arguing? Her deliverance would have ended in a fight. Once God has set you free, don't let anybody trap you into religious arguments.

When this woman began to bless the Lord, she literally built walls around her own deliverance. This is so important. When you've just been through surgery, don't mess around with things that can contaminate or infect you. She protected herself by entering into defensive praise! That's the strategy which says, "I will not allow myself to be sidetracked by majoring on minors, I won't allow my attitude to be influenced by negative opinions or spirits." When God delivers you, don't stop what you're doing to answer your accusers, or expose yourself to their moods and attitudes.

---

**JUST KEEP PRAISING THE LORD, AND
YOU'LL COME OUT ON TOP.**

# *Mud or Stars?*

**Although he was a son, he learned obedience
from what he suffered. (Hebrews 5:8, NIV)**

A young soldier married a woman and brought her to his post in the California desert. From the moment she arrived, she hated it. The temperature was 115 degrees, the sand blew over everything, and her only neighbors lived in an Indian village nearby. But worst of all was the loneliness, with her husband gone much of the time. Finally, she wrote to her mother and said, "I hate it! I'm coming home." Her mom wrote back these words: "Two men looked through prison bars, one saw mud, the other stars." She got the message! She decided to "look for the stars." She began to learn all she could about the desert, the language, the folklore, and the traditions of the Indians. She became so engrossed in it that she finally wrote a best-selling book on the subject. What had changed? Not the desert; not the Indians. No! The key was she changed her attitude and transformed a miserable experience into a highly rewarding one.

Jesus learned obedience from what He suffered. Some of the things you are trying to avoid are the very things that will nurture and shape you into the person God wants you to be.

OVERCOMERS WELCOME PROBLEMS, KNOWING THAT THEY'LL DRIVE THEM CLOSER TO GOD TO MAKE THEM OF MORE USE TO THE PEOPLE THEY'VE BEEN CALLED TO SERVE.

# God Really Cares

**Cast all your anxiety on him because he cares for you.
(1 Peter 5:7, NIV)**

In his book *He Still Moves Stones*, Max Lucado writes, "What matters to you, matters to God. You probably think that's true only when it comes to the big stuff, like death, disease, sin, and disaster. But what about the smaller things? Flat tires and lost dogs? Broken dishes, late flights, toothaches or a crashed hard disks? Do these matter to God? I mean, He's got a universe to run and presidents and kings to watch over. He's got wars to worry about and famines to fix. Who am I to tell Him about my ingrown toenail? I'm glad you asked! Let me tell you who you are—you are His child—as a result, if something is important to you, it's important to Him."

If you grew up hearing "go away, don't bother me," you might just think your heavenly Father feels the same way, too; but you'd be wrong! Fixing big problems doesn't require any more effort on His part, and handling little ones doesn't require any less. There are no degrees of difficulty to a God who is all powerful. Listen: "The Lord is good, a refuge in times of trouble. He cares for those who trust in Him" (Nahum 1:7, NIV).

—⚹—

THE SITUATION MAY BE TOO BIG FOR YOU, BUT IT'S NOT
TOO BIG FOR HIM. HE CARES ABOUT YOU TODAY.

## In Need of His Help

**My help comes from the Lord.
(Psalms 121:2, NIV)**

I smiled as I read this prayer: "Dear Lord, so far today I've done all right. I haven't gossiped, lost my temper, been nasty, greedy, grumpy, overbearing, selfish, or obnoxious. I'm really glad I've accomplished all these things on my own. But in a few minutes, Lord, I'm going to have to get out of bed—and from that point on, I'll need all the help I can get from You."

For the last five years, I've tried to find something fresh to write each day. Often I pray, "God, speak to me, or I'll have nothing to say that will help anyone else." Peter said, "Men of God spake as they were moved by the Holy Spirit" (2 Peter 1:21).

That's it! Without God, what do any of us have to say that makes any real difference? We can't even begin to make progress until we humbly acknowledge that we're powerless over people, places, and things. We are, but God's not! Whatever you're facing today, listen to these words and claim them by faith. "He will never let me stumble, slip or fall. For He is always watching, never sleeping. Jehovah Himself is caring for you! He is your defender. He protects you day and night. He keeps you from all evil and preserves your life. He keeps His eye upon you as you come and go and always guards you" (Psalms 121:3-8, TLB).

**HIS HELP IS AVAILABLE TO YOU TODAY. REACH FOR IT!**

# Give What You've Got

**I chose you and appointed you to go and bear fruit—
fruit that will last. (John 15:16, NIV)**

One morning, when the Berlin Wall was still standing, some East Berliners came and dumped a truckload of garbage on the west side of the wall. Greatly angered, the people there thought they would return the favor. Instead, they had a better idea! They filled a truck with canned goods, medicine, clothes, and other nonperishable items, then took it over to the east side. They stacked it up neatly beside the wall and put a sign near it, which read, "Each gives what he has to give!" If garbage is what you've got, garbage is what you'll give; but if love is what you've got, love is what you'll give! Love is the "fruit of the Spirit" (Galatians 5:22) and you can bear fruit only as long as you "abide in the vine" (John 15:4).

God's purpose for you is that your fruit should remain long after you've gone! To settle for second best is a terrible sin. God gave everything He could give, so that you could become everything you were designed to be. Paul says, "The fruit of the Spirit is love, joy, peace, patience, kindness, goodness, faithfulness, gentleness and self-control" (Galatians 5:22-23, NIV). No self-help book can teach you to live like this—He's the source of it all! The secret of fruitfulness is giving God the first part of every day, the first day of every week, the first portion of your income, the first consideration in every decision, and the first place in your life.

—⟡—

**DO IT AND SEE WHAT HAPPENS.**

# One-Note Players

**Whatever your hand finds to do, do it with all your might.**
**(Ecclesiastes 9:10, NIV)**

Have you heard about the "one-note musician"? She inspected her violin, took her seat in the orchestra, arranged her music, and tuned her instrument. As the concert began, the conductor skillfully cued one group of musicians, then another, until finally the crucial moment arrived. It was time for her note to be played! The conductor signaled her, she sounded her note, and the moment was over. The orchestra played on and the "one-note musician" sat there quietly for the remainder of the concert, not disappointed that she's played only one note, but with a sense of fulfillment and peace that she'd played it in time and with great gusto!

Have you heard of Ananias? He suddenly shows up in Acts 9, leads Saul of Tarsus to Jesus, and promptly disappears from the Bible. He's a "one-note player"—but what a note! Romans 16 is a doxology to the obscure "one-noters" who gave their lives to spread the Gospel and build the Church. All over the world, an army of devoted followers of Christ is helping to change nations—one life at a time. They are "one-note players."

———ᗰ———

THEY'VE FOUND THEIR PLACE.
THE QUESTION IS—HAVE YOU?

# Going It Alone

**Lengthen your cords, strengthen your stakes. For you will spread out to the right and to the left.
(Isaiah 54:2-3, NIV)**

Alex Haley, the author of *Roots*, has a picture in his office of a turtle sitting atop a fencepost. Under it, the caption reads, "You can be sure he didn't get up there by himself." You can't either! Paul said, "I am a debtor" (Romans 1:14). Barnabas got him into the right church; Titus encouraged him when he was going through rough times (see 2 Corinthians 7:5-6); Priscilla and Aquila risked their necks to protect him (see Romans 16:3-4). There were others who helped Paul along the way. Myles Munroe says, "Each one of us is just a sentence, and it takes a lot of those to make a complete paragraph."

What got you to this level won't get you to the next—you need new revelation, new resources, and new relationships. Why would a world that never stops changing listen to Christians who stopped learning and growing years ago? God has got to bless His people if we're to carry the message to a lost world. He's got to show us a better way if we are to get there on time. To do it, He'll shake up our tested relationships, our proven methods, and our comfort zones.

His word to us is, "Lengthen your cords, strengthen your stakes. For you will spread out to the right and to the left."

—⚏—

**THAT WORD WON'T LET US QUIT,
TURN BACK, OR STAND STILL!**

# Ready to Meet God?

**Believe on the Lord Jesus Christ, and thou shalt be saved.
(Acts 16:31)**

The Sunday morning after Princess Diana died, a man in Ireland sat weeping in front to of his television. He couldn't believe it—a life with such promise, suddenly was taken away! As he watched them towing the mangled remains of her car from the scene, he found himself praying, "O God, if that could happen to her, it could happen to me, and I'm not ready to die!" He asked God to have someone call him and invite him to go to church. A half-hour later the phone rang, and a friend invited him to attend a morning service. Though no invitation was given to come to Christ, on his way out someone gave him a copy of *The Word for Today*. At home he read it and came to the page with "the sinner's prayer." Kneeling down, he prayed it word for word, then call the United Christian Broadcasting prayer lines for help.

The question has never been, "Is death coming?" The only question is, "Will you be ready when it does?" If you're not ready, don't live that way another day. Stop what you're doing right now and pray this prayer: "Jesus, I receive you now as my Savior. I repent and turn from my sins. Come into my heart today. By faith I receive the cleansing of Your blood and Your gift of eternal life. Amen."

Now there's one more thing you need to do—tell somebody! If you're not sure whom to tell, call us.

—∿—

ONCE YOU'VE BROKEN THE "SILENCE BARRIER,"
YOU WILL GROW STRONGER AND STRONGER.
DON'T PUT IT OFF—DO IT TODAY!

# The "Rest House"

**Blessed is the man who perseveres under trial ... he will receive the crown of life. (James 1:12, NIV)**

About halfway up one of the mountains in the Alps, there's a popular "Rest House." It's a good day's climb from the bottom to the top, but you can usually get to the "Rest House" by lunchtime. That's where you "separate the men from the boys." When some of the amateur climbers feel the warmth of the fire and smell the good cooking, they say to their companions, "I'll just wait here while you go on to the top. When you come back down, I'll join you, and we'll go to the base together." A glaze of satisfaction comes over them as they sit by the fire or play the piano and sing mountain-climbing songs. But about 3:30 in the afternoon, everything changes. They start looking toward the top of the mountain, as their friends reach the goal. Suddenly the atmosphere in the house changes, and they realize—they settled for second best.

What happened? Comfort caused them to lose sight of their purpose! It can happen to any of us. We all have those sheltered places in our lives, where we retreat from the climb. Child of God, are you discouraged? Are you thinking of retreating? Don't do it! Listen: "Hold fast to the Lord your God, as you have until now" (Joshua 23:8, NIV).

HANG IN THERE, FOR THE CROWN GOES TO THE MAN WHO PERSEVERES UNDER TRIAL. JUST KEEP CLIMBING!

# How God Works

**I make known the end from the beginning.
(Isaiah 46:10, NIV)**

Do you know how a good director makes a movie? I'm told he shoots the last scene first, then goes back to the beginning and makes every scene move toward it. That's how God works with us. First, God establishes purpose, then He decides procedure. That's why He's not nervous when you are; He's already set your end. You may be struggling today and wondering if you're going to make it, but God knows you will because He's already planned it all out. (Read Jeremiah 29:11.)

It works like this: Before there's a building, there's a blueprint. The architect has already put every detail on paper. When you're confused, all you have to do is check with the specifications and look at what the architect has designed. At times we all ask, "Why am I going through this? Why have I had to wait so long?" Then the answer comes back, "What does the blueprint say? What do the specifications call for?" What God builds will take the pressure and stand the storm. Anything that is made well is made slowly; with God, the quality goes in before the name goes on.

———ɱ———

WHEN YOU'RE ASSURED OF YOUR PURPOSE,
YOU CAN'T BE INTIMIDATED BY YOUR CIRCUMSTANCES,
BECAUSE YOU KNOW THAT THEY'LL ALL BOW TO
GOD'S PURPOSE FOR YOUR LIFE.

# Going Places

**By faith Abraham ... went out, not knowing where he was going. (Hebrews 11:8, NASB)**

When you make a radical commitment to follow God, you'll go where you've never been before! If you're still looking at the same ground ten years later, you're going in circles. God said to the Israelites, "You have compassed this mountain long enough; turn you northward" (Deuteronomy 2:3). Today, God's saying to you, "Take the car out of park, put it in gear, and let's go!" Learn from your crisis, glean from the experience—but let's get going! Abraham didn't have to know where he was going—God did. All Abraham had to do was focus on his relationship with God, and everything else fell into place.

Helen Keller was asked, "Is anything worse than being blind?" She replied, "Yes, to have sight but no vision." Steven Covey, author of *The Seven Secrets of Highly Successful People*, said, "The risk of riskless living is the greatest risk of all." Don't end your life wishing you'd stepped out and followed God—go ahead and do it! You won't be rewarded for "well said"—you'll be rewarded for "well done" (see Matthew 25:21). Your dream will always be tested; its value is in how much you're willing to pay for it. Abraham was willing to give up everything and go where he'd never been. How about you?

—◈—

**ARE YOU WILLING?
IF YOU ARE, IT CAN ALL BEGIN TODAY!**

# Listening to God

**He goeth before them, and the sheep follow him:
for they know his voice. (John 10:4)**

What Jesus was to His disciples when He walked and talked with them, the Holy Spirit is to you right now. Let that sink in! He spoke to them through His flesh; now He speaks to us through His Spirit. He said, "I will ask the Father and He will give you another Helper" (John 14:16, NASB). Whatever you're facing today, you're not alone; He's there to help you. Because you're a child of God, you're being "led by the spirit of God" (Romans 8:14). Even though you are not aware of it, He's guiding every step you take. But you say, "There's so much I don't know!" Don't worry, the Holy Spirit will "teach you about all things" (1 John 2:27, NIV). He will take the Scriptures and tell you what they mean to you individually and what they mean to you right now. What a privilege!

A. W. Tozer says, "He is not a silent God who suddenly begins to speak in a book and, when the book is finished, lapses back into silence again. No, we must approach our Bible with the idea that it is … God speaking to us right now."

The prophets habitually said, "Thus saith the Lord." God is continually speaking in the present. What is a disciple? One who follows Jesus. To do that, you must "know His voice." That calls for a time, a place, a hunger, a discipline, a pure heart, a listening ear, and a determination to settle for nothing less.

---

**TODAY HE WANTS TO SPEAK TO YOU.
DON'T MISS WHAT HE HAS TO SAY!**

# Check Their Spirit

**For God has not given us the spirit of fear.
(2 Timothy 1:7)**

You don't need a lot of people in your life; you just need the right people. Let God pick your friends! Gideon was greatly outnumbered by the Midianites, so he chose 32,000 men to fight. God kept 300 and sent the rest home because they didn't have the "right spirit." Listen: "Whosoever is fearful and afraid, let him return and depart from Mount Gilead" (Judges 7:3). Fear is a "spirit," and it's contagious.

God told Moses He would take "the spirit that was upon him" and put it upon seventy others so that they could carry the load with him. (See Numbers 11:17.) Just because somebody is gifted doesn't mean they're called. Bill O'Neill points out, "If the gifts are the standard by which we measure, Balaam's donkey goes to the top of the list, because he prophesied."

Don't worry about numbers—God can still do more with less! Just get ready to lose some friends, for where God is taking you, they can't go. They don't have the right spirit! They will tell you you're too young, too old, too uneducated, it'll cost too much, it'll take too long. You'll have to love them and leave them.

—⚬⚬⚬—

DON'T ARGUE; SIMPLY TELL THEM, "THE JUST SHALL LIVE BY FAITH" (ROMANS 1:17) AND KEEP FOLLOWING GOD.

# Cleansed and Circumcised

**Blessed are the pure in heart for they shall see God.**
**(Matthew 5:8)**

If your heart is pure, your perception of God will be clear, and your communication with Him will be good. The word *pure* means "without contamination." That means old concepts have been abandoned, and self has been crucified. The difference between forgiveness and cleansing is similar to the difference between cutting off a weed at the ground or pulling it up by its roots. Forgiveness deals with the *results* of sin; cleansing deals with the *cause* of sin. Forgiveness comes by confession, cleansing comes by walking in the light. "If we walk in the light … the blood of Jesus Christ His Son cleanseth us [continually] from all sin" (1 John 1:7, author's insertion). Do you keep asking God to forgive the same sins over and over again? That's because you've never experienced cleansing. The cause has got to be dealt with!

Paul says our hearts must be circumcised. (See Romans 2:29.) This means cutting away everything that is of the flesh. It means removing the food if it hinders best. Some things may not be wrong in themselves, but if they take God's time and God's place, then they have got to go! God told His ancient people, "The Lord your God will circumcise your hearts … so that you may love Him with all your heart and with all your soul and live" (Deuteronomy 30:6, NIV).

—⁂—

CHILD OF GOD, DO YOU HAVE A HEARING EAR AND A PURE HEART? ASK HIM TO GIVE YOU BOTH TODAY!

# Be Thankful!

**I will remember the deeds of the Lord; Yes I will remember.
(Psalm 77:11, NIV)**

In some parts of Mexico, hot and cold springs are found side by side. Local women often boil their clothes in hot springs, then rinse them in cold springs. Recently, a tourist said to her guide, "These people must think Mother Nature is pretty good to supply them with hot and cold water side by side, all free of charge." The guide replied, "Not really. They grumble because she doesn't supply soap too; and not only that, they've heard that there are machines that do this kind of work in other parts of the world!" Contentment isn't getting what you want; it's enjoying what you've got!

If you want to be miserable, focus on what others have and forget what God has given you. Comparing will always leave you feeling left out, rejected, or shortchanged. If you don't put the brakes on those negative emotions, you'll become negative and critical. An entire generation of God's people died doing just that. "The complainers" finished up going in circles, but the "attitude of gratitude" people entered the land of blessing. How's your attitude these days? Hasn't God been good to you? Where would you be today without Him? David said, "I will remember the works of the Lord; surely I will remember" (Psalm 77:11).

**BEFORE YOU GO A STEP FURTHER TODAY,
CHECK YOUR ATTITUDE, AND THEN TAKE SOME TIME
TO GIVE THANKS TO THE LORD!**

# You Are God's Solution

**For I will give you words and wisdom that none of your adversaries will be able to resist. (Luke 21:15, NIV)**

In 1903, Horace Rockaway tried to borrow $5,000 to invest in a new company called "The Ford Company." The bank president refused, saying, "No! The automobile is only a novelty; the horse is here to stay!" In 1977, the president of Digital Corporation said, "There's no reason to believe that any individual would ever want a computer in their home." He just couldn't see it. However, Bill Gates, founder of Microsoft, *could* see it. The rest is history. God knows more than either Henry Ford or Bill Gates, and He's willing to share His knowledge with "those who walk uprightly" (Psalm 84:11, NASB).

Listen: "We have the mind of Christ" (1 Corinthians 2:16). Now if this is true, shouldn't we be able to do a better job than anybody else should? Solomon says, "To the sinner God gives the task of gathering and storing up wealth to hand it over to the one who pleases God" (Ecclesiastes 2:26, NIV). You say, "Why would they?" The answer is *solutions*! Elijah's prayers ended a drought and changed the food supply of a nation. How much would you pay a consultant for doing that? Jonah's preaching changed one of the wickedest nations on earth. Think how that would affect drugs and violence in any community! Child of God, you have been called to excel, to bring solutions to a world that is staggering in darkness.

GOD STILL HAS A LOT TO DO IN THIS WORLD, AND
HE WANTS TO DO IT THROUGH YOU.
MAKE YOURSELF AVAILABLE!

# The Kingdom of God

**Thy kingdom come. Thy will be done in Earth, as it is in Heaven. (Matthew 6:10)**

Before the colonialists imposed national boundaries in Southeast Asia, the kings of Laos and Vietnam had already reached an agreement about who was Laotian and who was Vietnamese. Those who ate short-grain rice, built their houses on stilts, and decorated their homes with Indian-style serpents were considered Laotians. Those who ate long-grain rice, built their houses on the ground, and decorated their homes with Chinese-style dragons were Vietnamese. The kings taxed the people accordingly; hence they had no need for "boundaries." It was simple; each person belonged to the kingdom whose values they shared.

Any time the will of God is done in your life, the Kingdom of God has come. When you adopt His values, live by His standards, and obey His commandments, the prayer of Jesus is answered: "Thy will be done in Earth, as it is in Heaven." You ask, "How do the citizens of His Kingdom act?" In His Sermon on the Mount, Jesus says they're humble in spirit; submitted to doing His will; hunger and thirst for God; show mercy to others; have a pure heart; are peacemakers; and rejoice in hardship, for they know their reward is waiting for them. (See Matthew 5:3-12.)

WHAT THE WORLD WILL KNOW ABOUT THE KINGDOM OF GOD IS WHAT THEY SEE DEMONSTRATED IN YOUR LIFE. THAT'S A BIG RESPONSIBILITY, SO YOU'LL NEED GOD'S HELP TO FULFILL IT!

# Get Back!

**We ... will confine our boasting to the field God has assigned to us. (2 Corinthians 10:13, NIV)**

God had a different message for each of the seven churches, so when He says something to you personally, don't try to impose it on everyone else. When Joshua met the Lord at Jericho, he cried, "What saith my Lord unto His servant?" (Joshua 5:14) You've got to hear from God for yourself. You can't conquer your Jericho on a word God gave to somebody else. Furthermore, stop trying to get "a word" for others just because they happen to be bothering you. Let God straighten them out, and you get to where *you* belong!

A policeman in Atlanta has no authority to make arrests in Amsterdam. He's out of his jurisdiction. Once you leave the place of your anointing, you lose your influence with God and with people. Paul said he was confined to the field God had "assigned" to him. If you're assigned—you're confined! You can't just go where you like and do as you please, expecting God to bless you. You have to discover your assignment and confine yourself to it; otherwise you're out of place. No matter how far down the road you go, it'll never become the *right* road. You've got to go back to where you missed the turn and get back on the right road; otherwise you'll lose everything.

DISOBEDIENCE MAY HAVE GOTTEN YOU THERE; DON'T LET PRIDE KEEP YOU THERE. PLEASE, GET BACK TO WHERE YOU BELONG!

# Time to Repent

**I have given her time to repent … but she is unwilling.
(Revelation 2:21, NIV)**

God's patience is amazing! In one of the most extraordinary examples of His love, He gave Jezebel time to repent, and when Ahab, her wicked husband, humbled himself and repented, God healed and restored him. Humbling yourself before God will turn things around in your life when nothing else will work. Consider these words carefully: "Humble yourselves in the sight of the Lord, and He will lift you up" (James 4:10). Did you hear that? *Humble yourself—don't wait for God to do it!* Again the Bible says, "My son, do not make light of the Lord's discipline and do not lose heart when He rebukes you, because the Lord disciplines those He loves" (Hebrews 12: 5-6, NIV).

To repent is not just to feel sorry about your sin, but to change your way of thinking and acting. You must learn to take every thought captive, then make them obedient to Christ. (See 2 Corinthians 10:5.) You're no longer your own, you're His bondservant. Bondservants can't just decide to do what they want to, they belong to their master. They don't live by their impulses; they live by His commands. If you don't live in obedience to the Lord you will continually drift out of His will.

**BEFORE YOU GO A STEP FURTHER, GET ALONE WITH GOD, REPENT OF YOUR DISOBEDIENCE, AND LET HIM RESTORE YOU TO FULL FELLOWSHIP. HE'S WAITING FOR YOU.**

# Maintain Your Joy

**Because you did not serve the Lord your God with joy …**
**you shall serve your enemies.**
**(Deuteronomy 28:47-48, NASB)**

When you lose your joy, you end up in legalism or license. "Legalists" struggle to be perfect, so generally they're miserable to be around, whereas "license" will tempt you to go back to look for joy in all the wrong places. Sherman Owens says, "Happiness is of the mind, but joy is of the spirit. Happiness has to do with your circumstances, but joy has to do with your outlook." One is an *effect you feel*, the other is a *decision you make*, because you know God's got everything under control.

Peter says that you were "called out of darkness" (1 Peter 2:9). Do you remember how dark some of your days used to be? Sometimes you have to talk to yourself and say, "Bless the LORD, O my soul, and forget not all his benefits" (Psalms 103:2). Have you started taking them for granted? Or worse, maybe you feel you deserve them. Listen: "It is of the LORD'S mercies that we are not consumed, because his compassions fail not. They are new every morning: great is thy faithfulness" (Lamentations 3:22-23). Don't ask God for one thing more until you have learned to rejoice in what He has already given you. Nehemiah said, "The joy of the LORD is your strength" (Nehemiah 8:10).

—⟨⟨⟨—

**WHATEVER YOU'RE FACING TODAY,**
**HIS JOY WILL CARRY YOU THROUGH IT!**

# Develop Strong Roots

**Let your roots grow down into Him and draw up nourishment from Him. See that you go on growing in the Lord. (Colossians 2:7, TLB)**

My friend David Robinson says, "Faith grows only in the soil of adversity!" He's right! When young plants get too much rain, even a short drought can kill them. Why? Because it was too easy! During frequent rains, they didn't have to push their roots deeper into the soil in search of water; they didn't develop any strength. They have a weak, shallow root system and die quickly.

How's your "root system"? When stress and adversity enter your life, do you hold up or fold up? Do you find yourself thinking God has abandoned you or do you start doubting Him? Look out! Ease is your enemy! When you become too comfortable, you stop "digging deeper" in the Word. You allow others to spoon-feed you rather than develop your own personal relationship with God through prayer and Bible study. Thank God for the rain, but you have to develop a "root system" that will sustain you in the hard times.

You won't prepare for a fight you're not expecting, so, Paul says, "Put on God's complete armor, that you may be able to resist and stand your ground on the evil day [of danger] and, having done all [the crisis demands], to stand [firmly in your place]" (Ephesians 6:13, AMP).

NOW THERE'S SOMETHING TO THINK ABOUT!

**A man's wisdom gives him patience; it is to his glory to overlook an offense. (Proverbs 19:11, NIV)**

I heard about a couple celebrating their golden wedding anniversary. Somebody asked the wife the secret of their marital success. She answered, "On my wedding day, I decided to make a list of ten of my husband's faults, which, for the sake of our marriage, I would always overlook. I figured I could live with at least ten!" When she was asked which faults she had listed, she replied, "I never did get around to listing them. Instead, every time he did something that made me mad, I'd say to myself, 'Lucky for him that's one of the ten!'" She got it right; Paul says, "Love does not hold grudges and will hardly even notice when others do it wrong" (1 Corinthians 13:5, TLB).

Every relationship will experience storms from time to time, but you have the power to decide how you'll react. When things must be dealt with, speak the truth in love—not anger. If you can't, pray, cool off, and wait until you can. The longer you live, the more you'll understand what Solomon meant when he said, "A man's wisdom gives him patience; it is to his glory to overlook an offense" (Proverbs 19:11). Can you remember any of the stuff you argued about last month or last year? Was it worth it? Don't you wish you'd handled it better?

—◊◊◊—

**TODAY GOD'S GOING TO GIVE YOU ANOTHER OPPORTUNITY TO DO JUST THAT!**

# Discerning People

**If you love someone you will ... always expect the best of him.
(1 Corinthians 13:7, TLB)**

Mike Murdock says, "We rarely discern others accurately! Almost every conclusion we have about them is flawed and inadequate. We give up on them too soon, because we can't see what God is looking at. Someone close to you right now has a great future—God has already determined it. In fact, if you knew their destiny, you might withhold your words of judgement and invest more time and energy into them." Remember Joseph? The one who aggravates you the most could become the next prime minister. So treat him well.

Look beyond appearances. Clothing can be deceptive. Remember Ruth? She is a peasant in the fields, gathering "leftover" barley, but she'll soon become the wife of Boaz—your boss. Someday she might be signing your paycheck. So when you meet her in the field, be sure to leave handfuls "on purpose" to bless her. (See Ruth 2:16.)

Take another look at the situation you don't understand—Mary, the mother of Jesus, looking for a place to spend the night and have her baby. Here's the "opportunity of a lifetime"—don't miss it! Why did Jesus say, "Love your enemy" (Luke 6:27)? Because Saul of Tarsus (the one who's giving you so much trouble today) will become Paul the Apostle and bring multitudes into the Kingdom. (See Acts 9.)

**TODAY ASK GOD TO HELP YOU SEE IN OTHERS WHAT HE SEES. YOUR FUTURE DEPENDS ON IT!**

# Showing Kindness

**Be kind and compassionate to one another.**
**(Ephesians 4:32, NIV)**

One morning, before William McKinley became President of the United States, he was riding to his congressional office on a streetcar. A sick woman got on and, unable to find a seat, she clutched an overhead strap next to one of McKinley's colleagues. Pathetically, this colleague hid behind his newspaper to avoid offering her his seat. Immediately, McKinley rose, gave her his seat and took her place in the aisle. Years later, when he was president, this same colleague was recommended for the position of ambassador. McKinley refused his appointment! He said, "If his kindness is of the quality he showed that morning on the streetcar, I fear what he might do representing us in a foreign land." The disappointed congressman never did learn why McKinley chose someone else for the job. Paul said, "Love is kind" (1 Corinthians 13:4, NIV). You'll never be God's ambassador without it!

Mother Teresa said, "We cannot do great deeds, but we can do small deeds with great love." That's it! What good are tireless efforts fueled by personal ambition or a willingness to serve rooted in a desire to rule? If you're not kind, what does it all mean? Listen: "If I had the gift of faith so that I could speak to a mountain and make it move, I would still be worth nothing at all without love" (1 Corinthians 13:2, TLB).

---

**IF KINDNESS IS THE STANDARD,
HOW DO YOU MEASURE UP?**

# Three Judgments!

**The fire will test the quality of each man's work. If what he has built survives, he will receive his reward. If it is burned up, he will suffer loss. (1 Corinthians 3:13-15, NIV)**

As sinners, we were judged at the Cross. Listen: "The Lord has laid on him the iniquity of us all" (Isaiah 53:6). Had you been the only sinner who ever lived, Jesus would have suffered and died just for you. The question is what are you going to do about it?

As sons, we are judged daily. Why? In order to bring maturity and produce in us the character of Christ. Listen again: "Whom the Lord loveth, he chasteneth [judges]" (Hebrews 12:6, author's insertion). When I was young, my mother used to say to me, "I'm whipping you because I love you." In those moments, I wished I were big enough to return her love. But now I understand. The "pruning" process is to make you more fruitful.

As servants, we will be judged at the judgment seat of Christ—not for our sin, but for our service. Listen: "For we must all appear and be revealed as we are before the judgement seat of Christ, so that each one may receive [his pay] according to what he has done in the body, whether good or evil, [considering what his purpose and motive have been]" (2 Corinthians 5:10, AMP). You will be "audited." Again, Paul says, "The work of each [one] will become [plainly, openly] known [shown for what it is]" (1 Corinthians 3:13, AMP). Live without reservation!

**GIVE YOURSELF COMPLETELY TO HIM TODAY, AND WHEN THE DAY COMES, YOU'LL HAVE GREAT JOY AS YOU STAND IN HIS PRESENCE.**

81

## Contentment

**Be content with such things as ye have.
(Hebrews 13:5)**

Recently, I saw a cartoon picturing two fields divided by a fence. Each field had a mule and each mule had his head stuck through the fence, eating the grass from the other mule's pasture. Although more grass than he could eat surrounded each, the other field just looked better. In the process, the mules had got their heads caught in the fence, and they were braying furiously. The caption on the cartoon read, DISCONTENT. That says it all, doesn't it?

Contentment is not having what you want, it's wanting what you have and enjoying it. Life is not built on things; it's built on relationships. How's your relationship with God? How's your relationship with your family? If you don't want to get "caught in the fence," learn to enjoy your own field. Behind some of the world's success stories are the other stories of emptiness and discontent. When Marilyn Monroe committed suicide at age 36, she was at the height of her career. Debbie Reynolds said at her funeral, "Poor Marilyn; happiness eluded her all her life." There's nothing wrong with wanting more if you get it in the right order. Jesus said, "Seek ye first the Kingdom of God . . . and all these things shall be added unto you" (Matthew 6:33).

**IS GOD SAYING SOMETHING TO YOU TODAY
THROUGH THIS?**

# Have You Consulted God?

**And they did not ask for the counsel of the Lord.
(Joshua 9:1, NASB)**

It's hard to be humble when you've just walked through the Red Sea without getting wet and conquered the biggest city in Canaan. But overconfidence can be deadly! In the afterglow of victory, they thought they didn't need to seek God or listen to what He has to say. It's quite a story!

The crafty Gibeonites realized they couldn't win against God's people, so they sent a committee to meet them to try making peace. Even though they were lying, Joshua presumed they were telling the truth, and he made a peace treaty with them. It was one of the biggest mistakes of his life. From that day on, the Gibeonites would become a constant thorn in their side, and Joshua would live to regret "not asking the counsel of the Lord." The songwriter says, "Oh, what peace we often forfeit. Oh, what needless pain we bear. All because we do not carry everything to God in prayer."

Yesterday's victories don't guarantee tomorrow's—only God does. It's too easy to move from relying on God to relying on yourself, or trusting in a method just because it worked in the past or because everybody is using it in the present.

---

ASK GOD FOR A "RED LIGHT" IN YOUR SPIRIT
TO LET YOU KNOW IF YOU'RE MOVING IN YOUR
OWN ABILITY RATHER THAN IN HIS.

# Showing You Care

**Be kind to strangers, for some ... have entertained angels without realizing it. (Hebrews 13:2, TLB)**

On a bitter cold Virginia night, an old man waited on a path near the river. He was hoping somebody on a horse would come by and carry him across. His beard was glazed with frost, and his body was numb before he finally heard horses coming. Anxiously he watched as several horsemen passed without even noticing him. Finally, when only one rider remained, the old man caught his eye and asked, "Sir, would you mind giving me a ride to the other side?" Graciously, the rider helped him on to his horse and, sensing he was half-frozen, decided to take him all the way home, which was several miles out of his way. As they rode, the horseman asked, "Why didn't you ask one of the others to help you? I was the last one; what if I'd refused?" The old man said, "I've lived awhile son, and I know people pretty well. When I looked into the eyes I saw no concern at all for me, so I knew it was useless to ask. But when I looked into your eyes, I saw kindness and compassion." At the door of the old man's house the rider stopped, looked up and silently prayed, "God, may I never get so busy with my own affairs that I fail to respond to the needs of others."

AND WITH THAT PRESIDENT THOMAS JEFFERSON TURNED AND DIRECTED HIS HORSE BACK TOWARD THE WHITE HOUSE!

# Hearing From God

**He that hath ears to hear, let him hear.
(Matthew 11:15)**

It's not only possible to hear from God, it's absolutely necessary! Mary took the time to sit and listen to Jesus. (See Luke 10:39.) Later, while Peter attempted to persuade Him not to go to the cross, she anointed Him with oil in preparation for it. *Mary heard Him; Peter didn't!* Have you learned yet how to hear God?

Fifteen times in the New Testament our Lord says, "He that hath an ear let Him hear." That tells you three important things. First, you were born into God's family with spiritual ears; second, you have to learn how to use them; third, hearing from God must become the highest priority in your life. A baby is born with the ability to hear, but he doesn't know what he's hearing. Understanding takes time; it takes intimacy with his parents. Listen: "Then he opened their minds so they could understand" (Luke 24:45, NIV). He'll teach you!

Why is it that we can hear from God in times of crisis, yet not at other times? Because we have to! Until that changes, we'll keep living from crisis to crisis, so we'll never learn to hear from Him, either quickly or correctly. Jesus said, "I can of mine own self do nothing: as I hear, I judge" (John 5:30). Jesus did only the things placed in His mind by the Father.

—m—

HE WANTS YOU TO LEARN TO LIVE THAT WAY, TOO.
JUST TRY IT FOR ONE DAY; YOU'LL NEVER WANT TO
LIVE ANY OTHER WAY!

# Patience's Perfect Work

**But let patience have her perfect work, that ye may be perfect and entire, wanting nothing. (James 1:4)**

The problem with most of us is that we're too impatient! We're like the man who prayed, "God, give me patience, and I want it *now*." If God doesn't speak in the first five minutes, we get up, shake ourselves, and decide that "He isn't talking today." Where's the tenacity of the old saints, who would take hold of God in prayer and refuse to let go until they received "a sure word" from Him? (See 2 Peter 1:19.) Blighted with a microwave mentality, we want everything overnight, including Christian maturity. We've deleted from our Bibles—and from our thoughts—those passages of Scripture that command us to wait on God through the turbulent times.

There's a work going on in you right now. You may not be fully aware of it, but without it you'll never be qualified to handle what God has for you in the future. When the pressure's on and the answer doesn't seem to come, how do you handle it? Are you secure enough to trust Him, regardless of how bleak the situation looks? James says, "Let patience do its work!" Has God given you certain promises and assurances? The prophet said, "The vision is yet for an appointed time … though it tarry, wait for it; because it will surely come" (Habakkuk 2:3).

ASK GOD TODAY TO GIVE YOU FAITH AND PATIENCE. HE'LL DO IT!

# Grace and Tribulation

**Grace wherein we stand, and … tribulation [that] worketh patience. (Romans 5:1-3)**

There are two things you can count on as you walk with God: Tribulation that "works for you" and grace to "stand" while you're going through it. Have you been praying for patience lately? Get ready for tribulation! There is absolutely no other God-given way to get it. You can't grow oranges in Alaska—the climate isn't right. Patience will grow only in a climate of adversity. How do you test the strength of an anchor? Expose it to the blast of the storm. Some of the people you can't stand are the very ones who'll mature you and get you to your destiny! The problem is that we pray for things, but He also has a process. As you get to know Him better, you begin to recognize it.

Here's how it works: You ask God for strength, and He allows you to go through things that stretch you. You ask Him for wisdom, and you get to deal with problems and find solutions. You ask Him for prosperity, and He gives you the ability to work and wisdom to produce. You ask Him for favor, and you get responsibility. Salvation is a gift, but patience is a reward for overcoming.

STAY WHERE HE HAS YOU TODAY AND
LEARN WHAT HE WANTS TO TEACH YOU;
TOMORROW YOU'LL BE GLAD YOU DID!

# Wash Basins

**Moab is my wash basin.**
**(Psalm 60:8, NIV)**

The Moabites were Israel's troublesome next-door neighbors. When God's people got "dirty," He used the Moabites to clean them up. You say, "What does this have to do with me?" A lot!

A pastor I know prayed earnestly for his son who was on drugs. This man had a very successful church and was in great demand as a speaker all across the nation. But having an "addict" for a son was an embarrassment to him. So every day he prayed for God to change his boy. One day in prayer God told him He would not only change his boy, but through this situation He would radically change some things in him, too—things like pride, insecurity, and self-centeredness. He was more concerned with how his son's behavior affected his career than in what it was doing to his son's own life and future. David cried, "How can I ever know what sins are lurking in my heart? Cleanse me from these hidden faults" (Psalm 19:12, TLB).

Who is your wash basin? Who brings you to your knees? Who stretches your faith? Who develops in you a new level of compassion? Be encouraged, for God is working on both ends of the line.

---

BEFORE HE'S THROUGH, YOU'LL REJOICE NOT ONLY IN WHAT GOD'S DONE FOR THEM, BUT EVEN MORE BECAUSE OF WHAT HE'S DONE IN YOU. THAT'S GOD'S WAY.

# Worry

**Therefore do not worry for tomorrow.
(Matthew 6:34, NIV)**

If you're worried today, let's take another look at the feeding of the 5,000. (See Matthew 14:13-21.) There are some important lessons here for you. First, the disciples tried to get rid of their problem. They said to Jesus, "Send them away so that they may go … and buy themselves something to eat." But Jesus said, "Give ye them to eat" (Mark 6:36-37, NASB). You grow by dealing with the problem, not by avoiding it. Your faith increases when you place a demand on it. Lazy, inactive faith will fail you in the hour of need, so live in the Word of God and keep your faith strong. Next, Jesus asked them, "What have you got?" (Mark 6:38). He'll always ask you that, because you always have enough to create what you need. In your hands it's only a seed, but in His hands it becomes a harvest. So, put it into His hand and watch it multiply. (See 2 Corinthians 9:6-11.)

Finally, when Jesus gave them His plan, they explained to Him why it wouldn't work. Have you ever done that? The other day a friend in his 50s said to me, "I'd have to work for 30 more years to have enough to retire." I said, "That's true if the future is in your hands, so why don't you put it into God's hands?" Your security is not your job, your investments, even your pension—it's in His riches. (See Philippians 4:19.)

HAS HE EVER FAILED YOU? NO! AND HE NEVER WILL,
SO STOP WORRYING, START TRUSTING AND
HAVE A GOOD DAY!

# Busy People

**As thy servant was busy here and there, he was gone.
(1 Kings 20:40)**

Are you living a lifestyle that doesn't allow you to stop and listen to God? Has the unspoken attitude of your heart become, "If God has anything to say, He'd better hurry up and say it"? It's so easy to get caught in this trap. That's why today's word is for busy, overcommitted, let's-hurry-up-with-the-prayer-so-we-can-get-on-with-it-people.

A soldier who had been given charge of an important prisoner was told, "If he's missing, it will be your life for his" (1 Kings 20:39, NIV). Amazingly, he lost his prisoner—not because he was lazy or lacked commitment to the cause. No, he lost him because he got too busy with other things. Sound familiar?

God is saying to you today, "And ye shall seek me, and find me, when ye shall search for me with all your heart" (Jeremiah 29:13). Intimacy can't be rushed; it must be worked on day by day. The Bile says, "Jesus often withdrew to lonely places and prayed" (Luke 5:16). There's a price to be paid for hearing from God and walking in His will. There's no short cut to any place that's worth going to. If prayer was such a big part of His life, how come it's such a small part of yours? Today, take some time and think about these things.

GET INTO HIS PRESENCE AND ASK HIM TO GIVE YOU THE DESIRE AND THE DISCIPLINE TO BUILD A LIFE OF PRAYER. IF YOU DO, IT'LL BE THE BEST MOVE YOU'VE EVER MADE.

# Call It What God Does

**God ... speaks of the non-existent things ... as if they already existed. (Romans 4:15, AMP)**

God calls you in the present to what you're going to be in the future, then He initiates the process that will bring it to pass. Embrace what God has said about you over what anybody else has said about you. His Word is right, and they're wrong, no matter how sincere they are. If God has revealed it to you, it will come to pass if you'll only walk by faith and obey Him. Jesus fulfilled His promises and proved His critics wrong on Easter morning by conquering demons, disease, and death; and the same Spirit that raised Jesus from the dead is alive and at work in you right now. (See Romans 8:11.)

Renounce the past and renew your mind with His Word today. Believe God in spite of your feelings. Don't believe the lying prophecies of those who claim you'll never amount to anything. Turn a deaf ear to the racist who says that because you're a woman, you're not important. The Bible says, "Let God be true, and every man a liar" (Romans 3:4, NIV). Get up in the Name of the Lord and get going.

**YOUR DESTINY IS WAITING AND IT'S BETTER THAN ANYTHING YOU'VE EVER IMAGINED!**

# Behold the Lamb

**Behold the Lamb of God, which taketh away the
sin of the world. (John 1:29)**

When Adam sinned, God took a lamb and shed its blood to cover his sin. That day the principle of substitution was established: "The just for the unjust" (1 Peter 3:18). God told Noah to take two of each unclean animal, but seven of each clean animal, so that there would be a blood sacrifice when the world started again. In the Old Testament tabernacle, God arranged the furniture (the altar, the laver, the mercy seat, etc.) in the shape of a cross: four pieces down and three pieces across. Then He told Moses to sprinkle each piece with the blood of a lamb. For 1,400 years God looked down and saw a blood-stained cross in the midst of His people. How wonderful!

But one day John the Baptist pointed to Jesus and said, "Behold the Lamb of God which taketh away the sin of the world" (John 1:29). Did you hear that? Not just the sin of an individual or a family or a nation—but the sin of the whole world! That includes you and me. Listen: "For God so loved the world, that he gave his only begotten Son, that whosoever believeth in him should not perish, but have everlasting life" (John 3:16).

—⚬—

TODAY HE'S WAITING TO SAVE YOU FROM YOUR SINS;
ALL YOU HAVE TO DO IS CALL ON HIM—
HE'LL DO THE REST!

# *Breaking Out*

**Jabez cried out to … God, "Bless me and enlarge my territory!
Let your hand be with me and keep me from harm so that
I will be free from pain." God granted his request.
(1 Chronicles 4:10, NIV)**

The name Jabez means, "a source of misery." But it was a label he refused to wear and a prophecy he refused to fulfill—and you should too. Just because someone called you "illegitimate" doesn't make it so. God says you were in His mind before you were in your mother's womb. (See Psalms 139:13-16.) So whom are you going to believe? Who are you going to quote?

Jabez refused to allow his beginnings to dictate his end! He refused to allow his family to keep him down or his borders to keep him in. He took his case to a higher court and got God's verdict. You can too! Listen to him: "Bless me! Enlarge my territory! Let your hand be on me! Keep me from harm! And God granted his request." That's a prayer God's just waiting to answer for you also.

It's time for you to break out; become a "boundary-crosser." Start believing God for more, instead of settling for less. Paul says, "Eye hath not seen, nor ear heard, neither have entered into the heart of man, the things which God hath prepared for them that love him. But God hath revealed them unto us by his Spirit" (1 Corinthians 2:9-10).

———

GOD HAS SOME THINGS HE WANTS TO SHOW YOU,
SO GET INTO HIS PRESENCE AND STAY THERE
UNTIL YOU SEE THEM.

# The Devil's Waterloo

**But now is Christ risen from the dead.
(1 Corinthians 15:20)**

During the Battle of Waterloo, signalmen flashed news of the battle from hilltop to hilltop, until it reached London. There they had erected a great bulletin board for the people to read. At a critical point in the battle, two words appeared on the bulletin board, "Wellington defeated." Suddenly a heavy fog settled down and nothing more could get through. Fear gripped people everywhere. Some locked themselves in their homes, refusing to come out. Others made plans to get out of the country. After a while, the fog lifted and another word came through from the signalmen—"Napoleon." Now the completed message read, "Wellington defeated Napoleon! Fear turned into celebration and the streets filled with people, rejoicing because the enemy had been destroyed.

On Good Friday, Satan's "bulletin board" read, "Jesus Christ defeated," and a terrible darkness settled over the world. But three days later, on Easter morning, the darkness lifted, and the word "Satan" had been added. Now the bulletin board read, "Jesus Christ defeated Satan!"

REJOICE TODAY, HE'S ALIVE, AND BECAUSE HE'S ALIVE—
YOU CAN FACE TOMORROW.

**I was glad when they said unto me, Let us go into the house of the LORD. (Psalm 122:1)**

Do you love God's house? You should! There you can find salvation for eternity and solutions for every day of the week. Where else could you go to find that? Jesus went regularly (see Luke 4:16); so did the disciples (see Acts 2:46). But nobody loved God's house like David did. Listen: "My soul yearns, even faints, for the courts of the Lord ... Better is one day in Your courts than a thousand elsewhere" (Psalms 84:2, 10, NIV).

Yale University just concluded a twenty-eight year survey which found people who go to church are happier, enjoy better health, and live longer than those who don't. Imagine that! The survey, involving 28,000 older church attendees, found that they have lower blood pressure, less depression, and stronger immunity to disease. Furthermore, the non-churchgoers had a shortened life span, roughly equal to that of smokers. An interviewer asked an eighty-year-old woman, running on a treadmill, what her secret was. She said, "When you walk with God you have purpose, so you live longer, and you have peace, so you live better."

Now, if you could find all that in a pill, how much would you pay for it? And would anybody have to force you to take it? Listen again: "I was glad when they said unto me, let us go into the house of the LORD" (Psalm 122:1).

—◊◊◊—

**MAKE SURE YOU'RE THERE THIS SUNDAY!**

# Too Far to Turn Back

**If they had been thinking of the country they had left, they would have had opportunity to return. Instead, they were longing for a better country. (Hebrews 11:15-16, NIV)**

Any pilot will tell you that there is a "point of no return." The runway has all been used up, and there's no turning back—it's fly or die! In Hebrews 11, you have a list of ordinary people who did extraordinary things for God, because they never lost the vision, and in the worst of times they refused to turn back. When you follow God, not everybody will go with you; your vision can be their nightmare. After all, if you succeed, how will they ever explain it? Often, the first place you'll feel this will be at home. Joseph did, and so did Jesus. That's a risk you must take. If failure is not a possibility, then success doesn't mean anything. When Abraham decided to follow God and leave home, he had no idea where that journey would take him; neither will you, when you leave your comfort zone.

It begins with God stirring up your nest. (See Deuteronomy 32:11.) Until your misery factor exceeds your fear factor, you won't move. If you're comfortable, don't expect God to give you any more—you don't need it. When you start taking some risks, however, you'll pray like you've never prayed before, and you'll stay in the Word until you get answers, because your life depends on it.

THE MOMENT YOU DECIDE, "I'VE COME TOO FAR WITH GOD TO TURN BACK," YOU'LL BEGIN TO SEE HIS HAND AT WORK IN YOUR LIFE. THE QUESTION IS— WHEN ARE YOU GOING TO START?

# Waiting on God

**But if we must keep trusting God for something ... it teaches us to wait patiently and confidently. (Romans 8:25, TLB)**

One of my closest friends, a gifted minister, is battling against a serious illness. He's preached "faith" and seen God heal others; I'm learning a lot watching him. It's easy to have all the answers when you don't have any of the problems. He told me recently, "I've discovered a level beyond faith—that's trust." "Faith is the substance of things hoped for" (Hebrews 11:1). Faith is usually about what we want, but trust is about what God wants—a relationship. The place that John had at the Last Supper, leaning upon Jesus' breast, is available to you. But—it comes at a price.

At one point, my friend got so discouraged that he just prayed for God to take him home. But his prayer was rooted in pride. His real concern was, "What will people say?" Then God directed him to this Scripture, "We are troubled on every side, yet not distressed; we are perplexed, but not in despair; persecuted, but not forsaken; cast down, but not destroyed; always bearing about in the body the dying of the Lord Jesus that the life also of Jesus might be made manifest in our body" (2 Corinthians 4:8-10).

My dear friend has now reached the place where the material things that faith can obtain have faded away, and intimacy with Jesus has become his goal. Now, he often wakens in the night with the words ringing in his mind, "His strength is perfect when your strength is gone. He'll carry you, when you can't carry on."

**IS GOD SAYING SOMETHING TO YOU THROUGH THIS?**

# Gideon's God

**The Lord is with thee, thou mighty man of valor.
(Judges 6:12)**

If you've been under attack lately, get ready; God is about to show you what the fight is all about! Nobody brings heavy equipment to build a chicken coop. The level of warfare over your life tells you what God is going to build in and through you. Sometimes the devil is more aware of who we are than we are! Gideon was hiding in a cave, yet God was calling him "a mighty man of valor."

Somewhere in your life, you should have a vision from God that, humanly speaking, makes absolutely no sense. Something you know could never happen without Him. When you get it, something inside you will say, "I will," while everything else is saying, "I can't." It will take you beyond your own competency and make you realize that it's "not by might nor by power, but by My Spirit saith the Lord" (Zechariah 4:6).

Quit asking people who they think you are! Ask God! When He defines you, what difference does their opinion make? He'll show you what you've got, and then He'll anoint it and use it. When Gideon told God, "I don't have what it takes!" God said, "You're just what I'm looking for!" God wants to raise up people He can trust with success. People who can remember what they were when He found them. Not celebrities, but channels who refuse to touch the glory. He doesn't need anything you know or anything you've polished or anything you're proud of; He uses "foolish things" (1 Corinthians 1:27).

SO YOU'RE QUALIFIED! ALL YOU NEED IS TO
HEAR FROM GOD, SO GET INTO HIS PRESENCE TODAY
AND LET HIM SPEAK TO YOU.

# Double-Minded?

**That man should not think he will receive anything from the
Lord; he is a double-minded man, unstable in all he does.
(James 1:7-8, NIV)**

When you're double-minded, it may be because you haven't
made up your mind to do God's will or accept His Word on
the matter. You say, "I want to hear from God." Hear what? Have you
done what He's already told you to do? If you haven't, why would He
say anything else to you? God won't issue you further instructions
until you obey the ones He's already given you. You don't get to
vote on whether you like what God is saying or whether it suits
you. John says, "Whatsoever we ask, we receive of him, because we
keep his commandments, and do those things that are pleasing in
his sight" (1 John 3:22).

You'll never be able to approach God with confidence while there's
an area of your life you're not willing to surrender. Have you been
praying about a relationship that's in trouble? What if God says to
you, "The problem is you—your attitudes, your actions, and your
words. I want you to go to them in humility and ask them to forgive
you, without saying a word about their part in it"—could you do
it? You could, but only if you were willing to die to self. Paul says,
"I have been crucified with Christ and I no longer live" (Galatians
2:20, NIV). It's time to go back to the Cross.

TODAY ASK GOD TO HELP YOU TO BE SINGLE-MINDED,
FOCUSED, AND DETERMINED TO DO ONE THING ONLY—
HIS WILL! IF YOU MEAN IT—REALLY MEAN IT—
HE'LL HELP YOU.

# Caring for the Hurting

**She opens her arms to the poor and extends her hands
to the needy. (Proverbs 31:20, NIV)**

During Christmas 1989, Carol Porter saw a group of children searching for food in a McDonald's trash can. First, it broke her heart, and then it moved her to do something about it. She says, "I saw Third World conditions a stone's throw from where I live." Instead of asking, "Why doesn't somebody do something?" she asked, "Why don't I?" So she founded Kid-Care Inc., a non-profit group of volunteers who deliver thousands of free meals to needy families. Every meal is prepared in her tiny Houston home. You should see it! She has extra stoves and refrigerators installed in what used to be her living room and den. She receives no public funding; most of her $500,000 budget comes from donations.

Carol says, "When people ask what's in it for me, I tell them the look on the faces of those children! We give them more than food; we give them hope and dignity. We tell them they're worth loving, and when they start believing that, they have a future." John says, "If anyone has material possessions and sees his brother in need but has no pity on him, how can the love of God be in him?" (1 John 3:17, NIV).

YOU'LL NEVER BE MORE LIKE JESUS THAN WHEN YOU
REACH OUT IN LOVE TO TOUCH SOMEONE
WHO IS HURTING.

# God Has a Strategy

**And he said unto him … I am the least in my father's house.
And the LORD said unto him, Surely I will be with thee.
(Judges 6:15-16)**

For every battle God has a strategy, so stop praying about the problem and start praying for the strategy. The vision will always be greater than the one who is called to fulfill it! David said, "Except the Lord build the house, they labor in vain that build it" (Psalms 127:1). Jesus is a carpenter; He knows the weight-load you can handle, the materials required and how it will all fit together in your life. Could it be that He's already been speaking in your head for months? Has He been revealing His plan to you, but you've been afraid to act on it? Stop collecting opinions and get alone with Him. Shut the door and wait in His presence until you receive a "clear word."

Remember, if God is giving you blueprints, then you're about to go under construction. That means getting "hammered" and "nailed." It's not enough to be called; you have to be equipped. But don't be discouraged, the God who landscaped the Earth has already designed every detail of your future. Just step out and follow Him. You're built for it; you're designed to handle the pressure.

**THE ONE WHO SAID TO GIDEON, "SURELY I WILL BE WITH THEE" IS SAYING THE SAME THING TO YOU TODAY.**

## Encouragement

**If you are afraid … listen to what they are saying … You will be greatly encouraged. (Judges 7:10-11, TLB)**

God sent Gideon down to the enemy camp to hear what they were saying to encourage him. When he arrived, a Midianite soldier was telling a friend about his dream: "A round loaf of barley bread came tumbling into the Midianite camp. It struck the tent with such force that the tent overturned and collapsed!" His friend responded, "This can be nothing other than the sword of Gideon. God has given the whole camp into his hands." When Gideon heard the dream and its interpretation, he worshiped God. (See Judges 7:13-15.)

When you need motivation, listen to what your enemies are saying about you! It's a class for your enrichment! You're making a difference; otherwise they wouldn't even notice you! Turn their opposition into inspiration. Use their attack to fuel your faith and rekindle your vision. Paul said, "Who shall separate us from the love of Christ? Shall trouble or hardship or persecution or famine or nakedness or danger or sword? No, in all these things we are more than conquerors" (Romans 8:35-37, NIV). You must be doing something right to warrant this much attention. Listen again: "With him is only the arm of flesh, but with us is the LORD our God to help us and fight our battles" (2 Chronicles 32:8, NIV).

**THE WORD FOR YOU TODAY IS—"YOU'RE COMING OUT VICTORIOUS!"**

# Skiing Blind

**You shalt guide me with thy counsel.**
**(Psalm 73:24)**

When he was skiing in Colorado, Peter Lord says he saw some people wearing red vests with the words BLIND SKIER emblazoned on them. He thought, "I've a hard enough time skiing with two good eyes; how can they ski successfully with none?" How did they do it? The answer is that they had a guide, whose instruction they totally trusted and obeyed. As the guide skied beside them, he'd tap his poles together to assure them that he was there. Then he'd say to them, "Go right! Turn left! Stop! Slow! Skier coming up on your right." What a picture!

The Christian life is like skiing downhill blind. We can't see even five seconds into the future. We can't see the struggles to come or all the other "skiers" who might run into us or over us. But Jesus said that the Holy Spirit will be our Guide through life (see John 16:13), so our only responsibility is to listen and obey. Before we can obey, we must listen. To listen, we must learn to know His voice. That means saying "no" to lesser things and getting alone with God. David cried, "Teach me thy way" (Psalm 27:11).

**PERHAPS THAT'S A PRAYER YOU NEED TO PRAY TODAY ALSO.**

# *Unlock Your Potential*

**Greater is He who is in you than he who is in the world.**
**(1 John 4:4, NASB)**

Michelangelo worked on forty-four statues and completed fourteen of them. The unfinished ones are in a museum in Italy—the unfulfilled potential of a great genius. What's sadder to see are people who could become masterpieces—if only they were developed. You say, "How do I discover and develop my gifts?" First, look up. Find somebody who's a little bigger and a little better than you are, then spend time with them. That's what Joshua did with Moses and Timothy did with Paul. It's still God's way.

Next, give up. You've got to be willing to give up what you are, in order to be what you can become. Abraham gave up his home to seek a better country. Moses gave up the riches of Egypt to identify with the people of God. Paul gave up the comfort of being a Pharisee to pay the price of being an apostle. Every achiever has a "give up" story. Nothing comes free.

Finally, show up. If you want to win the game, you must face your opponent! Jephthah said, "I have opened my mouth unto the LORD and I cannot go back" (Judges 11:35). In spite of his terrible family background and his personal problems, he became Israel's youngest judge and finished up with the heroes of faith in Hebrews 11.

**GOD CAN DO IT FOR YOU, TOO—IF YOU'LL LET HIM.**

# A Picture of Unity

**Each part ... helps the other parts, so that the whole body is healthy and growing. (Ephesians 4:16, TLB)**

Next time you're in the woods, try to imagine what's taking place under you feet. When the roots of tress come into contact with one another, they actually form an underground network. If one tree has access to water, another to nutrients, and a third to sunlight, then a sharing takes place that strengthens them all. What a picture! Paul says that in the Body of Christ, "Every joint supplieth" (Ephesians 4:16). Not just the prestigious joints—every joint! There's a degree of glory in you that is not in me. I need you to release the purpose of God that is within me.

In this age of personal kingdom-building, I wonder, is anyone interested in unity? Jesus prayed, "... that they may all be one; even as Thou, Father, art in Me, and I in Thee ... that the world may believe" (John 17:21, NASB). Jesus prayed that we would have the same unity with each other that He had with the Father. You say, "But how?" Listen: "That the love You have for Me may be in them" (John 17:26, NIV). Jesus prayed that we would have the same love for Him that the Father had. Think about that for a moment. That love would never do anything to hurt any part of His body. If God calls a man His son, start calling him your brother! Share with him the deposit God has placed within you and receive with humility what he has to give back.

WHEN THIS HAPPENS, THE CHURCH WILL BE A FORCE FOR GOD TO BE RECKONED WITH. DON'T YOU THINK SO?

# The Still, Small Voice

**But the LORD was not in the wind;… the LORD was not in the earthquake;… the LORD was not in the fire; and after the fire a still small voice. (1 Kings 19:11-12)**

Have you heard of the Reticular Activating System (RAS)? We all have it. It's the part of the brain that filters out what's not important and focuses on what is. Here's how it works. First, there's positive focusing. A mother is so in tune with her baby's needs that even when she's sleeping, she still hears and responds to the baby's voice. Next, negative filtering. My grandmother lived beside railroad tracks, yet she could sleep through the noise of the train and the shaking of the house. She filtered it out. Then, there's individual perception. If five people see an accident or look at the same scene, they all have completely different perceptions.

Here's the point. When you decide that hearing God is vital, your RAS starts putting God through to you whenever He speaks; like a mother, you hear and always respond immediately. When God spoke to Elijah, it was just a "still, small voice," but it changed everything. When hearing God becomes your priority, things will begin to change in your life, too. As you learn to listen and respond, you'll start to hear from Him more and more.

THAT'S NOT BECAUSE GOD IS SPEAKING MORE,
BUT BECAUSE YOU'VE DEVELOPED THE ABILITY
TO HEAR WHAT HE IS SAYING.

# Contentious People

**The servant of the Lord must not strive;
but be gentle unto all men. (2 Timothy 2:24)**

Contentious people are not born, they are raised. Mostly, they use the tools they were given; tools like accomplishment through intimidation. We call these people bullies! Paul says, "Mark them which cause divisions" (Romans 16:17). The law of agreement is one of the greatest laws of success in the Word of God. Jesus said, "If two of you shall agree on earth as touching anything that they shall ask, it shall be done for them of My Father which is in heaven" (Matthew 18:19). Contentious people ignore every point of agreement and focus only on the differences. If you let them, they'll rob you of the blessings that come only through agreement.

You ask, "How can I identify them?" First, when you confront a contentious person, their spirit will always surface. Solomon said, "Reprove not a scorner, lest he hate thee. Rebuke a wise man and he will love thee" (Proverbs 9:8). Note, also, contentious people usually discuss what's wrong with others—never what's wrong with themselves. Listen again: "He who, passing by, stops to meddle with strife that is none of his business" (Proverbs 26:17, AMP). These people have the right answers—they just have the wrong spirit. James says, "The wisdom that comes from heaven is first of all pure and full of quiet gentleness. Then it is peace loving and courteous. It allows discussion and is willing to yield to others" (James 3:17, TLB).

**IF YOU FIND YOURSELF CRANKY AND CONTENTIOUS
TODAY, YOU'LL KNOW IT'S TIME TO PRAY.**

## Overcoming

**I can do all things through Christ which strengtheneth me.
(Philippians 4:13)**

How many times did you fall down before you finally got up and learned to walk? Life is about overcoming! Twice, General Douglas MacArthur was refused admission to West Point, but the third time he was accepted and marched into the history books. Rudyard Kipling received a rejection letter from the San Francisco Examiner saying, "Sorry, Mr. Kipling, but you just don't know how to use the English language." After a lifetime of defeats, at 62, Winston Churchill became one of Britain's greatest prime ministers. Enrico Caruso's teacher told him he had "no voice at all and couldn't sing." Albert Einstein couldn't speak until he was four years old, and he couldn't read until he was seven. His teacher described him as "mentally slow, unsociable, and adrift forever in his foolish dreams."

By age 46, Beethoven was completely deaf, yet he wrote five of his greatest symphonies without hearing a note. Thomas Edison tried over 2,000 experiments before the light came on. A reporter asked how it felt to fail so often. Edison replied, "I never failed once. I invented the light bulb—it just happened to be a 2,000-step process." Remember Peter? And Jonah? And David?

**DON'T WORRY ABOUT FAILING; WORRY ABOUT WHAT YOU'RE GOING TO TELL GOD IF YOU DON'T EVEN TRY!**

# Stay Connected

**I am the vine, ye are the branches: He that abideth in me, and I in him, the same bringeth forth much fruit: for without me ye can do nothing. (John 15:5)**

Your potential for fruitful living is unlimited because of your source. Jesus said, "I am the true vine" (John 15:1). What a source! A little boy in Sunday school was learning Micah 6:8 (NIV): "What does the LORD require of you? ... to walk humbly with your God." Suddenly he looked at his teacher and said, "It wouldn't be hard to be humble if you were really walking with God now would it?" I think he saw it! When you truly begin to understand who you're walking with—God Himself—you start believing that you can do anything He calls you to do.

My sister, Ruth, tells of a mouse and an elephant crossing a bridge. When they got to the other side, the mouse said, "Boy, we really shook that bridge, didn't we?" You may smile, but when you walk with God, you become "Mighty Mouse," and there's absolutely nothing you can't accomplish.

Hudson Taylor, the great missionary to China, once said, "Many Christians estimate difficulty in the light of their own resources, thus they attempt very little, and they always fail. The real giants have all been weak men who did great things for God, because they reckoned on His power and His presence to be with them."

The key is found in the words, "Abide in Me" (John 15:4). Ten times in just six verses, Jesus tells us to "abide in Him." Stay connected in prayer; stay connected in the Word; stay connected in fellowship with His people.

TELL YOURSELF TODAY, "I'M IN PARTNERSHIP WITH GOD HIMSELF, SO MY POTENTIAL IS UNLIMITED."

# It's the Law

**Bear ye one another's burdens, and so fulfill the law of Christ.
(Galatians 6:2)**

Years ago at the Special Olympics in Seattle, nine physically and mentally challenged children took off running in the 100-yard dash. As they rounded a corner, one little boy fell and lay there crying. Suddenly, the other eight stopped and went back. A little girl with Down's syndrome bent over and kissed him and said, "There, that'll make it all better." They then lifted him up and all of them, with their arms linked together, walked toward the finish line. Thousands of people stood and cheered for the next several minutes.

The choice is yours. You can just keep on running, or you can stop to help that one who has fallen. Paul says, "Brethren, if a man be overtaken in a fault, ye which are spiritual restore such an one … Bear ye one another's burdens and so fulfill the law of Christ" (Galatians 6:1-2). This is not just a good idea, it's "the law" for those who follow Jesus.

In his book *Man's Search for Meaning*, Victor Frankel says, "We who lived in concentration camps can remember the men who walked through the huts comforting others, giving away their last piece of bread. They may have been few in number, but they offer sufficient proof that everything can be taken from a man but one thing, the last of human freedoms—to choose one's attitude in any given set of circumstances."

———

TODAY, WHEN YOU SEE SOMEONE WHO HAS FALLEN,
STOP AND HELP THEM BACK UP.

# A Cause

**And David said . . . "Is there not a cause?"**
**(1 Samuel 17:29)**

Little minds have great wishes; great minds have causes. Why else would David have gone out to fight Goliath with only a sling in his hand and faith in his heart? His God was being ridiculed, and his people were afraid to tackle their problem. When you're confronted with giant problems, what is it that makes you to rise up and say, "I won't accept that!" The answer is—having a cause you believe in, a cause worth living for. Not long ago, I read a survey of people who lived to be over 100 years old. I expected to read about healthy diets and strenuous exercise programs. But that wasn't it; the one thing all these centenarians had in common was—purpose. They had a compelling reason to live. Paul said, "For me to live is Christ" (Philippians 1:21). For Paul, that was it! To do His will, to exalt His name, and to spread His Kingdom to the four corners of the Earth. Now there's a cause to live for!

Too many of us are like the man who said, "No matter what I'm working on, I'd rather be doing something else." Are you like that, or have you found a purpose great enough to hold you steady in the storm, strong enough to keep you going when everything is against you? Behind every great accomplishment, there's a purpose—not a wish!

TODAY, ASK GOD TO REVEAL TO YOU HIS HIGHEST
PURPOSE FOR YOUR LIFE. UNTIL YOU FIND IT,
YOU HAVEN'T LIVED; UNTIL YOU FULFILL IT,
YOU'RE NOT READY TO DIE!

# Don't Frame It!

**Every branch in me that ... beareth fruit, he purgeth it, that it may bring forth more fruit. (John 15:2)**

God doesn't look at you through the eyes of an observer. He sees you through the eyes of an investor. He's looking for fruit, and He'll "cut off" anything that stands in its way. He knows that if He doesn't cut back the "dead wood," all our resources will go toward producing wood instead of fruit.

You may bring to your office and put in a frame, a motto as fine as its print;

But if you're dishonest while playing the game, that motto won't make you a saint.

Put up lots of placards and cover your wall, but here is a word I announce:

It isn't the motto that hangs on the wall; it's the motto you live that counts.

If the motto says, "Smile" and you carry a frown, "Do it now" and you linger and wait;

If the motto says "Help" and you trample men down,

If the motto says "Love" and you hate,

You'll stand before God and be judged for your deeds,

You'll know as the evidence mounts,

It wasn't the motto you hung on your wall, but the motto you lived that counts.

THE DIFFERENCE BETWEEN GOD AND YOU IS THAT HE KNOWS WHAT NEEDS TO BE PRUNED FROM YOUR LIFE— YOU DON'T.

# The Ice Cream Man

**When you are tempted, he will also provide a way out so that you can stand up under it. (1 Corinthians 10:13, NIV)**

Sally was desperately trying to save all her pennies, so she could buy a doll's carriage. She collected empty soda bottles and did jobs around the house—anything to make money. One night, her mom overheard her praying, "O Lord, please help me to save all my money for that doll's carriage. That doll is so beautiful, and I know it would be very happy with me. If I get it, I promise I'll let my friends play with it, too." Sally's mom smiled approvingly, but just when she thought the prayer was over, Sally added one more line, "… and please, God, don't let the ice cream man come down our street this week!"

As sure as Satan is called "the tempter," you can expect him to come down your street this week. For Sally, it was the ice cream man, for David, it was Bathsheba, and for Demas, Paul's traveling companion, it was the lure of the world that caused him to turn his back on God. (See 2 Timothy 4:10.) But the good news is that God will provide a way out. Even if you have failed, remember that failure is not final. Don't let one of those failed attempts go to waste. Turn them into learning experiences today and let them drive you into the arms of Jesus. The Bible says, "He himself was tempted" (Hebrews 2:18, NASB).

THAT'S WHY HE'S WILLING AND ABLE TO HELP YOU, IF YOU'LL JUST REACH FOR HIM TODAY.

# Learning to Love

**Above all, love each other deeply, because love covers over a multitude of sins. (1 Peter 4:8, NIV)**

Someone has said, "Nobody cares how much you know, until they first know how much you care." Imagine being weighed on those scales! Have you ever noticed that when others are set in their ways, they're obstinate; but when you are, you're just being firm? When they don't like someone, they're prejudiced; but when you don't, it's good judgment? When they treat someone extra well, they're buttering them up; but when you do, you're just being thoughtful? When they take time to do things well, they're slow or lazy; but when you do, you're meticulous? When they find fault and pick flaws in things, they're critical; but when you do, you're perceptive? When they're gentle or mild-mannered, they're weak; but when you are, you're gracious? When they dress well, they're extravagant; when you do, you're tasteful? When they say what they think, they're spiteful; when you do, you're just being honest? When they take risks, they're reckless; but when you do, you're just being brave?

Today, when I read the words, "Above all, love each other deeply, because love covers a multitude of sins," I prayed, "God, help me to grow in that kind of love and show it wherever I go."

—m—

**HOW ABOUT YOU?**

# Crickets

**I was asleep, but my heart was awake. A voice! My beloved was knocking; open to me. (Song of Solomon 5:2)**

A friend who was visiting Peter Lord's home told him he has discovered eighteen different kinds of crickets in his garden. Peter had lived there for years and never heard one! The difference was this man was a professor of entomology and had learned to distinguish over 200 different types of cricket calls with his natural ear. Imagine learning to listen to crickets! Looking back, Peter wrote, "I suddenly understood that a person *learns* to hear and that there were many sounds I was not hearing." Imagine what you've been missing all these years because you haven't learned how to hear God for yourself. Listen: "Your ears will hear a voice behind you saying, 'This is the way, walk in it'" (Isaiah 30:21, NIV).

Thank God for books, broadcasts, services, even good counselors, but the very gifts God speaks to you through can weaken your desire to hear from God for yourself. The children of Israel said to Moses, "You hear from God for us." The problem is that when you only hear through secondary sources, it's easier not to make any real commitment to obey what you've heard. But when you hear from God for yourself, you must make a clear-cut decision.

THAT'S WHY YOU NEED TO GET INTO GOD'S PRESENCE AND ASK HIM TO GIVE YOU EARS THAT HEAR. NOTHING WILL CHANGE IN YOUR LIFE UNTIL YOU DO.

# Shipwreck

**Thou shalt guide me. (Psalm 73:24)**

If you want to avoid shipwreck, study Acts 27 carefully. First, they were dissatisfied with where they were. Listen: "Since the harbor was unsuitable ... the majority decided that we should sail on" (Acts 27:12, NIV). God doesn't guide us by "dissatisfaction" or by "opinion polls," He guides us by His Spirit. (See Romans 8:14.) When things get difficult, you're called to overcome them, not try to escape them. Next, they were impatient to get where they were going. Sound familiar? I don't know of a single Scripture that tells us to hurry up or we'll miss God. Israel learned that when the cloud moves, you move. But, when the cloud stops, stay where you are and wait on God!

Then they failed to heed the Word. Listen: "The centurion was more persuaded by the pilot ... than ... by Paul" (Acts 27:11, NASB). Be careful; if you look long enough, you'll find someone whose opinion confirms what *you* want to do. That's a dangerous place to be. Finally, they looked to the circumstances, instead of God, to guide them. (See Acts 27:13.) The idea that circumstances will always line up favorably with God's guidance is not scriptural. God often leads through the wilderness, and He'll never lead you anywhere that doesn't require His provision and protection. If you can get there without God—He didn't send you.

TODAY GET INTO HIS PRESENCE AND ASK HIM TO SHOW YOU THE RIGHT WAY. REFUSE TO LIVE EVEN ONE DAY WITHOUT HIS GUIDANCE.

# Out of the Storm

**In all these things we are more than conquerors through him.
(Romans 8:37)**

First, prepare for the storm before you get into it! The wise man built his house upon the rock, because he believed in storms. (See Matthew 7:24.) Where did we ever get the idea that Christians shouldn't have problems? God is more interested in your character than He is in your comfort. Listen: "To you it has been granted ... to suffer for His sake" (Philippians 1:29, NASB). This is warfare—not welfare!

Next, stay calm! Panic kills more pilots than bad weather, because it destroys your ability to function properly. In the storm, Jesus said to His disciples, "It is I; be not afraid" (Mark 6:50). Get your eyes on Jesus and keep them there; otherwise, your fear will hurt you more than your circumstances.

Finally, never abandon your purpose! They threw cargo—the purpose for their journey—overboard! Don't do it! Never let go of the purpose for which God has called you, for it will sustain you in the storm. Paul said, "We know that all things work together for good ... to them who are called according to his purpose" (Romans 8:28).

BE STRONG TODAY; THE STORM DOESN'T CONTROL YOUR DESTINY; GOD DOES! HE'S STILL IN CHARGE.

# Want It? Give It!

**Be merciful, just as your Father is merciful.**
**(Luke 6:36, NIV)**

Hemingway tells a wonderful story of a father and his teenage son who lived in Spain. Their relationship fell apart, and the son ran away from home. After some years, the father began a long journey in search of the lost and rebellious son, finally putting an advertisement in the Madrid newspaper as a last resort. His son's name was Paco, (a very common name in Spain). It simply read, "Dear Paco, meet me in front of the Madrid newspaper office tomorrow at noon. All is forgiven. I love you." The next day at noon in front of the newspaper office there were 800 Pacos all seeking forgiveness!

Who do you need to forgive today? Show me a man who truly walks with God, and I'll show you a man who's merciful and forgiving. Someone sent me this humorous Irish prayer—it's a prayer you shouldn't pray: "May those who love us, love us; and those who don't love us, may God turn their hearts; and if He doesn't turn their hearts, may He turn their ankles, so that we'll know them by their limping." When you don't forgive, you hurt yourself more than anyone else. You aren't built to carry the stress that goes with bearing a grudge. If you think you'll ever need mercy, show it, for Jesus said, "Blessed are the merciful, for they will be shown mercy" (Matthew 5:17, NIV).

**IF GOD IS DEALING WITH YOU ABOUT THIS, DON'T PUT IT OFF ANY LONGER.**

# Slow Down and Live

**This is the day which the LORD hath made.
(Psalms 118:24)**

In his great book, *Secrets of the Journey*, Dr. Mike Murdock says, "Today should be savored, not gulped down. If you don't learn how to stop and enjoy today, you'll never enjoy one day of the future either." James says, "What is your life? You are a mist that appears for a little while and then vanishes" (James 4:14, NIV). I'm told that when one of England's ancient queens was dying, she offered half of her kingdom to the royal physicians if they could give her six more months to live. They couldn't.

This morning God deposited 1,440 minutes into your account (the number in one day). You can invest them, but you can't save them. Take a look at yesterday's ledger; it's a prophecy of your future, unless you rise up and take control of your time. Have you any idea how much time you've spent watching TV lately? Relaxing is one thing, vegetating is another. Start your day the way you intend to continue it—prayerfully! David said, "In the morning, I lay my requests before you and wait in expectation" (Psalms 5:3, NIV). After you've talked to God, your whole outlook for the day will change. You have the same amount of time David did, so just set some priorities. If you don't like what you're getting—change what you're doing!

**TAKE SOME TIME TODAY AND ASK GOD TO HELP YOU
ENJOY EVERY MINUTE OF THIS DAY!**

# 3 Questions for You

**The LORD gave him success in everything he did.
(Genesis 39:3, NIV)**

Ask yourself these three questions:

1. Am I content with things the way they are in my life? John Maxwell says, "The only one who can stop you from becoming the person God intended you to be—is you." He'll never ask you to be what He won't enable you to become.

2. Am I afraid of success? Afraid of the commitment required? Leadership is lonely; perhaps you'd rather be with the crowd. Have you been knocked down, and now you're afraid to get up and try again? When Edison was asked why he was successful, he replied, "I start where other men leave off!" When World Heavyweight Champion Jim Corbett was asked what it took to be a champion, he said, "Just fight one more round." Paul said, "We get knocked down, but we get up again and keep going" (2 Corinthians 4:9, TLB).

3. Do I believe people can't be successful and spiritual at the same time? Somehow we've equated humility with poverty and assumed that successful people just couldn't be humble. Listen: "As long as he sought the LORD, God made him to prosper" (2 Chronicles 26:5). When successful people speak, other people listen—look at Joseph and Daniel! We have a message that the world is dying to hear, but if we don't have the money, the means, and the motivation to tell them, who will?

**IF YOU'VE BEEN SETTLING FOR LESS,
ASK GOD FOR A NEW FOCUS, THEN START AIMING HIGH!**

# Stretch or Shrink

**Straining toward what is ahead, I press on toward
the goal to win the prize. (Philippians 3:13-14, NIV)**

All rubber bands work on the same principle: They must be stretched to be effective! Every person who has ever achieved anything for God has learned to stretch. There are no exceptions. One of the most common mistakes is thinking that success is due to some genius or some magic something or other that you don't possess. Get rid of that thinking! Success comes only when you stretch to meet the challenge; failure comes when you shrink back from it. Stretching will make you vulnerable. When a rubber band is taut, it's much easier to break. Is that why you're afraid to stretch? Have you tried it before and been hurt? You'll always have critics, for Jesus said, "The servant is not greater than his Lord" (John 15:20).

Dr. Jonas Salk, who developed the polio vaccine, was attacked continually for his pioneering work in this field. He found that criticism came in three stages. First, they'll tell you, "It won't work!" Then, when you begin to succeed, they'll say, "What you're doing really isn't that important!" Finally, after they see that it's important, they'll say, "We knew you'd do it all along!" Don't look at the way things could be and ask, "Why not?" Through the power of God's Spirit you can make a difference.

**JUST MAKE YOURSELF AVAILABLE TO GOD AND
LET HIM SHOW YOU WHAT HE CAN DO WITH YOUR LIFE.**

# Forgive and Forget

**Bear with each other and forgive whatever grievances you may have against one another. Forgive as the Lord forgave you.
(Colossians 3:13, NIV)**

Jimmy drank too much at the party and really embarrassed his wife, Lisa. He did it all—flirting with every woman in the room, putting a lampshade on his head and wearing it as a hat, then passing out on the floor. Finally, some friends took him home and put him to bed. The next morning he felt humiliated and asked his wife to forgive him. She promised to "forgive and forget" the whole thing. But, as the months went by, she kept bringing it up, till one day in discouragement he said to her, "I thought you were going to forgive and forget." She said, "I have, I just didn't want you to forget that I have forgiven and forgotten." Do you forgive like that?

Paul said, "Forgive as the Lord forgave you." Think carefully about those words. Isaiah says, "He will not remember your sins" (Isaiah 43:25, NASB). He wipes the slate clean and lets you start over again. Sometimes forgiveness requires a healing process, but until you make the decision to forgive, that process can't even start. Forgiveness (God's kind) will turn your heart away from what *was* to what *can be*. The one who said, "I make all things new" (Revelation 21:5) will help you to close the door on the past and move on. If you knew you only had a short time to live, how important would this be?

—✦—

**YOU KNOW THE ANSWER—
SO START DOING SOMETHING ABOUT IT!**

# The Will of God

**If you keep My commandments, you will abide in My love.
(John 15:10, NASB)**

Gladys Aylward was just a simple woman who did what she believed God called her to do. A movie, *The Inn of the Sixth Happiness,* was produced showing what was accomplished through her. In 1920, she sailed to China, where she opened a home for orphaned children who'd been left to starve or wander the streets until the government placed them in warehouses. She'd read the words, "If you spend yourselves in behalf of the hungry and satisfy the needs of the oppressed, then your light will rise in the darkness, and your night will become like the noonday. The Lord will guide you always; He will satisfy your needs" (Isaiah 58:10-11, NIV).

When the Japanese invaded China, Gladys was forced to flee, and she ended up on the island of Formosa with over 100 children to care for. In the face of extreme difficulty and danger, she devoted her life, becoming a mother to each of them. Years later, when she was honored, she explained her amazing work like this: "I did not choose this. I was led into it by God. I'm not really more interested in children than I am in other people. But God gave me to understand that this is what He wanted me to do—so I did it!"

**HAVE YOU DISCOVERED YET WHAT GOD HAS CALLED YOU TO DO? ARE YOU DOING IT?**

# Plan Ahead

**We should make plans—counting on God to direct us.
(Proverbs 16:9, TLB)**

Someone asked the captain of the Queen Mary how long it would take to bring his ship to a stop. He replied, "A little over a mile." Then he added, "A good captain thinks at least a mile ahead." Listen to these verses from the Living Bible: "A sensible man watches for problems ahead and prepares to meet them. The simpleton never looks and suffers the consequences" (Proverbs 27:12). "Any enterprise is built by wise planning, becomes strong through common sense, and profits wonderfully by keeping abreast of the facts" (Proverbs 24:2-4). Plan ahead, and if God's your partner—make your plans big!

And be sure to stay with it! Paul says, "Be steadfast, immoveable, always abounding in the work of the Lord, knowing that your toil is not in vain" (1 Corinthians 15:58, NASB). Napoleon Hill studied 500 of the most successful people in the world and concluded that they all had one thing in common—they were persistent. When Winston Churchill went back to his old school to speak, the audience anticipated a great speech from the prime minister. But he stood before them and said just six words: "Never, never, never, never give up!" That was it; the speech was over, and it's probably the speech for which he is most remembered.

WHATEVER YOU'RE GOING THROUGH TODAY, STAND FIRM
ON YOUR COMMITMENT, STAY ON THE COURSE, TRUST
GOD, AND HE WILL CAUSE YOU TO TRIUMPH!

# Enjoy Today!

**Morning by morning, [He] wakens my ear to listen like one being taught. (Isaiah 50:4, NIV)**

"A lot of us have false notions about happiness," John Maxwell says. Some of us suffer from *destination disease*. We think that when we arrive at a certain point, we'll be happy—when we retire, take that trip, or reach that goal. Your happiest moments are along the way, not at the end of the trip. Isaiah says, "Morning by morning [He] wakens my ear to listen like one being taught" (Isaiah 50:4, NIV). Isaiah says that God has things to teach you every day!

Still others suffer from yesterday blues. A lady wrote to a newspaper editor and said, "Your newspaper's not as good as it used to be." He wrote back, "It never has been!" We like to crown the past with a halo and remember only the good times. As the saying goes, "If *ifs* and *buts* were candies and nuts, we'd all have a merry Christmas." Be glad where you are! David said, "This is the day the LORD hath made, let us rejoice and be glad in it" (Psalm 118:24, NIV).

**NOW, THAT'S LIVING!**

# *Whatever It Takes*

**Let us run with perseverance the race marked out
for us. (Hebrews 12:1, NIV)**

Listen to these verses: "So we continued the work with half the men holding spears, from the first light of dawn till the stars came out" (Nehemiah 4:21, NIV). That's hard work, and that's what it took for Nehemiah to build the wall and win the war. Listen to this: "Try to excel in gifts that build up the church" (1Corinthians 14:12, NIV). That's excellence, and that's what it's going to take to convince the world that we have what they need.

It's time for Christians to take some risks! When Charles Lindbergh was flying over Newfoundland, he recalls looking down for places to land in case of problems. But when he reached the coast, he said, "In that moment, I realized that there was no turning back." We've all got to reach that place! Lindbergh did it because he had a vision of being the first man to fly the Atlantic. What's your vision? Sure, you'll make mistakes; that's part of learning and growing. But God's more interested in your development than He is in your mistakes. Stop selling yourself short! Forty-eight years ago Johnny Weismuller was the greatest swimmer in the world; he held fifty world records. Today, 13-year-old girls break his record every time they go into the pool. Don't limit your potential—you can do better!

LET GOD SHOW YOU—LET GOD EQUIP YOU, AND
LET GOD USE YOU.

# Contentious People

**For lack of wood the fire goes out, and where there is no whisperer, contention ceases. (Proverbs 26:20, AMP)**

Your attitude is a personal decision. Your mood is a choice. A person with a "contentious spirit" is often the door through which Satan comes to do his work. James says, "Where envying and strife is, there is confusion and every evil work" (James 3:16). This spirit will submit to no one. John had to deal with it. Listen: "I wrote unto the church; but Diotrephes, who loveth to have the preeminence among them, receiveth us not" (3 John 9). Contention is usually about *control*. Most problems in the church come down to one question—who's in charge? A contentious person can never lead, because he has never learned to follow. A true leader has a "servant spirit."

And when you meet somebody who's constantly finding fault, just say to them, "God will turn this for our good! I am so thankful for what He is about to do! Isn't He wonderful?" Go ahead, do it! It will be like throwing cold water on a destructive fire. When there's no demand, the suppliers go out of business. Paul says, "Finally brothers, whatever is true, whatever is noble, whatever is right, whatever is pure, whatever is lovely, whatever is admirable; if anything is excellent or praiseworthy; think about such things" (Philippians 4:8, NIV).

A CONTENTIOUS SPIRIT IS LIKE A MALIGNANT CELL; IF LEFT UNCHECKED, IT CAN DESTROY YOU.

# Responding to God

**Blessed is the man who listens to me.**
**(Proverbs 8:34, NIV)**

When you were growing up, did you wait until your parents said something the third of fourth time? Be warned; if God has to raise His voice to you and speak repeatedly, you could be heading for trouble. God isn't a weak, indulgent parent. With Him, obedience is everything. David said, "When thou saidst, Seek ye my face; my heart said unto thee, Thy face, LORD, will I seek" (Psalm 27:8). That's the response He is after. Jesus said, "If any man is willing to do His will, he shall know" (John 7:17, NASB). What God really wants to know is—are you willing? If you are, He can teach you the rest. There's grace for the immature. Jesus said His sheep, not His lambs, know His voice. (See John 10:4.) Baby sheep just follow the adult sheep until their senses have been trained. Don't be afraid of missing God. If your heart is willing but your spiritual ears are not yet developed, He'll walk with you and work with you until you get there.

For 40 years, Samuel heard from God and guided the nation. When he first started, it took time for him to learn to know God's voice. You say, "How will I know His voice? Listen: "The wisdom [leading] that is from above is ... peaceable" (James 3:17, author's insertion). No matter what's going on around you, when God speaks, you'll experience a peace within you that will hold steady and bring you through victoriously.

—m—

**TODAY, HE WANTS TO TALK TO YOU—**
**TAKE TIME TO LISTEN.**

# The Power of Vision

**For whoever wants to save his life will lose it,
but whoever loses his life for me will save it.
(Luke 9:24, NIV)**

The happiest people in the world are those who are living out their dreams. If you want to know real happiness, get a dream that's bigger than you, then lose yourself in it! Go ahead, try it—it'll give you the strength and motivation to rise above the problems you're facing. Isn't there something better than just settling for average? Average doesn't look so good when you realize it's just the worst of the best and the best of the worst. Talk to people and you'll discover that their number-one problem is they've lost their dreams, their goals, and their purpose.

Joel 2:28 says, "Your old men shall dream dreams." Look at the great men and women who continued to pursue their dreams into old age. Moses was 80 when he started to lead Israel out of captivity. Colonel Sanders was 70 when he developed Kentucky Fried Chicken, and he donated much of his profits to the work of God. John Wesley was still traveling on horseback and preaching at 88. When he turned 90, he complained that he could preach only twice a day and had an inclination to sleep until five in the morning! Paul says, "But life is worth nothing unless I use it for doing the work assigned me by the Lord Jesus" (Acts 20:24, TLB).

**LOSE YOURSELF IN THE WILL OF GOD,
BUT NEVER LOSE YOUR DREAM.**

# Dogged and Determined

**As you know, we consider blessed those who have persevered.
(James 5:11, NIV)**

One day a woman who was dying got out of bed and pushed her way through a crowd until she reached Jesus. The moment she touched Him, she was healed. It was faith that healed her, but it was vision that brought her to Jesus. (See Luke 8:43.) When Caleb was 85, he went to Moses and said, "Give me this mountain." For 40 years he had held onto his dream and wouldn't let go. The Bible says, "Then Joshua blessed Caleb son of Jephunneh and gave him Hebron as his inheritance … because he followed the LORD, the God of Israel, wholeheartedly" (Joshua 14:13-14, NIV). Note the word "wholeheartedly." The poorest person in the world is not the person who doesn't have a penny; it's the person who doesn't have a vision. Once you've had a glimpse of what God can make of you, you'll never be satisfied to remain the same.

If you want a thing badly enough to go out and fight for it, to work day and night for it, to give up your time and sleep for it; if all that you dream and scheme is about it; if life seems useless and worthless without it; if you'd gladly sweat for it, fret for it, and plan for it; if you lose all your terror of the opposition for it; if you're willing simply to go after the thing you want with all your capacity and tenacity, faith, hope, confidence, and stern personality; if neither cold, famine, poverty, sickness, nor pain of body and mind can keep you from the thing you want …

IF DOGGED AND DETERMINED YOU BESIEGE AND
BESET IT; WITH THE HELP OF GOD—YOU'LL GET IT!

# Send for the Foreman

**He will call upon Me, and I will answer him.**
**(Psalm 91:15, NIV)**

My mother once worked as a weaver in west Belfast. It was hard work. A big sign overhead read, "If the threads get tangled, call for the foreman!" One day a new worker got her threads all tangled up. The more she tried, the worse it got. Finally, in despair, she sent for the foreman. He said, "Why didn't you send for me earlier?" Defensively she replied, "I was doing my best." He told her, "No, your best would have been calling for me!"

The best thing you can do today is call on God! Prayer shouldn't be your last resort; it should be your first. No matter what you are facing today—Pray! Pray! Pray! God longs to be your helper, but He comes by invitation only. God can work without prayer, but He has chosen to operate through it.

Leonard Ravenhill wrote, "One might estimate the weight of the world, tell the size of the Celestial City, count the stars of heaven, measure the speed of lightning, and tell the time of the rising and setting of the sun—but nobody can estimate the power of prayer. It's as vast as God—because He's behind it and it's as good as God—because He's committed himself to answering it." Jesus said, "Whatever you ask for in prayer, believe that you have received it, and it will be yours" (Mark 11:24, NIV).

**CHILD OF GOD, HAVE YOU PRAYED TODAY?**

**If we are faithless, He will remain faithful.**
**(2 Timothy 2:13, NIV)**

After dating Bill for several months, Lila was head over heels in love and wanted to marry him. The only thing that bothered her was his drinking. He's use any excuse: "I had a rough day at work!" "It's miserable outside." Despite her pastor's warnings, she went ahead and married him. Within two years, it was a living hell. By now, he was drinking every night and becoming physically abusive. Heartbroken, Lila filed for divorce, and they went their separate ways. She'd ignored all the warnings and made the biggest mistake of her life. Any time a child of God marries a child of the devil, they're going to have trouble with their father-in-law! (See Amos 3:3.)

Lila told her pastor, "I thought I knew what was best for me." Sound familiar? We all think that sometimes. We forget that God knows us better than we know ourselves. But the good news is that He never gives up on us. Listen: "I have loved you with an everlasting love; I have drawn you with loving-kindness. I will build you up again" (Jeremiah 31:3-4, NIV). Just come to Him today, admitting your mistakes. He'll forgive you.

---

RECOVERING FROM THE BAD CHOICES YOU'VE MADE CAN BE HEART-WRENCHING, BUT GOD IS ALWAYS READY TO RESTORE YOU, THEN GIVE YOU A NEW START.

**He gives them to each one, just as He determines.
(1 Corinthians 12:11, NIV)**

A plain bar of iron valued at just $5 can be turned into a pair of horseshoes worth $50 or a carton of sewing needles worth $5,000 or a shipment of balance springs for fine Swiss watches worth $500,000. The raw material is not what's important—what you do with it is!

In Matthew 25, Jesus gave us the Parable of the Talents. He said that the master gave one steward five talents, another two talents, and another one talent. The five-talent man turned his into ten talents. The two-talent man turned his into four. But the one-talent man was afraid of failing, so he buried his talent. (See Matthew 25:25.) He didn't realize that the greatest failure of all is failing to try, and for that he was severely judged!

Child of God, there will be an audit, and you'll be at it! Things that seem so important to you now will look insignificant then. Paul says, "There is going to come a time of testing ... to see what kind of material each builder has used. Everyone's work will be put through the fire so that all can see whether or not it keeps its value and what was really accomplished" (1 Corinthians 3:13, TLB).

—ɷ—

GET YOUR EYES OFF THE TEMPORAL AND ONTO THE
ETERNAL, FOR, "HEAVEN AND EARTH WILL SOON PASS
AWAY AND ONLY WHAT'S DONE FOR CHRIST WILL LAST."

# Be Encouraged

**Have I not commanded you, "Be strong, vigorous, and very courageous. Be not afraid, neither be dismayed, for the LORD your God is with you." (Joshua 1:9, AMP)**

Napoleon called Marshall Ney the bravest man he'd ever known. Yet, one morning before a battle, the Marshall's knees trembled so badly that he had difficulty mounting his horse. When he was finally in the saddle, he shouted down at his limbs, "Shake away, knees. You would shake worse, if you knew where I was taking you!"

Courage is not the absence of fear; it's the conquest of it! It's Gideon with 300 soldiers going to fight an army of Midianites as big as the ocean, because God said, "Surely I will be with thee." (See Judges 6:16.) It's Peter stepping out of the boat in the middle of a storm to walk on the water. It's doing what you've never done before, in order to go with God where you've never been before to receive from Him what you've never had before. It's choosing to take the road less traveled—the hard path—because it's the right path.

Do you need strength today? Are you facing a difficult situation? You're not alone today! Jesus said, "I will ask the Father and He will give you another Comforter (Counselor, Helper, Intercessor, Advocate, Strengthener, and Standby) that He may remain with you forever" (John 14:16, AMP).

---

THAT'S THE POWER YOU HAVE LIVING WITHIN YOU
RIGHT NOW. USE IT.

# What Moves You?

**When he saw the multitudes, he was moved with compassion.
(Matthew 9:36)**

Martha Smith has been working with HIV-infected children since 1987. In her first few months, five of her tiny victims died. Heartache and despair almost overwhelmed her, but she made a commitment to stick with it for a few more months. Those few months turned into eleven years and she's still there. Today, she has a clinic and a staff who care for hundreds of families with AIDS children. They go into homes and teach families how to prevent infection. They try to help parents face the future and plan for it. They take the children on trips to the zoo, the park, even to summer camps. One baby, who wasn't expected to see her first birthday, recently celebrated her twelfth. It's been long-term successes like these that give her an indestructible sense of hope and keep her going. She has a strong faith that one day, with God's help, a cure will be found.

When I read this story, I thought of Matthew 9:36. How long has it been since you've been moved by the needs of others? Your life is like a coin; you can spend it any way you want—but you can spend it only once.

—⚬—

**HOW ARE YOU GOING TO SPEND YOURS?**

# Don't Cut People Out

**Love forgets mistakes; nagging about them parts the best of friends. (Proverbs 17:9, TLB)**

In her book *Learning to Forgive*, Doris Donnelly writes, "Some years ago I met a family very proficient in the use of scissors. They constantly scrutinized their friends to see if they measured up to the family's standards and expectations. One slip ... and you were 'out.' It could be for almost any reason—a look, a word, an opinion, or failing to respond properly. 'Snip, snip,' they'd just cut you out of their life."

Eventually, they cut Doris out of their lives, too. She never knew why for sure, but she knew that once you'd been cut out there was no hope of ever being sewn back in. Sadly, last year the mother died. The father and his daughters, expecting large crowds for the funeral, called on assistance from the local police to handle traffic; telegrams were sent; phone calls were made; local motels were alerted. In the end, only the father, his daughters, their husbands, and a grandchild or two attended the services.

Cutting people out of your life because they're not perfect is a prescription for loneliness. Keep doing it, and who will you have left? Jesus said, "My command is this: Love each other as I have loved you" (John 15:2).

IS THERE SOMEONE YOU NEED TO FORGIVE TODAY
AND BRING BACK INTO YOUR LIFE?

# Everything We Need

**His divine power has given us everything we need.
(2 Peter 1:3, NIV)**

Have you heard the story of the man who was honored as the town's leading citizen? At a banquet in his honor, he said, "Friends, I walked into this town thirty years ago on a dirt road with only a suit on my back and all my earthly possessions in a little brown bag. Today, I'm chairman of the bank; I own hotels, apartment buildings, and companies with branches in thirty-nine different cities. Yes, this town has been good to me." After the banquet someone asked him, "Could you tell me what was in that little brown bag?" He said, "I think it was about half a million dollars in cash and $900,000 in government bonds."

You may smile, but until you discover what's in your "little brown bag," you'll never fulfill your destiny. Peter said, "God has given us everything we need." Look what you've got going for you today—the indwelling power of the Holy Spirit. John says, "His anointing teaches you about all things" (1 John 2:27, NIV). With "His anointing," you should excel in whatever you do. Start looking at what He's given you to work with: His name, which is His "power of attorney"; His Word, which "shall not return unto Me void" (Isaiah 55:11); His blood, "which gives you access into His presence day and night."

—m—

**WHAT MORE COULD YOU ASK FOR?
WHAT MORE DO YOU NEED?**

# Pleasant Words

**Pleasant words are ... sweet to the soul and
healing to the bones. (Proverbs 16:24, NIV)**

It takes as much energy to say something positive as it does to say something negative—in fact, less. Doctors now say that when we speak positive words our bodies relax, the blood flow actually increases to our brain, and a well-oxygenated brain will always help you handle things better. Positive words will build good relationships and create an atmosphere in your home that's conducive of rest, relaxation, and sleep—and that's necessary for good health.

Contrary to what you may have heard, negative words don't release pressure. They keep your body in a state of tension, the root cause of all sorts of sickness from ulcers to heart attacks. Solomon says, "Pleasant words bring healing" (Proverbs 16:24). If you want to improve your health, change what you say and what you listen to.

A survey conducted by an insurance company recently found that husbands who kiss their wives every morning live an average of five years longer; they're involved in fewer automobile accidents, and they're sick only half as much as those who don't; and they earn 30% more money! Maybe you don't need a new prescription or a visit to your counselor after all. Maybe you just need a kiss, a hug, and the right words.

—m—

WHAT DO YOU THINK?

# Rahab and Sarah

**Through faith also Sarah herself received strength to conceive.
… By faith the harlot Rahab perished not.
(Hebrews 11:11, 31)**

Hebrews eleven is faith's "Hall of Fame." In it you'll find Sarah, Abraham's wife, and Rahab the prostitute. Now, I understand Sarah being there, but how in the world did Rahab get there? Because God saw in Rahab what He also saw in Sarah—faith, which is why He saved her. God's not looking at your present position or your past problems; He's looking at your faith. No matter how many mistakes you've made, if you'll just believe God, you can get to live next door to Sarah. Not only you, but He'll save your entire house, too. That's right! He saved Rahab's whole family—and her's alone.

You'd have thought that God would save some nice little old lady's house, with petunias growing in her garden. Instead, He saved the harlot's house. Why? Because she had faith, and that's what moves God. When it was all over, she was the richest woman in the city and the only person in town who owned property. Her faith saved her family, her finances, and her future. She even went on to become one of the great-grandmothers of our Lord. Often we settle for less because we didn't meet the best. But when you find the best, it gives you the power to let go of the rest.

AND THAT'S WHAT WILL HAPPEN TO YOU WHEN YOU MEET
JESUS AND PUT YOUR TRUST IN HIM.

# *Passionate Persistence*

**Thank God for you, brothers … because your faith is growing more and more, and the love every one of you has for each other is increasing. (2 Thessalonians 1:3, NIV)**

Today I prayed: "Disturb me, Lord, when my dreams come true, only because I dreamed too small. Disturb me when I arrive safely, only because I sailed too close to the shore. Disturb me when the things I have gained cause me to lose my thirst for more of You. Disturb me when I have acquired success, only to lose my desire for excellence. Disturb me when I give up too soon and settle too far short of the goals you have set for my life."

We're all talented. The problem is that we're not all disciplined, and that's what determines destiny. Doing something once is easy; maintaining it will be the challenge of your life!

Learn from others who have gone where you want to go. Picture yourself as a success in what God has called you to do, then by faith act accordingly. Be persistent; 99% of getting from here to there is the determination to do it, regardless of the road blocks in your path. Stay in the Word and keep your faith strong. Learn something new every day. Practice it until it becomes part of your nature. How long does it take to achieve excellence?

**NOT LONG—BUT IT WILL TAKE YOU A LIFETIME OF PASSIONATE PURSUIT TO MAINTAIN IT.**

# The First Step

**Be strong and of good courage, and do it.**
**(1 Chronicles 28:20)**

When the children of Israel came to the River Jordan, God told the priests carrying the Ark to step into the water. Then, and only then, would He dry up the river. They assumed it would happen immediately, but God dried it up sixteen miles upstream, so they had to wait for all that water to pass by before they could cross over. What you're going through right now is what you have to go through while you're waiting for your miracle. (See Hebrews 10:36.) Why didn't God open the river where they were? It was because they needed an opening wide enough to move two million people across. (See Joshua 3:17.) When God moves, it's not just for your benefit, it's for the benefit of others as well.

Note: Nothing happened till they stepped into the water. There's a song in you that's never been sung, a sermon that's never been preached, and a gift that's just waiting to be released. But nothing will happen until you move. The moment you quit holding back, God will move to meet you. The doors will open, the right people will come, and the "ways and means" will be provided. God's Word for you is: "Be strong and of good courage, and do it" (1 Chronicles 28:20).

HE'S JUST WAITING FOR YOU TO TAKE THAT FIRST STEP.

## Handling Weakness!

**When I want to do good, evil is right there with me.
(Romans 7:21, NIV)**

Become an enemy of your weakness; make it your target, or it'll become your taskmaster! When Samson awoke in the lap of Delilah, he'd lost his anointing. His next step was a dungeon. The battle of your life is always between your strength and your weakness. Listen: "These two forces within us are constantly fighting each other to win control over us" (Galatians 5:17, TLB). Nobody's exempt. Your struggles may be different from mine, but we're all on the battlefield.

If you think you can indulge your weakness today and just walk away from it tomorrow, you're deceiving yourself; your weakness has a will of its own. Paul said, "When I would do good, evil is present with me" (Romans 7:21). Your weakness plans to destroy you. Listen: "Sin, when it is finished, bringeth forth death" (James 1:15). Every time you justify your weakness, it rejoices, knowing that it will eventually get you.

But there's good news; God will give you the power to overcome! After his failure, Jesus told Peter, "Satan hath desired to have you ... but I have prayed for thee, that thy faith fail not" (Luke 22:31-32). You're not alone! He's interceding on your behalf! He also said, "Behold, I give unto you power ... over all the power of the enemy" (Luke 10:19).

—ɯɯ—

**REACH FOR THAT POWER TODAY AND
LIVE THE LIFE OF AN OVERCOMER!**

# Handling Failure

**Though I have fallen, I will rise. Though I sit in darkness, the LORD will be my light. (Micah 7:8, NIV)**

When you stop and think how many times you've "blown it," it seems a shame to let all those lessons go to waste. When you fail, treat it as a moment—not a monument! Don't spend the rest of your life paying homage to it. You do that when you say, "I tried it, but it doesn't work" or "they said it couldn't be done, and they were right." Dr. Mike Murdock says, "Failure is not an event, it is only an opinion." He's right! Don't be too quick to judge something as a failure. Thomas Edison once conducted 50,000 experiments in his search for natural rubber. When his assistant said to him, "All those experiments and not one result," Edison exclaimed, "No results! We've had wonderful results! We now know 50,000 things that won't work; soon we'll find the one that does." No wonder he lit up the world!

If you're discouraged today, read these words again: "Though I have fallen, I will rise. Though I sit in darkness, the LORD will be my light" (Micah 7:8). The One who said to Paul, "My strength is made perfect in [your] weakness" (2 Corinthians 12:9) will turn your defeat into victory.

JUST GIVE HIM A CHANCE.

# *Barriers*

**Sir, we would see Jesus.**
**(John 12:21)**

Don't let the disciples keep you away from Jesus! The very ones who were supposed to make Him accessible kept people away. They forbade the children to come. (See Luke 18:15.) They tried to send the crowd home hungry. (See Luke 9:12.) They even tried to silence blind Bartimaeus when he called out for help. (See Mark 10:48.) Why? Because they thought Jesus was too busy. Christian leader beware! When your "handlers" become your "controllers," it's easy to forget what God told you to do.

James and John, the "Sons of Thunder," wanted to call down fire on those who disagreed with them. (See Luke 9:54.) When they found others who didn't belong to their group casting out demons, they wanted to stop them. (See Luke 9:49.) Yet a few chapters earlier, they, themselves, couldn't cast the spirits out of a tormented boy. *Why do we always want to judge people who do what we are incapable of doing?*

When the Greeks said, "Sir, we would see Jesus," the disciples wanted to keep them away because they weren't Jews. Imagine racism among the twelve disciples! Yet Jesus called all of them to follow Him. If you're a disciple, make your prayer today: "Lord, let nothing I say or do keep people away from You." On the other hand, if you're a seeker—come in! The very fact that He loves us as we are should be a big encouragement to you.

AFTER ALL, IN A PERFECT PLACE WITH PERFECT PEOPLE, HOW LONG WOULD YOU LAST?

# Dying to Self

**For me to live is Christ, and to die is gain.**
**(Philippians 1:21)**

Y ou don't have to survive, but you do have to find and fulfill God's purpose for your life. The three Hebrew children of God could say "no" to the king because they placed no importance on their personal survival. The widow in 1 Kings 17 was willing to give her "only," her "last," and her "all" to Elijah, because she didn't have a "survival mentality." Nelson Mandela said, "I'd gladly go back to that island prison again, if it meant setting my people free."

You say you want to be like Jesus? Are you serious? Listen to Him pray: "Father, if thou be willing, remove this cup from me: nevertheless not my will, but thine, be done" (Luke 22:42). He gave up His own will to fulfill the Father's. Are you prepared to do that? He also gave up His reputation. Paul said, "He made Himself of no reputation" (Philippians 2:7). Can you handle that? John the Baptist said, "He must increase, but I must decrease" (John 3:30). The trouble is that when we reach a certain level, we begin to rest on our accomplishments. We're afraid to accept the next challenge, because we've too much to lose. That's dangerous! Listen again to Paul: "For me to live is Christ, and to die is gain." God's goal for you today is "the death of self-preservation."

**ARE YOU WILLING TO LET HIM ACCOMPLISH THAT**
**IN YOUR LIFE?**

# Learning to Understand

**Then the LORD God made a woman ... and He brought her to the man. (Genesis 2:22, NIV)**

Let God bring you the person you need! Trying to plan a lifetime relationship without consulting Him first is insanity. Find any couple who has been married for ten or twenty years, then look at their wedding album. If looks were all that held them together, it would be a short-term event. Nobody remains twenty-one forever. The problem is that we're only young once, but some of us manage to stay immature for a lifetime.

We men are shocked to find that our wives appreciate gifts, but they "go into orbit" over cards. My wife Debby has cards that are so old they've turned yellow. The point is—if you don't learn to understand each other and speak each other's language, you'll finish up living in a Tower of Babel. That's where all work ceased, and arguing began. Before it was over, everybody separated and went their own way.

If you want to change your partner, try this: Everything you are going to do for them when they change—start doing it now. Do it by faith, and God will turn your Tower of Babel into an upper room. That's where, "Each one heard them speaking in their own language" (Acts 2:26, NIV). Ask God today to help you understand rather than be understood.

IF YOU DO, YOU'LL GET BACK MUCH MORE THAN YOU'VE GIVEN. THAT'S STILL GOD'S WAY!

# Broken Things

**Unless a grain of wheat falls into the earth and dies, it remains by itself alone; but if it dies, it bears much fruit [wheat].
(John 12:24, NASB)**

Only when Gideon's army broke their pitchers could the light on the inside shine out. (See Judges 7:20.) Only when Mary's alabaster box was broken could its contents be poured out as an act of worship. (See Mark 14:3.) Only when the loaves and fishes were broken could the hungry multitude be fed. (See Matthew 14:19.) Are you getting the idea? We all have to be broken.

Anthony Lockett wrote a song called "The Upside Down Kingdom." Here's how it works: If you want to preserve life, you give it away (see Luke 9:24). If you want to be on top, humble yourself before God (see Matthew 23:12). If you want to be the greatest, learn to serve others (see Matthew 23:11). If you want to really live, die to self (see Romans 8:13). If you want to make a difference in this world, sow your life like a seed into the lives of others (see John 12:24).

Listen: "I counted dollars while God counted crosses; I counted gains while He counted losses. I counted my worth by the things put in store; He sized me up by the scars that I bore. I counted honors, and I sought degrees; He counted the time I'd spent on my knees. I never knew till one day by a grave, how vain are the things that we spend life to save."

---

**THINK ABOUT IT!**

# A Passion for God

**Repent and do the things you did at first.
(Revelation 2:5, NIV)**

Robert Murray McCheyne lived to be only twenty-nine, but he shook Scotland for God. One day a minister visited his church. Anxious to know "the secret of his success," he asked the sexton to show him the great preacher's study. When they got there, the sexton said, "Sit in this chair!" Hesitantly, the visitor sat down. On the desk before him was an open Bible. Then the old Scotsman said, "Now drop your head on that book and weep, for that's what Robert Murray McCheyne always did before he preached!"

Has your love for God grown cold? In *The Screwtape Letters* by C.S. Lewis, the devil instructs his nephew Wormwood on how to tempt people. He tells him, "I, the devil, will always see to it that there is a bad person. Your job, my dear Wormwood, is to provide me with the people who do not care." Jesus warned us about being apathetic. He acknowledged our hard work, our doctrinal purity, but then He said, in essence, "You're just going through the motions, but you don't really love Me anymore" (Revelation 2:1-6). What's His prescription? "Turn around! Repent and do the things you did at first!"

**DO YOU NEED TO SPEND TIME TALKING TO THE LORD ABOUT THIS TODAY?**

# Wisdom

**Let not a wise man boast of his wisdom,… but let him … boast of this, that he understands and knows Me.
(Jeremiah 9:23-24, NASB)**

A small factory had to stop its operation when a machine broke down. Nobody could fix it, so an expert was called. He simply took a hammer and tapped the machine at a certain spot, and immediately it began running again. But when he submitted a bill for $1,000, the supervisor hit the roof. "A thousand dollars for just tapping?" "No," said the man, "One dollar for tapping; $999 for knowing where to tap!" There it is. You can wear yourself out, or you can ask God for wisdom, and He'll show you how to do the right thing, at the right time, for the right purpose. He knows where to tap! Just ask Him.

James says that God's wisdom "comes" from above (see James 3:17). Note three things: First, it comes from God; second, you have to ask for it; third, it comes daily. Have you asked God for His wisdom today? The biggest mistakes I've ever made had one thing in common: They were mine, not His! If I had taken time to seek God, I'd have gotten an entirely different result. Sound familiar? Listen again to these words: "Let him who boasts boast of this, that he understands and knows Me" (Jeremiah 9:24, NASB).

**THE CLOSER YOU GET TO HIM,
THE BETTER YOU'LL UNDERSTAND.**

# *Never Quit*

**Through you we push back our enemies; through your name
we trample our foes. (Psalm 44:5, NIV)**

Only when you accept failure as final are you finally a failure.
Any time you learn from a mistake, you've taken a major step
towards success. You can't hit a home run unless you get out of the
dugout and face the pitcher. Baseball legend Babe Ruth hit 714
home runs, but he also struck out 1,330 times. During a low period,
an interviewer asked him how he overcame discouragement. He
replied, "If I just keep swinging the bat, the law of averages says
I'll catch up. In fact, when I'm in a slump, I feel sorry for the
pitcher, because I know that, sooner or later, he's going to pay for
it." What a great attitude!

It's your attitude that determines whether failure *makes* you or
*breaks* you. Imagine, Henry Ford actually forgot to put a reverse
gear into his first car. But instead of giving up, he just said, "Failure
is only a necessary step to success!" If Abraham could start out as
an idol worshiper and finish up as "the friend of God," then there's
hope for all of us. When Benjamin Disraeli attempted to speak
in Parliament for the first time, they booed him into silence. But
he said, "Though I sit down now, the time will come when you
will all hear me." He was right! His critics are forgotten, but his
words live on. David said, "Through You we [will] push back our
enemies" (Psalms 44:5).

THAT MEANS, THROUGH GOD, YOU CAN GET BACK UP,
YOU CAN PREVAIL, AND YOU CAN WIN!

# Do It While You Can

**Thou shalt be missed, because thy seat will be empty.
(1 Samuel 20:18)**

Since my father died, I've wept many times over the questions I wish I could have asked him and for the grandchildren he's never met. He left us so quickly; he left without saying good-bye. I sometimes envy those whose parents are still alive. My own children are now married and gone, but I still feel the need to call them at times and just say, "I love you and I'm proud of you!" I think that's important!

The ultimate absentee parent is one who is dead. There are no arguments to be had and no issues to be resolved. If you can fill the empty seat in your life, do it while there's still time. If your parents are gone, reach out to your children; overcome every obstacle and love them. When the prodigal son finally came home, he wasn't greeted with scorn or, "I told you so." He may have been a failure to everyone else, but not to his dad! His father's arms reached out to hold him, because he knew that when he touched his son, he was touching himself. So long as we're still alive, we'll disappoint each other. It's part of being human. But if God's love can't overcome our disappointments, then we're sure to die lonely.

**DON'T LET THAT HAPPEN TO YOU!**

151

# Born to Produce

**And God said unto them, be fruitful.**
**(Genesis 1:28)**

One day an ox said to a mule, "Let's play sick today." The mule said, "No, we need to get this work done." But the ox played sick, and the farmer brought him fresh hay and corn. When the mule came in from plowing that evening, the ox asked him how things went. The mule said, "We did OK." Then the ox asked, "What did the farmer say about me?" The mule replied, "Nothing." The next day the ox played sick again. When the mule came home, the ox asked again, "How did it go?" The mule said, "OK, but we didn't get much done." The ox asked, "Did the farmer say anything about me?" the mule replied, "Well, he said nothing to me, but he did stop and have a long talk with the butcher!"

You may smile, but you were born to be productive. When you're not, life becomes meaningless. *Paul didn't retire—he "finished"* (see 2 Timothy 4:7). Listen to what he says, "Whatever you may do, do all for the honor and glory of God" (1 Corinthians 10:31, AMP). Think about that! When you consider how little some people work, you wonder how they'll ever know when they retire. Honor God on your job! You may be the only Christian your fellow workers know, so a lot is riding on your performance. Go the extra mile. It'll do more to reach them than all your preaching.

**ASK GOD TO MAKE YOU AN EXAMPLE ON THE JOB TODAY.**

# Time to Praise the Lord

**By him therefore let us offer the sacrifice of praise to God continually, that is, the fruit of our lips. (Hebrews 13:15)**

Before you say another word, have you taken time today to praise the Lord? Listen: "From the rising of the sun unto the going down of the same the Lord's name is to be praised" (Psalm 113:3). Your first words in the morning, your last ones at night, should be words of praise to Him. Today's verse tells us three important things about praise. First, it should be continual, not occasional! Second, it should be sacrificial, not just when you feel like it! Third, it should be audible, not just silent! David said, "Let everything that has breath praise the Lord" (Psalms 150:6). If you're still breathing, you should be praising God.

An old man was given to outbursts of praise in church. You could never tell when he'd let loose. So, at the dedication of the new church, the pastor said, "Wilbur, if you'll just be quiet in the service today, I'll buy you a new pair of boots." Wilbur was delighted, and he promised to try. He made it safely through the hymns and the prayer, but halfway through the sermon, he couldn't stand it any longer. He jumped to his feet and shouted, *"Boots or no boots, I'm gonna praise the Lord!"* Go ahead; get over your inhibition. Open your heart, lift your hands, and begin to praise Him today.

---

**HE'S WORTHY OF IT!**

# Check Your Attitude!

**Have this attitude in yourselves which was also in Christ.
(Philippians 2:5, NASB)**

At lunchtime, a man said to his fellow worker, "I can't believe it! Baloney again! I'm sick of baloney sandwiches. This is the fourth time this week I've had baloney." His friend said, "Take it easy! Why don't you just tell your wife you don't like baloney and ask her to make you something different?" The fist guy replied, "What are you talking about? I don't have a wife. I make my own lunch!" Think about it. If there's a lot of baloney in your life today, guess who put it there? What you sow, you reap. (See Galatians 6:7.)

Listen to Paul: "Do not merely look out for your own personal interests, but also for the interests of others. Have this attitude in yourselves which was also in Christ" (Philippians 2:4-5, NASB). How's your attitude toward others? Remember the elder brother in the parable of the prodigal son? He wanted the privilege of being a son, but not the obligation of being a brother. Until you learn to love your brother, you'll always have a strained relationship with your father. The elder brother had no idea why his father would rejoice over his brother's return, so until you can celebrate God's blessing in somebody else's life—your future is "on hold." Ask God to reveal any wrong attitudes in your life today. Treat people not as they are, but as you wish they were.

THEN BELIEVE GOD TO CHANGE THEM. HE CAN DO IT!

# A Call to Holiness

**Let us turn away from everything wrong ... giving ourselves to Him alone. (2 Corinthians 7:1, TLB)**

Before his conversion, St. Augustine was a "party animal." After becoming a Christian, he often walked home past a bar he'd frequented every night. One night, a prostitute, who assumed he'd finally "come back to his senses," approached him. But when they met, he walked right by her. In amazement, she called to him, "Augustine, don't you recognize who you just walked by? It's me!" For a moment he stopped, turned to her and said, "Yes, but it's no longer me!" Paul says, "If any man be in Christ, he is a new creature: old things are passed away; behold, all things are become new" (2 Corinthians 5:17).

When I was young, many of those claiming to be holy seemed harsh to me. They looked like they were enduring, rather than enjoying, their religion. They were comfortable in church, miserable everywhere else. Deep inside I knew something was wrong. Peter says, "His divine power has given us everything we need for life and godliness" (2 Peter 1:3, NIV). God will help you in both areas! He also says that through His Word "you might become partakers of the divine nature" (2 Peter 1:4). You have His very nature within you, and that nature will cause you to grow up spiritually. You'll know you've grown up—when you're able to feed yourself! As you do, holiness will be a natural outgrowth of your relationship with God.

REMEMBER, YOU CAN'T BE HOLY IN A HURRY,
BUT YOU CAN START TAKING STEPS IN THAT DIRECTION
RIGHT AWAY.

## Paying the Price

**Which of you, intending to build a tower, sitteth not
down first, and counteth the cost?
(Luke 14:28)**

We know now that God shut the lions' mouths, but Daniel didn't know in advance that it would happen! He simply counted the cost and kept his commitment to God. So did a lot of others. In Hebrews eleven, it went both ways for committed believers—some were taken out, others were taken through, but all of them "obtained a good report" (Hebrews 11:39). To follow Jesus means to discover what you were born to be, pay the price required, and spend the rest of your life pursuing it to the point of excellence! Once you catch a glimpse of "the high calling," you'll get up earlier, stay up later, and say "no" more often, because you understand God's will for you. Is that how you live?

Sure, you'll make mistakes. Les Brown says, "When life knocks you down, fall on your back, for if you can look up, with God's help you can get up." Winston Churchill said, "Success is the ability to go from one failure to another with no loss of enthusiasm." Think about that! Successful people are just the ones who do what the rest of us only talk about, but never get around to doing. God doesn't measure you by others; He measures you by what you could have been if you'd paid the price.

ASK HIM TODAY FOR THE STRENGTH AND THE
WILLINGNESS TO MAKE THAT COMMITMENT.

# Learned Behavior

**I have learned to be content.
(Philippians 4:11, NASB)**

A joyful attitude is a learned behavior. Your attitude creates your environment. Look around at the jobs people have but hate; the marriage they endure, but never enjoy. Why? Because they're waiting for others to do something, instead of realizing they are responsible for their own lives.

Have you ever smelled Limburger cheese? It's awful! When grandpa was taking a nap, the kids put some of it on his moustache as a joke. When he awoke, he said, "This room stinks." So he went into the kitchen, and it stank, too. Finally, when he went out into the backyard to get some fresh air, he exclaimed, "The whole world stinks!" You may smile, but until you get rid of the Limburger cheese in your attitude, your world will always stink.

Which song is yours? "Make the World Go Away", "Raindrops Keep Falling on My Head", "I Did It My Way", or "Oh What A Beautiful Morning"? The song you choose is the song you'll sing! Paul was in prison when he wrote, "Rejoice in the Lord always" (Philippians 4:4). Notice, the one on the *inside* is telling the ones on the *outside* to rejoice! That's where he also wrote, "I have learned to be content" (Philippians 4:11, NASB). He's teaching us something he himself had to learn.

---

**ASK GOD TO HELP YOU LEARN IT, TOO!**

**Then said Mary unto the angel, How shall this be,
seeing I know not a man? (Luke 1:34)**

Has God been telling you certain things He wants to do in your life? Have you been questioning Him? Maybe you're a single parent raising children, and your circumstances don't seem to allow you time to accomplish much. Or you've been thinking you must have a husband or a wife to fulfil the will of God. Listen to what God told Mary, "The Holy Ghost shall come upon thee" (Luke 1:35). If you're wondering how God will make things come to pass in your life, put the Holy Spirit into the picture. He will accomplish the task. No man will get the credit!

Don't allow your vision to die because you've been called to walk alone! My father was an unbeliever for many years. However, my mother loved him and prayed for him faithfully. Before he died, he committed his life to Christ. In spite of the hardships she faced, both her sons are in the ministry today. Cling to the promise God has given you for your family! Sarah didn't stand on Abraham's faith; she stood on her own. Listen: "Through faith also Sarah herself received strength to conceive" (Hebrews 11:11). Don't just sit by the window waiting for God to send somebody.

IF HE DOES, THAT'S WONDERFUL; BUT UNTIL HE DOES,
MAKE YOUR LIFE COUNT FOR GOD.

# Get a Checkup

**I will take away sickness from among you.
(Exodus 23:25, NIV)**

My friend, Ron Dryden, pastors one of America's largest churches. Recently, he discovered he had cancer in its early stage. Providentially, the doctors found it in time, and he's back in his pulpit doing what God called him to do. Thank God he was sensitive to a strong "inner leading" to go and have a check-up. Think of the lives he will be able to touch tomorrow.

Can you imagine what 50 years of today's food and stress do to a healthy body? I know God heals, but if He miraculously flushed all the cholesterol out of your arteries tomorrow, would you change your eating habits, or would you just clog them up again? Good health is not a guarantee just because you're a Christian—it's a reward for being wise!

Because my dad died young, I spent much of my life fearing I would, too. I often told my family, "If I live to be 50, I'll throw a party and invite everybody I know." Well, I'm 54, and I'm making plans for the next 25 years; I'm also watching what I eat. God promised to take sickness away from our midst and help us live a long healthy life, but He expects us to cooperate with Him on it! (See Exodus 23:25.)

—⁓—

**DON'T YOU THINK SO?**

### Compassion

**The LORD is gracious and compassionate.
(Psalms 111:4, NIV)**

Dr. Karl Menninger, the famous psychiatrist, was once asked by someone in his audience, "What would you advise me to do if I felt a nervous breakdown coming on?" To their surprise, he replied, "Lock up your house, go across the railroad tracks, find someone in need, and do something to help them." That's great advice! The Pharisees spent their lives being good, but Jesus spent His *doing* good and Peter said, "You should follow in His steps" (1 Peter 2:21).

A good way to discern a person's character is to watch how they treat someone who can do them absolutely no good! Compassion doesn't give in order to "score points" or put others in debt to you. Instead of magnifying the bad, compassion looks for the good in others and builds on it. It warms but never burns and always knows how to disagree without being disagreeable.

There are people all around you who need the compassion of Jesus. Don't miss one of the opportunities God gives you today to show it. Mother Teresa said, "To be unloved and forgotten is a greater hunger and a greater poverty than to have nothing to eat. May God give us the compassion to find and care for each other."

---

**ASK GOD TO GIVE YOU A HEART OF COMPASSION.**

# Handling Temptation

**When you are tempted, He will also provide a way out so that you can stand up under it. (1 Corinthians 10:13, NIV)**

Listen carefully to this essay by Portia Nelson: "I walk down the street. There's a hole in the sidewalk, and I fall in. I'm lost; it isn't my fault. It takes me forever to get out. I walk down the street again. There's a hole in the sidewalk, but I pretend I don't see it, so I fall again. I can't believe I'm in the same place; still, it isn't my fault. I walk down the street again. There's a hole in the sidewalk. I see it, but I still fall in—it's a habit. But now my eyes are open, and I know where I am. It is my fault. I get out immediately. I walk down the street. There's a hole in the sidewalk. I walk around it! Finally, I walk down another street!"

If you're tired of walking down the same street and falling into the same hole, then God has provided "a way out" for you—another street! That's why Paul says, "Take all the help you can get, every weapon God has issued, so that when it's all over but the shouting you'll still be on your feet. Truth, righteousness, peace, faith and salvation are more than words. Learn how to apply them. You'll need them throughout your life. God's Word is an indispensable weapon. In the same way, prayer is essential in this ongoing warfare. Pray hard and long. Pray for your brothers and sisters. Keep your eyes open. Keep each other's spirits up so that no one falls behind or drops out" (Ephesians 6:13-18, TM).

—m—

**NOW THESE ARE WORDS WORTHY OF YOUR CONSIDERATION TODAY!**

*Dry Spells*

**As the deer pants for the water brooks,**
**So my soul pants for Thee, O God.**
**(Psalms 42:1, NASB)**

A traveler in Africa hired laborers from a local tribe to help him carry his load. The first day they moved fast and went further than he thought they'd get. But the next day, the tribesmen refused to move an inch. When he asked why, they told him they'd gone too fast the first day; now they were waiting for their souls to catch up with their bodies. Is that how you feel today—exhausted and spiritually drained? We all go through "dry spells." David said he once led the whole congregation into the presence of God, but now he couldn't even find God for himself (see Psalms 42:3-4).

Let me share with you some discoveries from my own "dry spells." First, at such times, God is usually demanding new growth and maturity from me. In that place I'm more honest, I pray harder and reach for Him more. Or perhaps He's teaching me that I've spent too much time in the wrong environment or watching television. The kids call it "vegging out." Sometimes God's just moving me from one season of ministry to another, and I feel dislocated. Other times, it's just plain disobedience to something He has told me to do, and I'm "holding out." It could be, too, that I'm on the verge of a greater revelation of Him, and He's creating within me a new hunger; not for what He can give me—but just for who He is.

—✳—

IF THAT'S WHERE YOU ARE,
THERE'S ONLY ONE PLACE TO GO—
BACK INTO GOD'S PRESENCE!

**Just as you excel in everything …**
**see that you also excel in this grace of giving.**
**(2 Corinthians 8:7, NIV)**

Dr. Martin Luther King, Jr. said, "There are three conversations we must all have with God. The first conversation is of the heart, the second is of the mind, and the third is of the purse." Most of us find the third the most difficult. Jesus said, "For where your treasure is, there your heart will be also" (Matthew 6:21, NIV). *Until God has access to your money, He doesn't have access to your heart.* David said, "We have given You only what comes from Your hand" (1 Chronicles 29:14, NIV). You don't have a thing God didn't give you!

Never apologize for God's blessings. Listen, "Let the Lord be magnified, which hath pleasure in the prosperity of His servant" (Psalm 35:27). God delights in blessing you, so let no one put you under pressure concerning what He's given you. And remember, giving proves you've conquered insecurity. If God is truly your source, you can stop worrying over the future. When you understand the law of sowing and reaping, you will become a "cheerful giver" (2 Corinthians 9:7) for the same reason a farmer rejoices when his seed is in the ground—he's anticipating his harvest. Paul said God's plan for you is to "be made rich in every way so that you can be generous on every occasion" (2 Corinthians 9:7, NIV). God wants to bless you, so that you can bless others.

—————

HOW'S YOUR SOWING?
HOW'S YOUR EXPECTATION LEVEL?
DO YOU NEED TO TALK TO GOD ABOUT THIS TODAY?

# God's Favor

**For it is time to show favour.
(Psalms 102:13, NIV)**

The favor of God will carry you from your present situation to your God-ordained destiny. You can't get there without it. It's that simple! In spite of his family's rejection and the lies Potiphar's wife told, the favor of God took Joseph from a prison to a palace in less than 24 hours (see Genesis 41). *God's favor can change your situation in an instant!* Look at Ruth; widowed, impoverished, and living in a foreign country, she remained faithful to God. Instead of giving in to despair and resentment, she decided to get up and start again. Before it was over, she became "the boss's wife" (see Ruth 4:13). That's favor! Your Bible is filled with such stories.

Favor is not an accident or "a lucky break." Listen: "All these blessings shall come on thee and overtake thee, if thou shalt hearken unto the voice of the Lord thy God" (Deuteronomy 28:2). *Obedience* brings the favor of God! Ask Him today to help you see the areas where His favor is already at work in your life. As you acknowledge it in small things, it will increase. Who is God using to bless you right now? Stop building walls to keep them out. Open your arms to them. If there is known sin in your life today, get rid of it!

—m—

**RELEASE ALL YOUR FEARS AND GET READY TO RECEIVE HIS FAVOR—HE LONGS TO SHOW IT TO YOU TODAY!**

# Get a Grip!

**Add to your faith goodness; and to goodness, knowledge;
and to knowledge, self-control.
(2 Peter 1:5-6, NIV)**

Recently I noticed a sign on an office which read, "If you could kick the person responsible for most of your troubles, you wouldn't be able to sit down for a week." It's true, isn't it? Consider carefully these words:

An enemy I strove to know, he dogged my steps where 'ere I'd go. My plans he balked and blocked my way. To lofty goals he answered, "Nay!" Till I from him the veil did draw, I looked and lo—myself I saw!

The Greek word for self-control means "to get a grip on." Child of God, get a grip on your life, especially those areas where you've been undisciplined and inconsistent. You see, what you do in the hour of temptation, will depend on what you already are! When John Wesley's students met each week, they would ask these four questions:

1. What sins have you committed since we last met?

2. What temptations have you faced?

3. How were you delivered?

4. What have you thought, said or done, of which you are uncertain whether it is sin or not?

---

THOSE ARE SEARCHING QUESTIONS. TAKE SOME TIME TODAY, GET INTO GOD'S PRESENCE AND ANSWER THEM. HOW YOU DO COULD WELL DECIDE YOUR DESTINY!

# *Want to Succeed?*

**This book of the law ... you shall meditate on it day and night,...
be careful to do according to all that is written in it;... will make
your way prosperous,... you will have success.
(Joshua 1:8, NASB)**

I smiled as I read about three people trying to come up with
a definition of success. The first said, "I'd consider myself a
success if I could talk personally with the president in the Oval
Office." The second said, "I'd consider myself a success if, while
talking with him, his hotline rang and he ignored it." The third
said, "I'd consider myself a success if, while I'm talking with him,
his hotline rang and he answered it and said, 'It's for you.'" What
would success be for you?

Listen: "So God created man in His own image ... and God said
... Be fruitful, and multiply" (Genesis 1: 27-28) God equipped
us to be successful, and He expects us to succeed. He gave Adam
instructions, and the only way failure could enter his life was if
Adam disobeyed them. There it is: Success is obeying God! What
has God told you to do? If you're still not sure, ask Him. Stay in
His presence until He tells you. There are no secrets of success.
Just do these three things, and you'll succeed anywhere:

1. Speak His Word over your life;

2. Think about it constantly;

3. Obey its instructions.

IF YOU DO, YOU'LL BE A SUCCESS AT WHATEVER YOU DO.
THAT'S HIS WORD TO YOU TODAY!

# New Goals

**I press on toward the goal to win the prize for which God has called me heavenward in Christ Jesus.**
**(Philippians 3:14, NIV)**

Some day you'll look back and realize how small your goals were. You'll ask, "Why did I settle for so little?" If you are changing, shouldn't your goals be changing, too? Remember, your present feelings and opinions are not permanent, so don't build your future on them. Thank God for His goodness to you in the past, but get ready for what He's got for you next.

For fourteen years I pastored and loved it. For the next sixteen years I enjoyed traveling and speaking around the world. But today, my greatest joy is staying at home and writing this devotional. What a change! And equally wonderful changes will happen for you, too. Others don't have to understand your goals or even agree with them. Permit them their individuality. Just make sure they don't persuade you to move away from your calling. Let yesterday's dreams die; they were fine for then, but this is now.

Beware of people who don't respect your goals. Life is too short to permit the carriers of discouragement to get you down. Unclutter your life, get rid of the unnecessary, and reach for the prize.

**IF YOU DO, GOD WILL HELP YOU TO REACH IT.**

**So if the Son sets you free, you will be free indeed.
(John 8:36, NIV)**

When your desire to go forward becomes greater than the memories of your past, you'll begin to live again. Purpose always overcomes pain! Solomon said, "Where there is no vision, the people perish" (Proverbs 29:18). Until you have a vision of tomorrow, you'll always live in yesterday's struggles. The very fact that God is putting desire back into your spirit again means that better days are coming. David said, "I had fainted, unless I had believed to see the goodness of the Lord in the land of the living" (Psalm 27:13).

When T. D. Jakes was a boy, he had a dog named Pup. He was a ferocious animal, so they kept him chained to a post in their back yard. Nobody believed he could break that chain, though he had often tried. One day, Pup saw something he really wanted, and suddenly the motivation before him became greater than the chain that held him. In that moment, the chain snapped, and he was free. God can do that for you, too! The chain that's held you back will snap, and you'll move from defeat to victory. When you finally understand that you're loose, you'll start behaving like it. You'll go wherever God takes you, and you'll become all that He wants you to be.

REJOICE, THAT PROMISE IS FOR YOU!

# *Don't Accept It!*

**Be on the alert. Your adversary, the devil, prowls about like a roaring lion, seeking someone to devour. But resist him, firm in your faith. (1 Peter 5:8-9, NASB)**

Receiver, be careful what you receive. When Satan brings a mood or an attitude to you, resist him. Tell him, "This is not for me, and I don't receive it." It's his job to offer it, and it's your job to resist it. Paul says, "Do not give the devil a foothold" (Ephesians 4:27, NIV). You must learn to discern his influence and rebuke him before he enters your life. Any mood that's not in agreement with God's Word is Satan trying to "plug in" to you. He wants you to believe that you can't change. When you say, "That's just the way I am" or "I'm in a terrible mood today," you're accepting what you ought to reject! Don't do it!

Settle for nothing less than the attitude God wants you to have: "If anything is excellent or praiseworthy think about such things" (Philippians 4:8, NIV). Don't let the devil have your day, your family, your moods, or your words. Nurture what you want to grow, and starve what you want to die.

---

FEED THE VISION GOD HAS PUT WITHIN YOU AND "PULL THE PLUG" ON ANY DOUBT, THOUGHT, OR ATTITUDE THAT ROBS YOU OF GOD'S BEST.

# The Roller Coaster

**He has made everything appropriate in its time.
(Ecclesiastes 3:11, NASB)**

My brother Neil says, "Sometimes life is a roller coaster; you just have to strap yourself in and hold on!" Solomon says, "God made everything appropriate in its time" (Ecclesiastes 3:11, NASB). You say, "Appropriate to what?" Appropriate to whatever God wants to work out in your life! He's not developing escape artists; He's developing overcomers. In times of trouble, God has promised to provide a way out, so that you stand up under it (see 1 Corinthians 10:13, NIV). We grow more "under it" than we do "out of it." In *The Screwtape Letters*, C. S. Lewis tells of Satan warning one of his junior demons, "We are never in greater danger than when they look around and all traces of God have forsaken them, yet they still choose to obey Him!"

When the three Hebrew children of God faced the fiery furnace, they said, "Our God is able to deliver us ... and He will ... but if not ... we will not serve thy gods" (Daniel 3:17-18). There are three levels of faith. The first level is: "Our God is able." Most of us can manage to believe that. The second level is: "And He will!" A lot of us wish we could believe that, but we're not sure. The third level is: "But if not." That's the highest level of all! It says, "But if not now or in the way I want or if not at all—I'll still trust God!"

—◦◦◦—

THAT'S THE KIND OF FAITH THAT GLORIFIES HIM MOST.
IT GROWS WHEN YOU LIVE IN HIS WORD
AND IN HIS PRESENCE.

# Your Destiny

**For this reason I was born.**
**(John 18:37, NIV)**

Without purpose, your life is just an experiment! Jesus could say, "For this reason I was born." Can you say that your present circumstances don't disqualify you? When God called Gideon "a mighty man of valor" he was hiding in a cave. (See Judges 8:12.) But God wasn't speaking to his circumstances; He was speaking to the destiny that was inside him!

You say, "How can I recognize my destiny?" First, it's a desire that won't let you go. Paul cried, "Woe unto me, if I preach not the Gospel!" (1 Corinthians 9:16). Being a queen was Esther's position, but saving God's people was her destiny. That's why she risked everything and said, "If I perish, I perish" (Esther 4:16). We're not what's important—God's purpose is!

Second, your destiny will be more than a job, it'll be a joy. Sure there'll be sacrifices, but through it all you'll say like David, "I delight to do Thy will, O my God" (Psalm 40:8). What a way to live!

Third, your destiny will unlock your creativity. It will open doors and bring the right people to you. God's purpose always carries with it God's favor! Finally, your destiny fulfilled is the only thing you'll want to face God with.

---

HE WON'T SAY "WELL DONE" OVER THE MONEY YOU'VE
MADE OR THE REPUTATION YOU'VE BUILT.
HE'LL ONLY SAY IT BECAUSE YOU FOUND AND
FULFILLED HIS PURPOSE.

## Winning Attitude

**You armed me with strength.**
**(2 Samuel 22:40, NIV)**

According to the law of aerodynamics, bumblebees can't fly. Their body is too big for their wings. But nobody ever told them, so they just fly anyway. When God says, "You can," it cancels out everybody else's, "You can't." God longs to find people who'll believe Him. Paul prayed that we would be "strengthened with might by His Spirit" (Ephesians 3:16). Micah declared, "But as for me, I am filled with power, with the Spirit of the Lord" (Micah 3:8, NIV). If you'll feed your spirit with Scriptures like these, you'll fly, even when your critics say you can't get off the ground. It's "the winning attitude," and everybody who makes a difference in this world has it.

When the great architect Frank Lloyd Wright was 83, somebody asked him which of his works he would select as his masterpiece. He replied, "My next one!" Imagine, 83 and still flying. Be like the elevator operator who greeted everyone who got on and hummed a tune between every floor. When an irritated passenger finally snapped, "What are you so happy about?" He replied, "Well, sir, it's like this; I ain't never lived this day before!" His grammar may have been off, but his attitude was "right on!"

ARMED WITH GOD'S STRENGTH, THIS DAY IS UNLIMITED.
GO AHEAD, LIVE IT TO THE MAX!

# Don't Lose Your Vision

**I was not disobedient to the vision.
(Acts 26: 19, NIV)**

When Alexander the Great had a vision, he conquered the world; when he lost it, he couldn't conquer a liquor bottle. When David had a vision, he conquered Goliath; when he lost it, he couldn't conquer his own lust. When Samson had a vision, he could defeat a thousand men; when he lost it, he couldn't handle one woman. When Noah had a vision, he built an ark and preserved the human race; when he lost it, he got drunk. It's your dream that keeps you on track; it's your vision that keeps you in focus.

The average man's lifetime includes twenty years sleeping, six years watching television, five years shaving and dressing, three years waiting for others, one year on the telephone, and four months tying his shoes. You say, "Surely there's got to be something more?" There is! It's the thing that kept Paul going, through shipwreck and starvation, beating and betrayal, persecution and prison—his vision! Listen: "I was not disobedient to the vision" (Acts 26:19). Do you have a vision? If you don't, get into God's presence today and ask Him to give you one.

—⚭—

**WITHOUT IT, WHAT'S YOUR PURPOSE FOR LIVING?**

## Watch What You Watch

**I will set no wicked thing before my eyes.
(Psalms 101:3)**

As a teenager, Marilyn got hooked on "soap operas." After years of watching them, her perspective changed, and she began to think the illicit shows were more exciting. As a college student, she found it easy to get involved in one-night stands. Finally, after a series of affairs, her marriage ended in disaster, and she sought help from a counselor. At first, he couldn't understand why she'd had the affairs. Finally, he discovered the source that had driven her into this "secret life." Years of exposure to the wrong thing! Paul says we are changed into what we behold. (See 2 Corinthians 3:18.) Think about that!

What you see on television becomes part of your memory bank, your frame of reference, and your value system. Ultimately, it becomes the justification for the way you behave. It's no coincidence that a generation that watches seven hours of television every day also has the world's lowest morals and highest divorce rate. Your eyes are the gateway to your soul. John warns us to beware of "the cravings of sinful man [and] the lust of his eyes" (1 John 2:16, NIV). It was after David's encounter with Bathsheba that he wrote, "I will set no wicked thing before mine eyes" (Psalms 101:3).

EITHER YOU LEARN FROM HIS MISTAKE OR YOU REPEAT
IT. THE CHOICE IS YOURS!

# Consecration

**Who is willing to consecrate himself to the LORD?**
**(1 Chronicles 29:5, NIV)**

From earliest childhood, two sisters talked about going to the mission field together. But, by the time they'd reached mid-life, each of them had built a successful career. One day, the younger sister gave up her job and moved to South America, where she spent the rest of her life helping to pioneer new churches and building a mission school. Still, her older sister lingered at home. She worried about the dangers of the mission field, and anyway, she was making too much money to go anywhere at the moment. Several times she wrote saying, "I haven't forgotten, it's still in my heart to go, but I'll go later." She never did. Two years later, she died in a tragic car wreck. She had "saved" her life, only to lose it.

That's how it is in God's Kingdom. If you try to preserve what's yours, you forfeit it, but if you put it into *His* hands, you'll always possess it. Safety is an illusion, apart from God. We trust in our jobs, yet companies go under every day. We trust the government, yet funds diminish, and laws change. We trust in our own abilities, only to be interrupted by accidents, sickness, or death. The most important question is, "Who is willing to consecrate himself today to the Lord?"

IF GOD HAS SPOKEN TO YOUR HEART TO GO, GET READY
AND WHEN HE OPENS THE DOOR, WALK THROUGH IT.
IF YOU DO, YOU'LL NEVER REGRET IT.

# Wake Up Your Mind

**But Daniel purposed in his heart that he would not defile himself with the portion of the king's meat, nor with the wine which he drank. (Daniel 1:8)**

Great people usually aren't smarter, richer or more talented—they're just more committed. Before you can make a real commitment to anything, you have to overcome three problems: First, the security trap. Insecure people don't take risks! They always have a "Plan B" in case God doesn't come through; they depend on things rather than on Him. Next, the success problem. When you've had some success, you want to guard it. You want people to continue thinking well of you, so you start living defensively. Then, there's the satisfaction problem. Listen, "I am rich and increased with goods, and have need of nothing" (Revelation 3:15). If your life is not touched by need, how can you be moved by the needs of others?

Great commitments are made in dark hours. When the Battle of Britain began, Churchill rose and said, "Upon this battle depends the survival of Christian civilization. Let us therefore brace ourselves to our duties and so bare ourselves that, if the British Empire lasts for a thousand years, men will say—this was their finest hour." Make your commitment because it's right—not because it's easy.

IT WAS AFTER DANIEL COMMITTED HIMSELF THAT
GOD DELIVERED HIM AND HONORED HIM.
HE'LL DO THE SAME FOR YOU.

# Your Way or God's?

**He guides the humble in what is right and teaches them His way. (Psalms 25:9, NIV)**

God had a plan, but Abraham had a good idea; as a result, Ishmael was born. Abraham and Sarah couldn't understand why God was taking so long, so they took the matter into their own hands. Sound familiar? Note that God blessed Ishmael and made him a great nation, and, in His mercy today, God is blessing a lot of things that we've given birth to "in the flesh." But, even though He blesses our Ishmaels, He won't *inhabit* them, and He can't fulfill His ultimate purposes through them. The only thing God will use in these last days is that which is born of His will, in His timing, and by His Spirit. God may bless your Ishmael, but you'll have to feed him, and, before you're through, you'll wish you'd done it God's way.

Some of you reading these words right now know from painful experience what I'm speaking about. But that's a price you don't have to pay if you'll just listen to God and follow His direction. David said, "He guides the humble in what is right and teaches them His way." (Psalms 25:9, NIV) God will show you what's right for you, if you'll seek Him. There are only two ways—His way and yours! If you're tired of trying things your way, get down on your knees today and humbly ask Him to show you His way.

**WHY WOULD YOU EVEN CONSIDER ANYTHING ELSE?**

*The Next Step*

**In his heart a man plans his course, but the LORD determines
his steps. (Proverbs 16:9, NIV)**

Have you been asking God for specific direction for your life?
You should, for He knows the next step you need to take.
When you're in His will, you can pray with greater faith, because
you know you're doing what He has told you to. John says, "We
have confidence before God and receive from Him anything we
ask, because we obey His commands and do what pleases Him"
(1 John 3:21,22, NIV).

God knows what it will take to turn you around and get you
moving in the right direction! For Jonah it took three days at the
bottom of the ocean. Listen: "But Jonah ran away from the Lord"
(John 1:3, NIV). Imagine, trying to run from God! Where are
you going to go? For the prodigal son, it meant losing every penny
and every friend he had. Has it occurred to you that nobody is
coming to bail you out this time? God won't let them. The pressure
you're feeling right now is just His way of getting you back in line.
The only thing that will truly make you feel good about yourself
again will be finding and doing God's will. Otherwise, your life is
pointless! Paul said, "I have finished my course" (2 Timothy 4:7).
Try to envision the finish! What will that scene be like? Will you
be able to look back with joy and say the same thing?

IF YOU CAN, THEN TRULY NOTHING ELSE WILL MATTER!

# Someone Special

**Enjoy life with your wife, whom you love.
(Ecclesiastes 9:9, NIV)**

If you're looking for someone who can be everything to you, don't look around—look up! God is the only one who can fill that bill. When you marry someone, you inherit their weaknesses as well as their strengths. It's a package deal. By expecting perfection, you're asking more from them than you can provide yourself. Nobody's always "there" or always "on target" or always anything.

On the other hand, when you get into trouble, you can count on your partner. Marriage is having someone to curl up with when the world seems cold. Someone who's as concerned as you are when the children are ill. It's having a hand that keeps checking your forehead when you aren't well and a shoulder to cry on when they lower your parent's body into the ground.

T.D. Jakes writes, "To the one you marry you're saying, 'When my time comes to leave this world, when the chill of eternity blows away my birthdays, and my future stands still in the night, it's your face I want to kiss good-bye. It's your hand I want to squeeze as I slip from time into eternity. As the curtain closes on all I have attempted to do and be, I want to look into your eyes and see that I mattered. Not what I looked like or how much money I made, even how talented I was. I just want to look into the eyes of someone who loved me, and see I mattered!'"

**IF YOU HAVE SOMEONE LIKE THAT TODAY, LET THEM KNOW YOU LOVE THEM AND APPRECIATE THEM.**

# Trust God

**Who is among you that feareth the LORD, that obeyeth the voice of his servant, that walketh in darkness, and hath no light? Let him trust in the name of the LORD.**
**(Isaiah 50:10)**

I heard about a man who received four long-distance calls before he could even get out of the house one morning. Everybody had problems, and they all wanted him to come and solve them "right now!" He told his wife to forget about breakfast and rushed out, only to discover his car wouldn't start—so he called a taxi. When he got into the taxi, he yelled, "All right, let's get going!" The driver asked, "Where do you want me to take you?" He replied, "I don't care where we go, I've got problems everywhere."

Do you feel like that today? Have you done all you know to do, but the situation hasn't improved? Here's your answer: "Trust in the name of the Lord" (Isaiah 50:10). God's character, God's faithfulness, and God's power are all wrapped up in His name. So, when you pray and claim the promises in His name, you're trusting in His character, His faithfulness, and His power. It's like standing on a rock! All of us have times when our faith is weak and we struggle to believe. But God is faithful to us even in those moments. Listen: "If we believe not, yet He abideth faithful: He cannot deny Himself" (2 Timothy 2:13). God knows what you are going through today, and He'll help you, if you'll just turn it all over to Him.

---

GO AHEAD; ALL IT REQUIRES IS ONE STEP OF FAITH
ON YOUR PART.

# A Sense of Peace

**Peace I leave with you, my peace I give unto you.**
**(John 14:27)**

Look at what Jesus left you in His will. Peace. He called it "My peace." It's a sense of well-being that transcends anything you've ever experienced before. The wonderful thing is that He didn't just die and leave it to you, He rose again to make sure you got it. This peace kept Paul through the worst storm of his life. Listen: "There stood by me this night the Angel of God, whose I am and whom I serve, saying, Fear not, Paul" (Acts 27:23,24). With Him on board, nothing—absolutely nothing—can happen to you.

And you can never overuse His peace or run out of it. It's like the loaves and fishes that Jesus multiplied—the more you use it, the more it increases. Isaiah said, "Thou wilt keep him in perfect peace whose mind is stayed on Thee: because he trusteth in thee" (Isaiah 26:3). He will become your peace only when He becomes your constant focus.

Jewish people greet one another with the word "shalom." It means peace, well-being, and wholeness. And your Heavenly Father is actually called Jehovah-Shalom—"The Lord is [my] Peace" (Judges 6:24, NIV). What a promise—and it's yours today! Isaiah says, "If only you had paid attention to My commands, your peace would have been like a river" (Isaiah 48:18, NIV).

---

IF YOU'VE LOST YOUR SENSE OF PEACE TODAY,
GET BACK INTO GOD'S PRESENCE IMMEDIATELY AND
ASK HIM WHAT YOU NEED TO DO TO PUT THINGS RIGHT.

# Words Breathe Life

**He who guards his mouth and his tongue
keeps himself from calamity. (Proverbs 21:23, NIV)**

If you want others to forget something—don't talk about it! If you don't want to hear about it for the rest of your life, don't sow the seeds of it into the minds of others. Words breathe life into everything. Arguments would cease, and memory would have no record, if only we had the wisdom to know when to be quiet.

Your words will either wound or heal. Listen carefully: "The words of a talebearer are as wounds, and they go down into the innermost parts" (Proverbs 18:8). Listen again: "A wholesome tongue is a tree of life" (Proverbs 15:4). The choice is yours.

Be careful about confessing your mistakes. You may be sincere, but the issues you raise can live longer than the explanations you give. You can't stop people from shooting at you, but you don't have to give them ammunition. Certainly there are times when public disclosure is right and wise, but not often. If you have sinned, ask God to forgive you, and He will. (See 1 John 1:9.) Then focus on the future and put everything else in God's hands. If He can deliver you, then He can defend you; if He doesn't do either right away, He'll develop you.

THE IMPORTANT THING TO REMEMBER TODAY IS THAT
HE'S COMMITTED TO YOU—HE'LL NEVER, NEVER
LET YOU GO! WHAT ASSURANCE!

# *Measurements*

**For with the measure you use,
it will be measured to you. (Luke 6:38, NIV)**

Has God blessed you financially? Have you increased your giving back to Him? When you started, you probably gave in teaspoons, for that was the level of your faith. But when God gave you more, did you change your measuring instrument? I'm talking about moving from a teaspoon to a cup, then to a bucket, then to a wheelbarrow, and, who knows, before you're through, you might even need a pick-up truck. The point is that the tithe (10%) is the least you should give to God. (See Malachi 3:10.) Only your faith can determine the limit.

Do you need a raise? How about giving God one? How about giving Him 10%—not of what you already have, but of what you need to fulfill your vision? This is not some get-rich-quick scheme. Before God will trust you with more, He'll examine your motives and your attitude. And if your giving doesn't require faith, it won't please Him anyway. (See Hebrews 11:6.) Furthermore, God will watch how you act in times of difficulty, to see whether you stretch or shrink. Isaac literally "sowed" his way out of a famine. Listen: "Then Isaac sowed in that land and received in the same year an hundredfold; and the Lord blessed him" (Genesis 26:12). Jesus said that whatever you give to spread the Gospel, you will receive back one hundred times, now, in this time. (See Mark 10:29-30, NIV.)

—m—

GOD LOVES TO FIND PEOPLE WHO'LL BELIEVE HIM AND
PUT THESE PRINCIPLES INTO PRACTICE.
WILL YOU BE ONE OF THEM?

# Hollow Inside

**Devote yourselves to prayer.
(Colossians 4:2, NASB)**

In his book, *The Power and the Blessing*, Jack Hayford says, "I had gone on vacation, and I needed it! It was delightful to get to the beach. But about the fourth day … I found I was feeling empty inside. Then it occurred to me that for four days, I hadn't read a word of Scripture, prayed a prayer, or sung a song of praise. It was just kind of 'let's get away from it all.' We were so involved with church that we didn't want to do anything 'godly' for a while. But suddenly I was called back by the inner hollowness that I felt. Through that experience, I learned that you can't recover at a physical or emotional level if you neglect the spiritual level." What insight!

Paul says, "Devote yourselves to prayer, keeping alert in it with an attitude of thanksgiving" (Colossians 4:2, NASB). Until you've been in God's presence and drawn strength from His Word, you're not equal to the challenges you'll face today. You may take a day off from reading and praying, but your enemy won't take time off! Jesus said, "Watch ye and pray, lest ye enter into temptation. The spirit truly is ready, but the flesh is weak" (Mark 14:38). Listen to this line from one of John Wesley's daily prayers: "O fill up all that is wanting and reform whatever is amiss in me. Perfect the things that concern me."

**ARE YOU SENSING AN INNER HOLLOWNESS TODAY?
IF SO, MAKE THIS YOUR PRAYER, TOO.**

# Made Whole

**Woman, thou art loosed from thine infirmity.
(Luke 13:12)**

Listen: "And He was teaching in one of the synagogues on the Sabbath. And behold, there was a woman which had a spirit of infirmity eighteen years and was bowed together and could in no wise lift up herself. And when Jesus saw her, He said unto her, 'Woman, thou art loosed from thine infirmity'... and immediately she was made straight and glorified God. And the ruler of the synagogue answered with indignation ... 'There are six days in which men ought to work: in them therefore come and be healed, not on the Sabbath Day.' The Lord then answered him and said, 'Thou hypocrite ... and ought not this woman, being a daughter of Abraham, whom Satan hath bound, lo, these eighteen years, be loosed?' ... and all the people rejoiced for all the glorious things that were done by Him" (Luke 13:10-17).

Are you like this woman? Do you know someone who is? No matter how much you try, you just can't lift yourself up or straighten yourself out. Don't despair; come to Jesus. When He's through with you, your adversaries will be ashamed, your accusers will be silenced, and those who contributed to your low self-esteem will be confounded at what God has done for you. Come just as you are! Your past doesn't matter. Her potential, bound for eighteen years, was released the moment she came face to face with Jesus.

AND WHAT HE DID FOR HER, HE'S JUST WAITING TO DO
FOR YOU, TOO. WILL YOU GIVE HIM A CHANCE?

# Don't Quit!

**I've got my eye on my goal … I'm not turning back.
(Philippians 3:13, TM)**

Get your eyes out of the rear-view mirror and start looking ahead. Celebrate the fact that you've survived! The devil tried to destroy you, but the good news is that he failed! In spite of all you've been through, you're a walking, talking, breathing "miracle of grace." Right? God must have kept you around for some reason, so try to find it! Look at David after his encounter with Bathsheba and Peter after he denied Jesus. They're the same men, just recycled and restored by grace! That's what God can do! Your last chapter has not been written yet. Refuse to accept the verdict of those who say you'll never amount to anything. Get up! Stand on God's promises, take off your grave clothes, and dare to live again!

Paul says, "Let's keep focused on that goal, those of us who want everything God has for us" (Philippians 3:14, TM). You may say, "But it's so hard." Sure it is—for all of us. But you'll never discover your potential for victory until you get into a battle. It's in your struggles that you discover your strengths and learn to deal with your weaknesses. The biggest sin of all is not failing—it's quitting!

WHEN YOU QUIT, THERE'S NOTHING MORE GOD CAN DO FOR YOU. SO, ASK HIM TO GIVE YOU THE STRENGTH TO GET BACK ON TRACK TODAY.

# Bring Down Goliath

**Those who trust in the LORD are like Mount Zion, which cannot be shaken but endures forever.
(Psalms 125:1, NIV)**

Are you facing a giant problem today? If so, read 1 Samuel 17 and notice two things. First, David spent enough time with God to know Him intimately. Until you know someone, how can you trust them? Prayer is how you get to know God and how His power is released into any situation. In prayer, you take hold of God's eagerness, not try to overcome His reluctance. Listen: "Call to Me, and I will answer you, and I will tell you great and mighty things, which you do not know" (Jeremiah 33:3, NASB). God will show you what to do, if you'll just call on Him.

Second, when David went out to meet Goliath—he went alone while the others stayed back in their tents. Before anything great is ever achieved in reality, it's first believed in somebody's heart. The applause may come later, but whoever steps out first will usually step out alone!

A missionary society wrote to David Livingstone in Africa saying, "Some people would like to join you. What's the easiest road to get to where you are?" Livingstone replied, "If they're looking for the easiest road, tell them to stay in England. *I want people who will come, even if there is no road at all!*"

Child of God, step out and follow the Lord.

—∞—

**THE ONE WHO BROUGHT DOWN GOLIATH WILL BRING DOWN THE GIANT YOU'RE FACING TODAY. JUST TRUST HIM TO DO IT!**

187

# Use Your Heart

**If I speak with human eloquence and angelic ecstasy,
but don't love, I'm nothing but the creaking of a rusty gate.
(1 Corinthians 13:1, TM)**

People don't care how much you know, until they know how much you care. If you love your opinions more than you love your friends, you'll defend your opinions and destroy your friends. Step back and look at what's really important. Paul says, "Love … always looks for the best" (1 Corinthians 13:7, TM). Give others the benefit of the doubt. When working with yourself, use your head; when working with others, use your heart! And learn to be flexible. Jefferson wrote, "In matters of principle, stand like a rock; in matters of taste, swim with the current." Don't major on minors, and stop fighting over things that will ultimately make no difference.

Be gracious with others in the same way God is with you. Mature love allows someone who has been defeated to ease out of the situation with their dignity and self-worth intact. Once the point has been made, back off! You're always going to have conflicts. They'll give you either ulcers or understanding; the choice is yours. Don't overreact; don't drop a bomb when a sling shot will do. When conflict arises, make it a time to learn, not to lose. Listen carefully: "Love never gives up. Love cares more for others than for self" (1 Corinthians 13:4, TM).

ASK GOD TO GIVE YOU THIS KIND OF LOVE TODAY.

# The Best Days

**With long life will I satisfy him, and show him my salvation.
(Psalms 91:16)**

Build your life around your personn not your role, otherwise when things change, you'll feel worthless. Being a good mother is a self-sacrificing job, but when those demands are over it's easy to feel like Naomi. Her name meant "my joy." But, after she lost her children and her husband, she changed it to "Mara," which means "bitterness." Don't allow changing times to change who you are. God still had a lot for Naomi to do. She would one day care for a little boy who was destined to become part of the lineage of Jesus himself. What an honor! When your circumstances change, remember your life isn't over. Redefine your purpose, gather up your assets, and keep on living and giving.

Look out for "The Mara Mentality." She allowed herself to become cynical; don't let that happen to you. Discouragement comes when we feel like we've seen and heard it all, and most of it is bad. That's not true! No matter how old you are, you can never say you've seen it all. You don't know what God will do with your life before it's over, but He does tend to save the best for last. He promised, through David, that we would bring forth "fruit in old age" (Psalms 92:14).

—m—

**IF YOU'LL GIVE GOD HALF A CHANCE,
HE'LL MAKE THESE THE BEST DAYS OF YOUR LIFE.**

# Point of View

**Joseph named his firstborn Manasseh ... "because God has made me forget all my trouble." The second son he named Ephraim ... "because God has made me fruitful in the land of my suffering." (Genesis 41:51-52, NIV)**

You can't change the events of the past, but you can change your perception of them. It's all in how you choose to look at it. If you can see God at work in it, you'll come out a better person. Even if you can't see Him clearly, at least trust Him until you can; He knows what He's doing. Begin to praise Him that He's working everything out for your good. (See Romans 8:28.) Before it's over, you'll be able to say, "If I hadn't experienced that, I wouldn't have received this." It all begins with a decision to let it go. Paul said, "This one thing I do, forgetting those things which are behind" (Philippians 3:13). If he could do it then, by God's grace, you can too.

Joseph's family betrayed him and broke his heart. But when he got through it, he realized they'd only positioned him for blessing and prepared him for his destiny. That's what's happening with you right now! Every day as he watched his sons, Ephraim and Manasseh, grow up, their names constantly reminded him that God can help you to forget everything you've been through and make you stronger and wiser because of it.

WHAT AN ASSURANCE!

# Don't Jump!

**I will guard my ways, that I may not sin with my tongue.
(Psalms 39:1, NASB)**

When John D. Rockefeller ran the Standard Oil Company, one of his senior executives made a mistake which cost them over $2 million. Most of the other executives thought Rockefeller would come down on him "like a ton of bricks." But they were wrong! Before he called the man in, he sat down, took a notepad, and wrote across the top of it *points in favor of this man!* Then he listed the man's virtues, including how he'd helped the company make the right decision on other occasions and earned them millions in profits.

One of the senior executives who witnessed it, later said, "Whenever I'm tempted to rip into someone, I force myself first to sit down to compile a list of the good qualities they have. By the time I've finished, I have the right perspective, and best of all, my anger is under control. I can't tell you how many times this habit has prevented me from committing one of life's costliest of mistakes—losing my temper. I recommend it to anyone who must deal with people."

Child of God, before you jump to conclusions about anyone, stop and pray for wisdom, then make a list of their good points. (See Philippians 4:8.) If you do, you'll probably come to a different conclusion, you'll approach them in the right spirit, and you won't say things you'll regret later.

**THERE'S A LITTLE DIVINE WISDOM FOR YOU TODAY.**

# Throw Your Shoe

**Pray without ceasing.
(1 Thessalonians 5:17)**

For several nights, a little girl threw her shoe under the bed before getting in. When her mother finally asked her why, she said, "My Sunday school teacher said, if I have to get down by the bed every morning to look for my shoe, I'll probably remember to say my prayers while I'm there." What a great idea! If it helps, throw your shoe under the bed! You'll never get on your feet till you first get on your knees. David knew that prayer was like oxygen to his soul. Listen: "Day and night I cry out before You" (Psalms 88:1, NIV). Nothing, nothing, nothing in your life will change until you start praying, until you bring God into the picture. That's why Paul writes, "Pray without ceasing."

Dr. Bill Hybels says in his book, *Too Busy Not to Pray,* "I knew more about prayer than I ever practiced in my own life. So I decided to study the subject until I finally understood it. I read every book I could get my hands on. I even memorized all the Scriptures that speak about prayer. Then one day I did something absolutely radical: I prayed! As a result, I've had a long list of miraculous answers, but the greatest result has been the difference it has made in my relationship with God."

IF YOU WANT A RELATIONSHIP WITH GOD,
YOU'VE GOT TO SPEND TIME WITH HIM IN PRAYER.
WOULDN'T TODAY BE A GOOD DAY TO START?

# Elizabeth and Mary

**For with God nothing shall be impossible.**
**(Luke 1:37)**

Your age is no problem to God. Elizabeth was too old, Mary was barely a teenager, but when God moved, they both became pregnant with a promise. Never forget, God will bless you in His own time and on His own terms! For six months Elizabeth had been a recluse. But one day she answered the door, and it was Mary. Suddenly everything changed. In that moment, the child leaped in her womb, and she was filled with the Holy Spirit. (See Luke 1:41.)

That's still how God works. When the Holy Spirit comes upon you, God's plan and purpose will begin to rise up within you. First, you'll receive the seed, then it will begin to grow, and finally, after the pain and the stretching, you'll give birth to your destiny. In that moment you'll rejoice, because you'll know why you were born. Your situation may look impossible today, but God says in effect, "You're about to have visitation! Don't just sit in your chair and die! Get up and answer the door!"

Look at Mary's response: "Be it unto me according to thy word" (Luke 1:38). That's it! Not according to your marital status, your age, your job, the color of your skin, even what you deserve, but according to His Word. When God speaks, the opinions of others simply don't matter anymore. His verdict settles the issues and determines the future.

—⦿—

**ALL YOU HAVE TO DO IS BELIEVE HIM AND**
**DO WHAT HE TELLS YOU TO DO.**

# Basic Survival Skills

**The LORD is my light and my salvation;
whom shall I fear? (Psalms 27:1)**

For seven years, Jeremiah Denton was a prisoner of war in North Vietnam. Most of that time he was in solitary confinement. As one of the highest ranking American prisoners, he was subjected to grueling torture. But he not only survived, he overcame it, and when he returned home, he was elected to the United States Senate. How did he ever do it? He says that one of his "basic survival skills" was quoting passages he had memorized from the Bible. Internalized Scriptures were his sword to defend himself against the cruelest weapons the enemy could use. He used them to build a wall of protection around himself. Memorized Scriptures literally became his prayers.

Try it today! Meditate upon His Word. Memorize it! Begin to pray it, and watch your faith grow and your fears melt. You pray differently when you're not sure you'll see the light of another day. David spent years on the run from King Saul. One night in a cave he wrote, "I will exalt you, O LORD, for you lifted me out of the depths and did not let my enemies gloat over me. O LORD my God, I called to you for help and you healed me" (Psalms 30:1-2, NIV). What a testimony!

GO AHEAD, CHILD OF GOD, START DECLARING
HIS WORD OVER YOUR SITUATION TODAY.
IT WORKED FOR JEREMIAH DENTON, FOR DAVID,
AND IT WILL WORK FOR YOU TOO!

**Even in old age they will still produce fruit.
(Psalms 92:14, TLB)**

Listen to these words: "If you have left your dreams behind, if hope is cold, if you no longer look ahead, if your innermost fires are dead—then you are old. But if to God you give your best, and if to life you give the rest, no matter how the years go by, no matter how the birthdays fly—you are not old."

It's not the loss of energy or health that makes you old; it's the loss of vision. Without it you can be old at thirty. With it, you can still be young at ninety.

Last year, almost 70% of the support that was given to God's work came from retired people. How interesting! They were wise enough to know that you can't take it with you, but you can send it on ahead. Solomon said, "He who wins souls is wise" (Proverbs 11:30, NIV). Daniel said, "Those who are wise will shine like the brightness of the heavens, and those who lead many to righteousness like the stars for ever and ever" (Daniel 12:3, NIV). Just because you're shut in doesn't mean you're shut out. You're a vital part of every soul that's won and every life that's touched when you stand by a man of God or a ministry He has raised up. You'll shine like the stars! Now there's a different definition of stardom—a true one! *Unless you are cheese or wine, age simply doesn't matter.* David said, "But the godly shall flourish like palm trees" (Psalms 92:12, TLB).

**DID YOU KNOW THAT A PALM TREE PRODUCES ITS BIGGEST HARVEST OF FRUIT IN ITS LAST YEARS? REJOICE, THAT'S YOU HE'S TALKING ABOUT!**

# What Have You Done?

**Give your entire attention to what God is doing right now, and don't get worked up about what may or may not happen tomorrow. (Matthew 6:34, TM)**

Here's a poem I think you'll want to ponder carefully:

You say you'll do much in the years to come, but what have you done today?

You plan to give wealth in a princely sum, but how much have you given away?

You'll heal broken hearts and dry every tear, bring to them hope and take away fear;

Carry His Word to those far and near; but what have you done today?

You say you'll be kind after a while, but what have you done today?

The lonely and hurting wait for your smile, you promised to light up their way;

Your aim is to give truth a grander birth and to steadfast faith a deeper worth,

To carry His love to the ends of the earth, but what have you done today?

You plan to reap much in the by and by, but what have you sown today?

You plan to build mansions up in the sky, but what have you built today?

It's nice to dream and in visions bask, but here and now have you done your task?

—m—

**THE ONLY REAL QUESTION THAT MATTERS, I ASK, IS WHAT HAVE YOU DONE TODAY?**

# *Tomorrow*

**Do not boast about tomorrow, for you do not know
what a day may bring forth. (Proverbs 27:1, NIV)**

We spend so much of our lives worrying about yesterday and tomorrow. Yet one's buried, and the other's unborn. There's not a thing you can do about either—except let them steal today right out of your hands. Don't do it! David said, "This is the day which the Lord hath made; we will rejoice and be glad in it" (Psalms 118:24). Get out of the grandstand; you can win only as you play the game. Don't die in the waiting room! Jesus said, "Until now, the Kingdom of Heaven has been forcefully advancing and forceful men lay hold of it" (Matthew 11:12, NIV).

Did you hear that? Seize this day with all its blessings and its challenges, and live every moment of it. There's only one way to overcome your past—learn from it. Let the very thing that others thought would destroy you, develop you into the person God has called you to be. Don't wait for "some day"—God is "a very present help" (Psalms 46:1). Never say, "I don't have enough time." You have exactly the same number of hours in your day as everybody else, including the people you most admire. There are two things you can count on God to do: First, to give you a clear understanding of His will and assignment for your life; second, to give you the time and the ability to carry it out.

**WHAT MORE COULD YOU ASK FOR?**

# New Things

**Forget the former things; do not dwell on the past.
See, I am doing a new thing! (Isaiah 43:19-19, NIV)**

It's dangerous to assume that you'll keep getting from life only what you've gotten before. God has wonderful ways of giving back purpose and meaning to our lives when we've lost it. He gave Jacob a new name, He gave Sarah a new baby (at 90), and He gave David a new song. For Naomi, it came through a relationship with Ruth (one she tried to discourage). Be careful when you avoid people or send them away. They may hold the key to God's blessing in your life. Listen: "And Ruth said, Entreat me not to leave thee or to return from following after thee: for whither thou goest, I will go; and where thou lodgest, I will lodge; thy people shall be my people, and thy God my God" (Ruth 1:16).

Naomi thought her only connection to Ruth was through her deceased son, but she was wrong. If you're very family-oriented, it's easy to build all your relationships within the family. Then when circumstances change, you feel lost and alone. There are bonds that are stronger than blood; I call them "God-bonds." The Lord wanted to bless Naomi and allow her to pass her wisdom on to someone worthy of it, so He gave her Ruth. Let God pick your friends!

JUST KEEP YOUR HEART OPEN, FOR HE HAS SOME NEW
THINGS HE WANTS TO DO AND SOME NEW PEOPLE HE'D
LIKE YOU TO MEET IN THE DAYS AHEAD.

# The Time Crunch

**There is an appointed time for everything.**
**(Ecclesiastes 3:1, NASB)**

Your life will go nowhere until you learn to value time, protect time, and use time wisely. Time management is not hyperventilating with calendars and stopwatches. It's learning how precious one hour is. Until you learn that, you'll waste days, months, and years. Stop agonizing over the time you don't have and organize the time you do have. If you don't, your days will endure without purpose, and your life will end without accomplishment. When you die, what will others remember you for—the good times you had or the difference you made? You, and only you, have the power to answer that question.

First, you always have enough time to do all that God wants you to do. If you don't, you're involved in things He never gave you to do. Get rid of them! (See John 17:4.) Second, learn to "come apart" before you "fall apart." Jesus did often. He said, "My yoke is easy" (Matthew 11:30). What kills us is the stuff we allow others to put on us. If your schedule is out of control today, get alone with God to ask Him to show you any problem areas.

ASK HIM TO TELL YOU WHAT HE THINKS YOU SHOULD BE
DOING. NOW THERE'S A PLAN THAT WILL WORK FOR YOU.

# Hearing God

**Blessed is the man who listens to me.**
**(Proverbs 8:34, NIV)**

A perfect day begins by hearing the voice of God. In his great book *Secrets of the Journey*, Dr. Mike Murdock says, "Hear the voice of God before you get your doctor's report, for He's your great physician. Hear His voice first, then the critical words of others will have little effect on you. 'Great peace have they which love Thy law; and nothing shall offend them' (Psalms 119:165). Hear the voice of God and you will not require the praise of others, nor will you be seduced by their flattery. His words will set you free to help others, but lean only on Him.

"Hear the voice of God, and your attitude will change instantly. You'll be able to face the future without anger or anxiety. His word settles every issue; time always proves Him correct. Don't be pressured by people's demands or intimidated by their complaints. Before you respond to anyone—hear from Him. Your time, your love, and your money is seed too precious to waste. It deserves a screening process. Qualify the soil. Is it stony ground, thorny ground, good ground? (See Matthew 13.) It's so easy to be persuaded by people—the wrong people. Finally, hear God's voice before you make any significant change in your life. You don't design the plan, but you must discover it."

---

GET INTO HIS PRESENCE TODAY, AND LET HIM
REVEAL HIS PLAN FOR YOUR LIFE.

# Get Over It!

**Finally, the Lord said to Samuel, "You have mourned long enough for Saul." (1 Samuel 16:1, TLB)**

Are you still trying to "get over" the past or "salvage" what you can from it? Are you trying to explain to people who aren't listening—and wouldn't care even if they could because they've moved on. The problem is, you haven't! My old mentor used to say, "More things are forgotten than are ever solved." Samuel was so "hung up" on Saul—the king God had rejected—that he couldn't see David—the king God had prepared. Saul was the past, but David was the future, and when he came to the throne, God's people would be blessed as they'd never been before.

One of the devil's most successful strategies is to get you focused on things that don't matter any more. If someone has hurt you, forgive them and move on. If it keeps coming up, keep forgiving them until it loses the power to hurt you any more. Why spend the only life you'll ever have trying to justify the past, when you can move forward into the blessings of God. If you win your point and miss your purpose, what have you gained? (See Philippians 3:13.)

**YOU'VE OBSESSED OVER IT LONG ENOUGH—MOVE ON!**

# You and Your Money

**Don't trust in uncertain riches, but in the living God.
(1 Timothy 6:17)**

Is God tapping you on the shoulder to remind you of a few important facts? First, command those who are rich not to be haughty! It is amazing what a little prosperity will do to some people. When I was growing up in Belfast, a family on our street suddenly came into money, bought a new car, added an indoor toilet, and promptly stopped speaking to the rest of us! My mom, with a touch of dry wit, remarked, "Same cat, just different whiskers!"

Whether you're "old money," "new money," or "no money," listen: Don't trust in uncertain riches but in the living God who gives us all things richly to enjoy. God wants you to succeed, and He wants you to enjoy everything He has given you. All He asks is that you remember who gave it to you and show some gratitude! By the way, He also said that when you have more than enough to meet your own needs, "be ready to give and willing to share" (1 Timothy 6:18).

TODAY, SOMEONE WHO IS NEEDY WILL WALK ACROSS
YOUR PATH. BE READY TO GIVE.

## Added Blessings

**Much is required from those to whom much is given.**
**(Luke 12:48, TLB)**

When God entrusts you with more, He'll let you get away with less! In his outstanding book, *The Assignment*, Dr. Mike Murdock says, "You will only succeed when your assignment becomes your obsession." Jesus refused to let anything or anyone break his focus. When Peter got in his way, Jesus said to him, "Get thee behind me, Satan; thou art an offense unto me" (Matthew 16:23). Imagine trying that today!

Refuse anything that weighs you down or distracts you from doing God's will. "Lay aside every weight" (Hebrews 12:1). Be careful with relationships that lessen your hunger for God or weaken your resolve to do His will. Listen: "No one serving as a soldier gets involved in civilian affairs—he wants to please his commanding officer" (2 Timothy 2:4, NIV). One day a man, who had not spoken to Mike in twenty years, called to say, "I have to meet with you urgently!" When they met, the man wanted to get him involved in a multi-level marketing program. The product and plan were both good, and the income potential was great. The trouble was the time involved would have taken away from other things. When Mike said, "No," he never heard from the man again. How interesting! When you build your life around your assignment, wrong relationships will die and right ones will be born.

**NOTHING IN YOUR LIFE TODAY IS MORE IMPORTANT THAN FINDING AND FULFILLING YOUR PURPOSE.**

# Failure Is Not Final

**For though a righteous man falls seven times, he rises again. (Proverbs 24:16)**

I'm told that successful people fail two out of every five times they attempt something, whereas unsuccessful people fail three out of every five times. That's not a lot of difference, is it? We all fail at something every day. The only people who don't are dead. Some of us are so afraid of failing that we try to "tiptoe" safely to the grave, without blowing it somewhere along the way. Why is it that failure destroys some of us, yet others thrive and become stronger because of it? The secret is that they turn failure into their teacher and their greatest defeats into learning experiences.

What do you believe God has called you to do with your life? Step out in faith and try it! God said He would strengthen and uphold you. (See Isaiah 41:10.) You can't do better than that! Recently, I read these inspiring words: "I'd rather be ashes than dust. I'd rather my spark burn out than that it should be stifled by dry rot. The proper function of my life is to live, not exist. So I shall not waste my days in trying to prolong them. I shall use every moment." Can you say that? Charles Kettering said, "Virtually nothing comes out right the first time. Repeated failures are just finger posts on the road to success."

THE IMPORTANT THING TO REMEMBER IS THAT
WHEN YOU FALL—FALL FORWARD.
NOW THERE'S SOMETHING TO THINK ABOUT!

# Close the Door

**A gentle answer turns away wrath,
but a harsh word stirs up anger. (Proverbs 15:1, NIV)**

You can't enter the next season of your life with integrity if you don't exit this season right. Close the door gently, for you just might need to walk back through it again some day. Close it with forgiveness. Bitterness will poison your attitude and your memories. It'll destroy you from within. Give to God those who have hurt you, and let Him do the correcting—you're not qualified.

Close the door with your promises and commitments fulfilled. Jesus didn't leave His work. He finished it. (See John 17:4.) Your character is on the line here; whatever it costs, honor your vows! Also, close the door with courage. It's not easy to face tomorrow when you feel all alone, but remember, you're not alone! Jesus said, "Lo, I am with you always, even unto the end of the world" (Matthew 28:20). He will bring you through this if you just stay close to Him.

Finally, close the door in God's timing. Go because He tells you to—not because somebody else does. Go in the knowledge that He has gone before you. He's promised. "The steps of a good man are ordered by the Lord" (Psalms 37:23). Be encouraged today—you're walking a prepared path.

---

WHEN GOD CLOSES ONE DOOR, HE ALWAYS OPENS
ANOTHER. AT THE MOMENT, ALL HE ASKS YOU TO DO
IS TO HAVE CONFIDENCE IN HIM.

# Get Rid of Excuses

**The steps of a good man are directed by the Lord. He delights in each step they take. If they fall it isn't fatal, for the Lord holds them with His hand. (Psalms 37:23-24, TLB)**

It's not what you do that makes you a failure, it's what you say to yourself about it afterwards. Some of the world's greatest successes were once labeled failures. For example: A banker in Iowa laughed and told Alexander Graham Bell to remove that "toy" (the Bell telephone) from his office. A supposedly great movie producer scrawled "Reject" on the screenplay of *Gone With The Wind*. In 1906, the man who was Henry Ford's greatest investor asked that his stock be sold because he didn't believe the company would go anywhere. Can you imagine how he felt later?

Mr. Roebuck sold his part of the Sears Roebuck company for $25,000 because he thought it would "never fly." The last I read, Sears is now selling $40,000 worth of goods every ten seconds. Think about it. You have everything every winner in history had—plus God! What a position to be in! The God of the Red Sea, the lions' den, and the walls of Jericho is your God. He's on your side today! (See Romans 8:37.) The only "up and down" that you should know is getting down to pray, then getting up in the strength of the Lord to go out and win.

---

**THAT'S HIS PLAN FOR YOU TODAY.**

# Damaged Goods

**He hath sent me to heal the brokenhearted,... to set at liberty them that are bruised. (Luke 4:18)**

Tamar was King David's daughter. She was also a rape victim. If you're like her, Jesus said He came to heal the brokenhearted and to set at liberty them that are bruised (see Luke 4:18). If you feel like "damaged goods," He's saying to you today, "I will heal you and deliver you; I will renew you and release you!"

Tamar's future was greater than her past—because she was a child of the King. So are you! You'll come through this and sing the song of the overcomer—because you're His child. Your recovery will begin when you learn to live in the present, not the past. Allow God's love to touch the hurting places inside you. Give all your secrets to Him, and leave them there. The enemy wants to destroy you through what happened, but God wants to restore you as if it had never happened. Like Tamar, you survived! That's a victory worth celebrating. Begin to thank God that you made it! Through Jesus' blood, you'll recover the loss you've suffered at the hands of your abuser.

YOU'LL GET BACK ALL THAT WAS STOLEN FROM YOU. GOD WILL HEAL YOUR BROKEN PLACES AND REBUILD YOUR SELF-ESTEEM. RECEIVE IT TODAY.

# Moving God

**I sought for a man among them, that should make
up the hedge, and stand in the gap before me.
(Ezekiel 22:30)**

In her book *Glorious Intruder*, Joni Eareckson Tada writes about Diane, who suffers from multiple sclerosis: "In her quiet sanctuary, Diane turns her head slightly on the pillow towards the cork board on the wall. Her eyes scan each thumb-tacked card and list. Each photo. Every torn piece of paper, carefully pinned in a row. The stillness is broken as Diane begins to murmur. She's praying. Some would look at her, stiff and motionless, and shake their heads, 'What a shame, her life has no meaning.' But Diane is confident, convinced that her life is significant and that *her labor of prayer counts.*

"She moves mountains that block the paths of missionaries. She helps open the eyes of the spiritually blind in Southeast Asia. She pushes back the kingdom of darkness that blackens the alleys and streets of the gangs in East L.A. She aids homeless mothers, abused children, despondent teenagers, and dying, forgotten, old people in the nursing home down the street from where she lives.

"Diane is an intercessor! She's on the front lines, advancing the Gospel of Christ, holding up week saints, inspiring doubting believers, and delighting her Lord and Savior." Miracles happen when somebody "stands in the gap." (Read Matthew 16:19, James 5:16, and Romans 1:9. )

---

BE ENCOURAGED TODAY, CHILD OF GOD;
YOUR PRAYERS WILL PREVAIL, AND
GOD WILL COME THROUGH ON YOUR BEHALF.

# Successful Failures

**He that overcometh shall inherit all things;**
**and I will be his God, and he shall be my son.**
**(Revelation 21:7)**

"Successful failures" are people who use their set backs to bring them out on top. You successfully fail when it stirs you up to keep on trying. It's like the old farmer whose mule fell into a well. Since he couldn't pull the mule out, he decided to bury him. He got a truckload of dirt and dumped it on top of him. But instead of lying down under the dirt, the mule started kicking and snorting until he worked his way to the top of it. This continued all afternoon, truckload after truckload, and the mule just kept tramping away. Finally, when the dirt reached the top, the mule just snorted and walked away, a dirtier but wiser mule. What was intended to bury him just "put him on top." *That's a successful failure!*

Also, you fail successfully when you discover your true self. When Nathaniel Hawthorne was fired from his job, he was devastated. But his wife said to him, "Now you can start that book you've always wanted to write. Out of that came *The Scarlet Letter.* James Whistler failed at West Point. He also failed in business, so he tried painting—*and the rest is history.* It's not over until God says it's over!

DON'T EVEN HINT OF QUITTING, FOR HIS WORD TO YOU IS,
"HE THAT OVERCOMETH SHALL INHERIT ALL THINGS."

# Survival Seekers

**However, I consider my life worth nothing to me,
if only I may finish the race and complete the task
the Lord Jesus has given me. (Acts 20:24, NIV)**

We were all born with the instinct to survive. We're fighters! But that creates a problem, for Paul says, "I am crucified with Christ" (Galatians 2:20). If your number-one goal is to survive, you're no longer free to make the right decisions. You'll keep doing things based on what feels good or what's acceptable to others, rather than doing what God wants you to do. Next, you'll talk a lot about being *faithful* to the Church, but very little about being *fruitful*. You can bring forth fruit only if you are willing to die. (See John 12:24.) Someone told me recently, "I'm not really accomplishing much, but at least I'm consistent." I asked, "Consistent at what?" If you're "spinning your wheels," you're busy, but you're going nowhere!

All the "survival seekers" in the Bible lost God's best by trying to "look out for number one." Without thinking of Abraham, Lot chose the well-watered plains of Jordan. (See Genesis 13:10.) In the process, he lost his family. The rich young ruler could have been numbered among the disciples of Jesus, but he had too much to lose. (See Mark 10:22.) Sometimes, the more we have, the more insecure we feel and the tighter we hold on. Are you doing that? Jesus said, "For whoever wishes to save his life shall lose it, but whoever loses his life for My sake, he is the one who will save it" (Luke 9:24, NASB).

**THE ONLY SAFE PLACE TO BE TODAY IS IN HIS WILL!**

# How's Your Faith?

**But I know, that even now, whatsoever thou wilt ask of God, God will give it thee. (John 11:22)**

Take a moment and visit the funeral of Lazarus. Heartbroken and distraught, Martha says to Jesus, "If You had been here, my brother would not have died." That's called "if only" faith. It says, "If only we'd lived in the days of Jesus." "If only we could be prayed for by a certain person." "If only" faith plans for an epitaph, not a resurrection.

When Jesus told Martha that Lazarus would live again, she replied, "I know that he shall rise again in the resurrection" (John 11:24). That's called "some day" faith. People who have it sing, "In the sweet by and by." With them, everything belongs to the future. But you need to know your rights, your privileges, and your authority—right now. When you do, your life will change radically.

Finally, Martha said, "But I know that *even now* God will give You whatever You ask" (John 11:21, NIV). That's it—"even now" faith! In spite of all you've been through, God has the power to raise you up again. You may have been married and divorced; be struggling with habits; be living in a prison or a penthouse; be black or white, gay or straight; it doesn't matter.

—m—

BY GOD'S GRACE AND POWER, "EVEN NOW" YOU CAN
COME OUT OF YOUR GRAVE AND LIVE AGAIN. ALL YOU
HAVE TO DO IS OPEN YOUR HEART TO JESUS TODAY.

# Melted Down

**Let us consider how we may spur one another on toward love and good deeds. (Hebrews 10:24, NIV)**

During the reign of Oliver Cromwell, the British government ran low on the silver used to make coins. So Cromwell sent his men to a local cathedral to search for some. They reported back to him that the only silver they could find was in the statues of the saints standing in the corners. Cromwell sent back word, "Good; let's melt down the saints and put them back into circulation." That's what we need—men and women who've been melted down, filled with God's Spirit, and put back into circulation. What good is our experience if we keep it in the church, enjoy it in the church, and leave it in the church?

For me, the highlight of last Christmas was providing gifts for a struggling single mother and her three children from our church. Working 10 hours a day, she could provide only the bare essentials. So we bought her 14-year-old boy Nike basketball shoes, a doll-set for her little girl, and clothes for the baby. When my wife and her mom delivered them to the woman, complete with a turkey, groceries, and all the trimmings, this mother broke down and wept with gratitude. It was the first time anyone had done anything like this for them. All around you today are people with genuine needs, who feel unloved and unwanted. Share with them what you've got, both materially and spiritually.

---

ASK GOD TODAY TO MELT YOU DOWN AND
PUT YOU BACK INTO CIRCULATION.

# Jawbones

**Put to death, therefore, whatever belongs to your earthly nature. (Colossians 3:5, NIV)**

David Robinson says, "The reason God was able to use the jawbone of an ass to give Samson victory over the Philistines was because it was completely dead, and there was no flesh left on it (see Judges 5:15). Consider that if you want to be used by God "the flesh" must go and you must die. That's not a popular message; we'd rather focus on the benefits and the blessings of serving the Lord. But there's a price to be paid. Jesus didn't tell us to make converts; He told us to make disciples. He made it hard to join, easy to leave. He wanted only those who ware committed unto death. He said, "Any of you who does not give up everything cannot be My disciple" (Luke 14:33, NIV). What a price tag! Are you truly His disciple?

*The Message* paraphrases Paul in these words: "Everything happening to me in this jail only serves to make Christ more accurately known, regardless of whether I live or die. They didn't shut me up; they gave me a pulpit! Alive, I'm Christ's messenger; dead, I'm His bounty. Life versus even more life! I can't lose" (Philippians 1:20, TM).

---

THAT WAS PAUL'S ATTITUDE TOWARDS LIFE. WHAT'S YOURS? PERHAPS IT'S TIME TO GO BACK TO THE CROSS.

# Love Others

**Bear ye one another's burdens, and so fulfill the law of Christ.
(Galatians 6:2)**

If you want to be transformed from a victim into an overcomer, find someone mature enough to share your struggles with. When you do, you've taken a giant step towards releasing the past—instead of constantly reliving it. Thank God for those who've been able to live victoriously all their lives. But most of us haven't. If we're not careful, we can easily become judgmental. Don't try to be super-spiritual in order to compensate for an embarrassing past. You can't earn salvation—so don't try. It's a gift you receive by faith. (See Ephesians 2:8-9.)

Get rid of your embarrassment over wounded people. Yes, we've got them in the Church. Sometimes they fail, and we have to re-admit them to the hospital to be treated again. That's what hospitals are for. And churches are spiritual hospitals. My struggle may not be yours, but don't judge me while you're wrestling with something equally as incriminating. Jesus was so different. Every time He saw a hurting person, He reached out and ministered to them. And you'll never be more like Him than when you accept people as they are, refusing to give up on them because you know what God's grace can do in their lives.

---

**ASK GOD TO GIVE YOU A GREATER LOVE FOR
HURTING PEOPLE.**

# Water Under the Bridge

**For you shall forget your misery; you shall remember it as water that passes away ... you shall lie down and none shall make you afraid. (Job 11:16-19, AMP)**

Can the pain of the past ever be forgotten? Yes! You can take the misery out of the memory—like you'd pull the stinger out of an insect bite—then healing will begin immediately. Job said, "You shall forget your misery; you shall remember it as waters that pass away." Go ahead, stand in the stream of God's love and release it. Let it all go. It was night, but now it's day! Nobody understood this better than David. He was humiliated before the world, yet when God healed him, he wrote, "Weeping may endure for a night, but joy cometh in the morning" (Psalms 30:5).

The only safe place to be is in the arms of God. It's there that you can allow the past to fall from you like a garment. You may remember it, but you don't have to wear it any more. Listen again: "You shall lie down, and none shall make you afraid" (Job 11:19). No more pacing the floor, no more bad dreams, no more fear of tomorrow. God says, "None shall make thee afraid." Rise up and take authority over every memory that keeps you linked to the past.

—⟶⟵—

LET THE PEACE AND THE ANOINTING OF GOD HEAL THE SCARS, BREAK THE CHAINS THAT BIND YOU, AND SET YOU TOTALLY FREE. Claim it today, for it's yours.

**Knowing God results in every other kind of understanding.**
**(Proverbs 9:10, TLB)**

The great Bible teacher Dr. Alexander Maclaren attributed everything he knew to one habit: spending an hour each day alone with God. Sometimes he allowed others into his prayer closet, but they were never allowed to speak. Maclaren would sit in a well-worn armchair with his big Bible lying across his knees. Sometimes he'd read its pages, but mostly he'd just sit with his hand over his face. During that hour he wouldn't read the Bible as a student or study it for sermons. One of his assistants noted, "He read it as a child would read a letter from an absent father, or a loving heart would drink in words of a loved one from far away." To know God, you must spend time with Him.

One night, a famous orator recited the 23rd Psalm to a packed house and great applause. Afterwards, he spotted his vicar in the crowd and called him to say a word. To their surprise, he too recited the 23rd Psalm. But when he was through, there was silence. People dried their tears all over the audience. At this point, the orator stood beside his pastor and simply said, "The difference is, I know the 23rd Psalm—but he knows the Shepherd!"

HOW WELL DO YOU KNOW THE LORD?
HOW CLOSE DO YOU REALLY WANT TO BE TO HIM?
NOBODY BUT YOU CAN ANSWER THAT QUESTION.

# In Partnership

**For we are laborers together with God.
(1 Corinthians 3:9)**

When Robert Morrison sailed as a missionary to China, the captain of his ship was very skeptical of his vision and gave him a rough time. As Morrison was leaving the ship, the captain said, "I suppose you think you're going to make an impression on China." Morrison replied, "No, sir, but I believe God will!" There it is: when you're in partnership with God, your potential for success is unlimited—so make your plans big!

I heard about a youngster who was selling five-cent pencils door-to-door to raise the money for a $30 million hospital in his community. One woman said to him, "Son, that's a mighty big goal for just one little boy selling pencils for a nickel." With a big smile he replied, "Oh, no, I'm not alone. See that boy across the street? He's my partner; we're really doing it together." You may smile, but if he had that kind of faith in a partner who was only his equal, shouldn't you and I have complete confidence in a God who is unequaled—one who's in partnership with us? Jesus said, "If ye abide in Me, and My Words abide in you, ye shall ask what ye will, and it shall be done unto you" (John 15:7). In other words, remain in Him, receive from Him, and you'll reproduce for Him. Then you can live like a "no limit" person.

NEXT TIME SOMEONE ASKS YOU WHAT YOU WORK AT,
TELL THEM, "I'M IN PARTNERSHIP WITH GOD,"
FOR YOU ARE!

## Commitment

**No man stood with me, but all men forsook me....
Notwithstanding, the Lord stood with me, and strengthened me;...
and I was delivered out of the mouth of the lion.
(2 Timothy 4:16-17)**

L isten to these words: "Until I am committed, there is a hesitancy, a chance to draw back. But the moment I definitely commit myself, then God moves also, and a whole stream of events begins. All manner of unforeseen incidents, meetings, people, and material assistance of which I never dreamed begin to move towards me—the moment I make that commitment." Have you made the commitment yet?

If I could pick one word to describe commitment, I'd pick the word *alone*. Daniel dined and prayed *alone*. Elijah sacrificed and witnessed *alone*. Jeremiah prophesied and wept *alone*. Paul said, "All men forsook me ... Notwithstanding, the Lord stood with me and strengthened me" (2 Timothy 4:16-17).

The place of commitment is the place where God intervenes on your behalf. When the three Hebrew children of God made their commitment, God brought them out of the fiery furnace without even the smell of smoke upon them. (You can't even do that well in non-smoking sections these days!) King Nebuchadnezzar was so impressed that he said, "There is no other God who is able to deliver in this way" (Daniel 3:29, NASB). That's what the world is waiting for—somebody who'll put everything on the line, get into the fiery furnace, and let the world see God's power.

—m—

**ARE YOU THAT PERSON?**

## Another Chance

**Then came Peter to him and said, Lord, how oft shall my brother sin against me and I forgive him? till seven times? Jesus saith unto him,... seventy times seven.**
**(Matthew 18:21-22)**

Always allow others room to turn around. Everybody deserves a chance to change, so allow them to do so. When the pressure's on, things come to the surface in all of us, and it's so easy to say the wrong thing, arrive at the wrong conclusion, and make the wrong decision. Slow down—ask God for patience and mercy. Don't force others to live by their past, while you expect yours to be forgiven and forgotten. Whatever you sow will come back to you a hundred times.

When it comes to relationships, everybody makes mistakes. Give them a chance to come back into the relationship with dignity. Jesus said, "Blessed are the merciful, for they shall obtain mercy" (Matthew 5:7). How long has it taken you to correct some of the mistakes in your life? Give people time. Give them an opportunity to explain themselves. They may not even know the right words at first. Be willing to listen a little longer. Jesus put up with Peter's weakness because He knew what Peter would become. While you're looking in anger at them today, they may be looking in hope at tomorrow. Don't extinguish that light. Allow them space to correct their mistake, and always give them room to turn around.

—⚹—

**THAT'S WHAT JESUS WOULD DO!**

# The Reputation Race

**It matters very little to me what you think of me ...
the Master makes that judgment.
(1 Corinthians 4:1, TM)**

For years, I was driven by the fear of failing. Every time I stood before an audience, my self-worth was on the line. No matter how well I did, I was terrified by the thought of having to go back and do it again next week. Eventually, all I tried to build collapsed like a house of cards. But out of ashes, God began building something more dependent on His anointing than on my ability. It's a relief to be out of the reputation race! Paul thought so, too. Listen: "I didn't try to impress you with polished speeches and the latest philosophy. I deliberately kept it plain and simple: first Jesus and who He is; then Jesus and what He did" (1 Corinthians 2:2, TM).

If you want to get out of the reputation race, first stop taking yourself so seriously. If you're worried about what others think of you—relax. They're probably not thinking about you at all! Lighten up! Learn to laugh at yourself. You'll be amazed at how much more people will enjoy you. Next, start loving people instead of using them. Remember the Golden Rule? "Therefore, however you want people to treat you, so treat them" (Matthew 7:12, NASB). Finally, turn your accomplishments into challenges. Use them as building blocks—not pedestals to rest on.

**YOU HAVEN'T "ARRIVED" YET, SO KEEP PRESSING ON!**

# The Choice Is Yours

**Choose for yourselves today whom you will serve …
but as for me and my house, we will serve the LORD.
(Joshua 24:15, NASB)**

Settle the issue of commitment before the challenge arises, or you'll falter in the hour of decision. The battle is won before the battle is begun. Before Joseph met Potiphar's wife, he'd already decided his values. Have you? The three Hebrew children of God already knew what they were going to do, fiery furnace or not, before they faced the king. Listen: "We are not careful to answer thee in this matter. If it be so, our God whom we serve is able to deliver us" (Daniel 3:16-17). What do you really believe about God? If you think He might fail you, you'll never make a strong commitment. But if you believe His Word, you'll say, like Joshua, "As for me and my house, we will serve the Lord" (Joshua 24:15).

Commitment grows! You can't make big commitments, until you first make small ones. The three Hebrew children of God couldn't have said "no" to the king's idols if they hadn't first said "no" to his food. You don't get that kind of courage suddenly. Most of us can look back over the years and identify a point at which our lives changed significantly. Because of a readiness within us at that moment, we made a choice that would affect us for the rest of our lives.

**TODAY, MAKE A DECISION THAT YOU WANT GOD'S BEST
FOR YOUR LIFE AND THAT YOU'LL SETTLE FOR
NOTHING LESS.**

# You Gotta Go!

**Though it cost all you have, get understanding.
(Proverbs 4:7, NIV)**

Jimmy's mother said, "Get up! It's time for school." He didn't answer. Again she said, "Get up! It's time to go to school." He said, "I am not going anymore; there are 1,500 kids in that school, and they all hate me!" Sharply she replied, "You've got to go to school!" "I can't," he said, "even the teachers hate me. Give me one good reason why I should have to go through that misery." Looking him in the eye, his mother said, "I'll give you two. First, you are forty-two years of age, and second, you're the principal!"

You may smile, but life is a school. It's a never-ending education. Pablo Casals, the great cellist, was asked why at eighty-five he still practiced five hours a day. He replied, "Because I think I'm getting better." Wow! What an attitude! Peter said, "Grow in grace and in the knowledge of the Lord" (2 Peter 3:18). The toughest decision you'll ever make is accepting responsibility for what you are—and what you can be.

Your mistakes are not the issue—what you learn from them is. Built into every painful experience is the wisdom to build a better future. All you need is the right teacher and the right textbook. When God found Gideon, he was hiding in a cave thinking, "There's nothing anybody can do." God showed him that he wasn't a captive to the Midianites; he was a captive to his own inferiority, fear, and the opinions of those around him. God had the power to do it; all He needed was Gideon to open his heart and cooperate, and the rest is history.

**GOD HAS THINGS HE WANTS TO TEACH YOU.
WILL YOU LET HIM?**

# The Star Thrower

**In everything set them an example by doing what is good.
(Titus 2:7, NIV)**

In his book, *The Star Thrower*, Loren Eisley tells of the day he was walking along a beach where thousands of starfish had been washed up. He noticed a boy picking up starfish one by one and throwing them back into the ocean. When he asked him why, the boy said, "If I don't, they'll die!" But how can saving so few make a difference when so many are doomed?" the author asked. The little guy picked up another starfish, threw it back into the ocean and said, "It is going to make a lot of difference for this one!" Eisley left the boy and went home to continue writing, only to find he couldn't type a single word. So he returned to the beach and spent the rest of the day helping the boy throw starfish back into the ocean.

How do you change the world? One life at a time. One life, one act of kindness, one step of faith. There's only one Moses, one Paul, one Shakespeare, one Lincoln, but it's the numberless acts of courage and commitment by ordinary people like you that make the difference.

**YOU BRING TO THE KINGDOM OF GOD SOMETHING SPECIAL THAT NO ONE ELSE HAS TO OFFER.**

# Know Your Heart

**Search me, O God, and know my heart: try me,
and know my thoughts:… lead me in the way everlasting.
(Psalms 139:23-24)**

Your character is not revealed by your *actions* but by your *reactions*. Actions can be planned—but reactions are spontaneous! They give you a glimpse of what is really in your heart so that you can look at it and deal with it. Child of God, you need the very storm from which you have been trying to run.

We all live in denial until we are brought face to face with the contents of our own hearts. Would you readily admit that you are greedy, lustful, fearful, and insecure? Or resentful of the blessing of God on the lives of others? Probably not! When David prayed, "Search me, O God, and know my heart," he was inviting God to create the circumstances that would surface in him all the "stuff" that was on the bottom of the lake, hidden from view—not only from the eyes of other people, but from his own eyes! The most dangerous lies are not the ones we tell other people; they are the ones we tell ourselves and learn to live with comfortably. The goal is, "Until Christ be formed in you" (Galatians 4:9). Do you realize what Paul is saying? To become so much like Him that, as Jamie Buckingham used to say, "When they cut you—you'll bleed Jesus!"

---

ASK GOD TODAY TO SEARCH AND SURFACE IN YOU
ANYTHING THAT SEPARATES YOU FROM HIM.

# Are You Willing?

**If you are willing and obedient, you will eat the best from the land. (Isaiah 1:19, NIV)**

Are you willing to learn? Willing to obey? Willing to change? Willing to work? Or are you at least willing to be *made* willing? If you are, that's a start! In his great book, *Ladder to the Top*, Sherman Owens says, "We want the fruit, but we are not willing to get out on the limb. We don't want to build an ark; we just want to know how to miss the flood." Nothing in your life will change for the better until you stop looking for an escape, and start looking for a solution. Escape is "the way out"; solution is "the way up"!

Some things take time. Often you'll have to "walk out your deliverance" day by day. The very stubbornness of your situation is what will drive you into the arms of Jesus—and keep you there. David said, "Before I was afflicted I went astray; but now have I kept thy word" (Psalms 119:67). Forced dependence—it's still God's way!

Salvation is the work of a moment—maturity is the work of a lifetime! You didn't get into this shape overnight, and you're not going to be transformed into His likeness overnight. (See 2 Corinthians 3:18.) You're going to be working on this for the rest of your life, so get rid of your "microwave mentality." Don't be in such a hurry to get to the top that you miss some of the rungs on the ladder. Remember, on each rung you learn different lessons and form different relationships which will ultimately sustain you when you get to the top. It's dangerous to arrive without them.

**TODAY ASK GOD TO GIVE YOU A WILLING HEART.**

# Close the Door

**Forgetting the past and looking forward to what lies ahead.
(Philippians 3:13, TLB)**

When a player begins to score, what does the opposing team do? They assign their best players to block him! The warfare over your life today is just an indication of your value to God. The attack you're sustaining is because you have the ability to score! If your assignment is of God, you'll attract attacks like a magnet!

Before Paul reached his destiny he wrote these words: "I have had to ford rivers, fend off robbers, struggle with friends, struggle with foes, I have been at risk in the city, at risk in the country, endangered by the desert sun and sea storm, and betrayed by those I thought were my brothers. I have known drudgery and hard labor, many a long and lonely night without sleep, many a missed meal, been blasted by the cold, naked to the weather. And that is not the half of it, when you throw in the daily pressures and anxieties of all the churches" (2 Corinthians 11:23-26, TM). Now listen to what he says as he looks back, "Forgetting those things which are behind" (Philippians 3:13).

I doubt if Paul forgot anything. He could remember the names, the places, the faces, and even record it. But there's a difference; Paul refused to let the hurts done to him affect his outlook or keep him from "finishing his course with joy." Don't let your past rob you of your future!

---

LET THE PAST BE THE PAST.
YESTERDAY ENDED LAST NIGHT AT MIDNIGHT.
CLOSE THE DOOR AND MOVE ON WITH GOD.

# Breakthrough!

**So he attacked them at Baal-Perazim and wiped them out.
That is why the place has been known as ... "the place of
breaking through." (1 Chronicles 14:11, TLB)**

Never forget, everybody you meet is fighting a battle of some
kind. They need a breakthrough! If you need one, too,
look at what David did. The enemy had come against him in
overwhelming force, but David did two things. First, he reminded
himself that "the Lord had made him king" (1 Chronicles 14:2).
Today remind yourself whose child you are, whose Spirit lives
within you, and on whose word you're standing. God didn't make
only David a king—He made you one, too, so don't let the enemy
push you around. (See Revelation 12:11.)

Next, David inquired of the Lord, "Shall I go up against the
Philistines?" (1 Chronicles 14:14). Have you talked it over with
the Lord? Did you stay in His presence long enough to hear what
He had to say? God doesn't respond to your need, He responds to
your obedience! When you've obeyed Him—you're invincible!

What happened next is a key for you! David said, "God hath used
me to sweep away my enemy" (1 Chronicles 14:11). Sometimes
God will do it for you; other times He'll use you to do it! That's
why you must hear from Him before you move. He'll provide the
harvest, but you have to plant the seed. You can't do God's part,
and He won't do yours! It's not a question of just doing something,
it's a matter of doing what He tells you to do.

THE MOMENT YOU DO, YOU'RE ON THE THRESHOLD OF
"A BREAKTHROUGH," AND THAT'S JUST WHAT GOD HAS
IN MIND FOR YOU TODAY!

# God's Obsession

**You can never please God without faith.
(Hebrews 11:6, TLB)**

God's greatest obsession is to be believed! His greatest pain is to be doubted! Think about it! Every effort of God has one focus—to find somebody who will believe Him! He wants you to approach Him when you have a need; He wants to be trusted! What parent doesn't? When you ask, you acknowledge His wisdom—and you also acknowledge your total dependence on Him. He likes that!

It is tough for some of us to acknowledge our limitations, especially in a world that prizes self-sufficiency. The most dangerous time in your life is when you don't have a need! Complacency will set in; smugness will grow like a cancer, and before you know it, you'll say, "I need the Lord," but you'll act like it all depends on you. Worse, your faith becomes unused—and when you're not using your faith you're not pleasing God. (See Hebrews 11:6.)

If your vision for the future doesn't require God, it's not of God! If God gets involved in your dream, He becomes the only means to achieve it. A friend recently said to my wife, "If God just gives me what I need, I'll be happy." Debby said, "If that's all God gives you, how can you bless someone else? What about those who are waiting to be blessed through you?"

---

THE GOD WHO SAID TO ABRAHAM, "I WILL BLESS THEE, AND ... I WILL MAKE OF THEE A BLESSING" (GENESIS 12:2) IS INVITING YOU TO COME TO HIM TODAY AND ASK!

# Straight Talk

**Let the LORD be magnified, which hath pleasure in the prosperity of his servant.
(Psalms 35:27)**

God truly cares about everything you need, and that includes your finances. Your needs matter to Him! Let that sink in! David said, "God is pleased when you prosper." Isaiah said, "God will teach you to profit" (Isaiah 48:17). How can someone condemn the teaching of "sowing and reaping" (2 Corinthians 9:6-11), yet live in a fine home, drive a new car, and have a "nest egg" in the bank? Beware of any man who manipulates people's giving for his own benefit, but beware also of any teaching that contradicts God's Word, cripples your faith, and leaves you wondering if it's all right to believe God for His blessings or if it's right to give, expecting something in return. The answer is a qualified, "Yes!" (See Luke 6:38; Proverbs 3:9.)

Do you want to be a "burden" or a "burden-bearer"? Prosperity is having enough to fulfill God's purpose for your life and having enough to bless others. What do you want? Just enough to take your family out to dinner on Friday night—or enough to feed hungry children in Romania, print Bibles for China, and help your pastor fulfill his vision? Listen: "Always having all sufficiency in all things, [you] may abound to every good work. As it is written, He hath dispersed abroad [that's missions]; He hath given to the poor [that's helping the needy]" (2 Corinthians 9:8).

**HOW CAN YOU HAVE A HEART FOR "OTHERS" AND SAY YOU DON'T WANT MORE? PLEASE TALK THIS OVER WITH THE LORD!**

# There Is a Rest

**Thou hast been a shelter for me, and a strong tower from the enemy. (Psalms 61:3)**

Blessed with success, but cursed with ambition, we self-destruct because we don't know how to rest. Samson could handle a thousand soldiers single-handed, but he couldn't handle the loneliness of an empty room, so he finished up in Delilah's lap. T.D. Jakes says, "Her weapons were not her lips, hips, and fingertips, but rather his tiredness, his numbness, and his inner void." David cried, "Thou hast been a shelter for me" (Psalms 61:1-3).

David found the answer in God's presence; Samson never did, and it killed him! Delilah's lap looked so good to Samson that he stayed too long, talked too much, and lost everything. When you're tired, you're vulnerable! I know! I built a successful church and became a familiar face on 200 television stations, but before it was over I "crashed and burned." I learned painfully that "He maketh me to lie down" (Psalms 23:2). He had to, because I didn't know how!

Your "Delilah" can be anything that comes into your life to deplete your strength. It can be a career, a relationship, or a habit. It's what you turn to when you need to escape. Don't be fooled—she may delight you tonight, but she'll destroy you tomorrow. Get up while you can and run—don't walk—run to the arms of Jesus. Listen: "He gives strength to the weary, and to him who lacks might He increases power" (Isaiah 40:29, NASB).

—m—

COME TO HIM TODAY; YOUR THIRST WILL BE SATISFIED,
AND ALL YOUR WOUNDS WILL BE HEALED.

# Listen, Parents!

## Suffer the little children to come unto me.
## (Mark 10:14)

Imagine how those children must have felt when Jesus rebuked the men who were pushing them away and said, "Come unto Me." How many destinies were changed that day because He loved them and He listened to them. He gave them something every child needs—self-worth and the dignity of their own thoughts and opinions. When you listen to me, it means that what I say matters, and that means I matter. After ten years (3,650 days) of being told, "Don't bother me", "Shut up!", "I don't have time for you", something dies—creativity and confidence. Imagine facing life without those things!

Nobody had more to do than Jesus, but He took time for children. Parent, are you listening? The pressure is rising! Our prisons are full of kids who commit adult crimes. When we study them, we find that they don't know how to express their emotions—so they explode!

As a child, he took a hammer and pounded his toy to pieces; now as a man, he drives his fist through the wall or batters his wife. His suit size has changed, but the messages inside are the same—nobody listens, nobody understands! Perhaps you think I'm making too much out of too little? Think again! Rearrange the priorities in your home.

—m—

DO IT RIGHT AND YOU CAN REJOICE FOR ETERNITY;
DO IT WRONG AND YOU'LL LIVE WITH
THE CONSEQUENCES.

# Heart Prayer

**The Lord looketh on the heart.
(1 Samuel 16:7)**

Don't avoid prayer because you're not articulate. God is not moved by vocabulary! He's only moved by an open heart that "spills" the burdens of the day across the altar, bearing every pain to the power of a God Who can! Can what? Can do whatever you have faith to believe Him for! (See Mark 11:24; Luke 11:9.) My faith is not in my ability to speak, it's in God's ability to hear and understand my heart! He already knows what I am trying to say: "In seasons of distress and grief, my soul has often found relief, and oft escaped the tempter's snare, by thy return, sweet hour of prayer." Child of God, either learn to pray—or learn to worry! What you give to Him—He maintains! What you keep—you maintain!

Everyone dumps their garbage on you, but where do you go for relief? Everything is "going out," but nothing is "coming in," and before you know it, you collapse under the weight of it all. Maybe that's where you are today. Prayer is your answer. It builds back up what life has depleted. When you pray, you're saying, "I believe You are competent to deal with the issues so much better than I, and I trust You to do it." In that moment the heart of your boss is in God's hand, the surgery you dread is in His hand, your children and your finances are in His hand. He is ready to intervene on your behalf—but you must learn to ask!

———

**TAKE SOME TIME TODAY AND TALK TO HIM ABOUT IT!**

# Close Enough

**By faith Noah, being warned of God, prepared an ark to the saving of his house. (Hebrews 11:7)**

Do you live close enough to God to hear His warnings when danger is present? Noah did, and he saved his entire family! Are you close enough to your family for them to have confidence in what God has spoken to you? You can literally change the direction of your whole family without argument or discussion—through prayer. Your loved ones need to be sheltered under the covering of your prayer life. No wonder the disciples of Jesus cried out, "Lord, teach us to pray!" (Luke 11:1).

We're emotionally overwhelmed and spiritually depleted because we have not learned the power of prayer. Lack of prayer has left us weak and anxious, and we blindly make decisions in our business, our homes, and our ministries, without taking any serious time to talk it over with the Lord. *You can't prepare an ark in time—without a warning from God.* That means staying close enough to Him to hear what He has to say. Listen: "If my people, which are called by My Name, shall humble themselves, and pray, and seek My face, and turn from their wicked ways, then will I hear from heaven, I will forgive their sin, and will heal their land" (2 Chronicles 7:14). God has promised to heal any situation that pertains to the man or woman who prays. Solomon was concerned about the things that were beyond his power. But God made it clear that nothing is beyond *His* power.

CHILD OF GOD, PUT PRAYER BACK AT THE CENTER OF YOUR LIFE AND WATCH WHAT HAPPENS.

# Tell on It!

**Confess your faults one to another, and pray one for another that ye may be healed. (James 5:16)**

It feels good to live above reproach. That doesn't mean you never stumble and fall, it just means you get back up immediately and start walking again. Some of us have given ourselves written permission slips to be weak and visas to fail, because we have become weary in the fight. It's a long fight, but you can win! Here's one of the great keys to victory: "Confess your faults one to another." I once struggled with a drug habit that almost destroyed me. One day I discovered that God never intended me to "do it alone." Whatever your "compulsion" may be, the moment it comes—tell on it! When you do, it begins to lose it's power! Tell who? Someone who has been through it, someone who is compassionate, someone who can stand with you in prayer, and someone you can trust to keep your confidence! The Bible says, "Pity the man who falls and has no one to help him up!... Though one may be overpowered, two can defend themselves" (Ecclesiastes 4:10-12, NIV). It's time to "double up!"

Remember, confess your faults, not your mate's faults! You can never be healed by confessing the faults of others! Confess your faults, and He will heal you. Today God wants you to be set free; He wants you to enjoy the blessings He has prepared for you.

**TAKE THE TIME TO GET INTO HIS PRESENCE, FOR THAT'S WHERE YOU WILL FIND THE ANSWERS!**

# Get Up and Go On

**Strengthen the things that remain.
(Revelation 3:2)**

Be like the man who said, "I'm never down; I'm either up or I'm getting up!" Strengthen the things that remain, and go on. You're in the ring with a formidable opponent who wants to "take you out!" He knows that God has a special plan for your life. But he doesn't have the power to "take out" the man or the woman who prays and stays close to God. Make a commitment to stand in God's strength regardless of what you're facing, or how hard you've been hit. Give him a clear message with fire in your eyes. Tell him you're not "throwing in the towel."

Paul says, "Be prepared! You're up against far more than you can handle on your own. Take all the help you can get, every weapon God has issued, so that when it is all over but the shouting, you will still be on your feet" (Ephesians 6:12, TM). You may have been to hell's door and back for yourself and your family, but you're going to win. Tell the devil you have been created in the image of his worst nightmare! You're a resurrected man! You've been renewed in your faith, and you're firm in you convictions!

**LET HIM KNOW, "I WILL BE KNOCKED DOWN NO LOWER THAN MY KNEES!"**

# Wrestling With God

**And Jacob was left alone, and there wrestled with him
a man until the breaking of the day.
(Genesis 32:24)**

When God decides to deal with you, He'll get you alone. Jacob was "left." They don't have guests in an operating room! When it's time for surgery, everyone has to go—even your wife and kids! Something in you must be dealt with, or you won't make it. Listen, "And there wrestled with him a Man until...." Others may confront and give up on you, but not God! He wrestles with you "until"! Until Jacob becomes Israel; until the deceiver becomes a prince with God; until he walks out of his tent and lives in such a way that everybody knows he's been touched by God.

God is not going to let you get by with all the little things He used to overlook; you are running out of time. He will wrestle with you to show you that you are wasting your life. He will wrestle with you over your careless attitudes, careless words, and careless actions. He will wrestle with you over your ingratitude and make you see how blessed you really are. He will wrestle with you over your instability and your unwillingness to make a commitment. You've worked at fourteen jobs! You've attended twenty-five different churches! When are you going to stand? When are you going to let Him plant you permanently and stay until you can "bear fruit?" If God is wrestling with you today, then stay in His presence until you are changed—into what He wants you to be.

FOR THEN AND ONLY THEN WILL YOU FIND HAPPINESS
AND FULFILLMENT (JEREMIAH 29:12).

# The Other Side

**Let us pass over unto the other side.
(Mark 4:35)**

The one thing the enemy doesn't want you to do is get through this and reach the other side! He doesn't care if you go to church, or slip into a robe and sing in the choir; he just doesn't want you to reach your destiny! But what's waiting for you on the other side is worth everything you are going through at the moment. Paul says, "Be careful for nothing, but in everything by prayer and supplication with thanksgiving let your requests be made known unto God. And the peace of God which passeth all understanding shall keep your hearts and minds through Christ Jesus" (Philippians 4:6). Change is not cheap, and it sure isn't easy! Before there is a resurrection, there must be a cross.

Paul said, "When I was a child,... I thought as a child; but when I became a man I put away childish things" (1 Corinthians 13:11). It's time to stop thinking like a child. You've got to put it away and grow up! No one can do it for you! You alone can make this painful sacrifice before God. Without it, you can't reach the blessings of God that are waiting for you on the other side. What do you need to change today? Your schedule, to make room for God? Your friends, because they're robbing you of your strength and spirituality? Your habits, because they're draining and defeating you? Your words, because you're speaking unbelief instead of faith?

**TODAY GET INTO GOD'S PRESENCE AND
ASK HIM TO HELP YOU GET THROUGH THIS AND
REACH THE OTHER SIDE. HE WILL!**

# The Process

**He will sit as a refiner and a purifier of silver.**
**(Malachi 3:3, NIV)**

It is hard to watch someone you love going through the Refiner's fire, but it is the only way to get silver or gold! It's tough watching the Refiner "turn up the heat" until everything on the bottom rises; until every impurity is removed, and He finally sees His face reflected on the surface. But that's God's goal for you! Do you know when you pray, "Make me more like Jesus," what you're authorizing the Holy Spirit to do? We don't change until the pain of staying the same becomes unbearable. For most of us, knowledge is not the bridge to progress—pain is!

No matter how much you love them, don't rescue someone with whom God is dealing. The worst thing you could have done for the prodigal was to have gone down to the pigsty, cleaned it up, and given him a "Big Mac." You would just have been enabling him to stay there longer! You'd have lengthened his valley! Let the Refiner do His work! Most of his life Jacob didn't need God. He'd have told you, "I'm doing just fine, thank you." Until it was time to go home and stand before his father, and face the wrath of his brother Esau. Then he was willing to wrestle with God to get what he needed. My friend Sherman Owens says, "Change comes when it hurts so much you *have* to change; when you learn so much you *want* to change, and when you receive so much you *welcome* change." David said that the way of the Lord is "in the sanctuary," and "in the storm" (Psalms 77).

THOSE ARE YOUR OPTIONS! WHY DON'T YOU TAKE THE EASY WAY, GET INTO GOD'S PRESENCE TODAY, AND LET HIM CHANGE YOU.

# *Run!*

**Let us throw off everything that hinders ... and let us run. (Hebrews 12:1, NIV)**

Wilma Rudolph was the twentieth of twenty-two children born into a poor family in Tennessee. As a child, she had polio and was forced to wear leg braces until she was nine. At twelve she tried out for her school's basketball team and failed. For the next year she practiced every day until she finally made the team. A college track coach spotted her one day and talked her into letting him train her to be a sprinter. Her persistence and prowess earned her a scholarship in Tennessee State University where she became a track star.

In 1960, she made the U.S. Olympic Team, and in the 100-meter sprint she had to face the world record holder, Yetta Mynie of Germany. But Wilma won! She did it again in the 200-meter event! Wilma's third race was in the 100-meter relay where she again faced Yetta. Just as the baton was handed to Wilma, she dropped it, giving Yetta the lead. But her never-give-up spirit made her pick up the baton and take off in desperate pursuit. She caught the German runner in the last few strides and won the third gold medal—more than any other woman had won at that time.

Today Wilma is a grandmother, and she travels the world for children's causes, motivating them with her life story. "I let them know," she says, "that they can achieve anything they want to, as long as they are willing to work for it."

---

CHILD OF GOD, WITH ALL YOU HAVE GOING FOR YOU, HOW CAN YOU EVEN THINK OF SETTLING FOR LESS?

# Forgiveness

**After Job had prayed for his friends, the LORD made him prosperous again and gave him twice as much as he had before. (Job 42:10, NIV)**

Remember Charles Dickens's Miss Haversham in *Great Expectations*? When the groom failed to show up on the day of their wedding, she dismissed the guests, locked the doors, stopped the clock, sat down in a chair, and resigned from life. Sometimes you just want to "stop the clock"! I received an inspiring letter from a lady in New Zealand whose husband, after 45 years of marriage, had left her for another woman. She has dealt with her grief and resentment, but she refuses to be a victim. She said that her Bible has become God's love letter to her every day, "leading, guiding, and comforting me." She now holds meetings in her home and ministers to others who've been hurt. She's got it right!

When Job prayed for his friends, God restored his health, his joy, and his prosperity. Do you know who Job's friends were? The very ones who caused him so much pain. There's the key! You can live in anger or live in blessing, but you can't live in both! When Job could pray for those who had hurt him, the blessings of God began to pour into his life. Jesus said we have the power to either remit the sins of others, or to retain them. (See John 20:23.) The choice is yours! The offense ceases the moment you decide to forgive it and wipe it off the books.

YOU ASK, "HOW CAN I KNOW I'M WALKING IN FORGIVENESS?" WHEN YOU CAN PRAY FOR THOSE WHO HURT YOU, AND MEAN IT!

# Jerry's Legacy

**The truth ... speaks highly of Demetrius.
(3 John 12)**

Bishop Jerry Kaufman died this morning. He pastored Love Gospel Assembly in the Bronx, New York. He had a passion for "the inner city." Like a character out of *The Cross and the Switchblade*, he ran with gangs in some of New York's worst neighborhoods. The night he was saved he was instantly delivered from heroin, and three days later was in Bible college studying the Word of God. When he graduated, he came back to his old neighborhood and started preaching. With an incredible heart of love he built a church in "one of America's ten worst neighborhoods" (according to *Newsweek Magazine*).

Many a Friday night I preached for him in the old synagogue that became home to the 1,500 people from every conceivable lifestyle whom he had won to Christ. He used to say with a smile, "Bob, we recycle them!" The services often went to midnight because Friday was their "night out." In the old days they never thought about time, so now they came to celebrate and to stay "until the job gets done!" I have stood with tears of joy, watching those faces. They didn't need to be coaxed; they'd been lifted from hell, and every breath was a song of praise. When I looked at what he'd built in the "devil's backyard" and the price he paid to do it, I felt, "Lord, I've done so little!"

TODAY JERRY'S ENJOYING A WELL-EARNED REST, AND THE TRUTH SPEAKS HIGHLY OF HIM. WHAT WILL IT SAY ABOUT YOU WHEN YOU GO?

# Free From the Law

**Free from the law of sin and death.**
**(Romans 8:2, NIV)**

Do you ever find yourself saying, "Why did I do that? How could I think such thoughts?" Because the law is still in force! Ignorance is no excuse. The cop you don't see will ticket you as fast as the one you do. If you're a Christian, you're in for the fight of your life, and the battle begins the moment your feet hit the floor in the morning. Listen to Paul: "Something has gone wrong deep within me, and it gets the better of me every time. It happens so regularly that it is predictable. The moment I decide to do good, sin is there to trip me up. I truly delight in God's commands, but it is pretty obvious that not all of me joins in that delight. Parts of me covertly rebel, and just when I least expect it, they take charge … I'm at the end of my rope. Is there no one who can do anything for me?" (Romans 7:21-23, TM). That sounds like a description of my life; how about yours? But there's an answer: "A new power is in operation. The Spirit of life in Christ … freeing me" (Romans 8:2, TM).

The "law of sin" can only rule if your flesh is alive. (See Romans 7:1, NIV.) So the answer is—die! Die to self-centered living and do it daily! That's the tough part, for just when you think you're dead, someone steps on your toes and your "old man" has a resurrection. Right?

—◊◊◊—

TODAY A NEW POWER IS IN OPERATION,
AND THE CLOSER YOU GET TO JESUS
THE MORE THAT POWER WILL WORK IN YOUR LIFE.

# Eating

**He shall bless thy bread, and thy water; and ... take sickness away from the midst of thee. The number of thy days [He] will fulfil. (Exodus 23:25-26)**

Recently I lost a dear friend, and God's army lost a great general because of a weight problem, which caused him to have a massive heart attack. I wish you'd seen the work he was doing for God and the struggle it's been to replace him. God says you have a "number" of days to fulfil, and an assignment to complete, but sickness can terminate you before you get there. My doctor, a leading cardiologist, recently told me to cut down on fatty foods and exercise regularly. He also told me his wife regularly forgets to service her car and keeps wondering why it always breaks down! Sound familiar?

Sherman and Mary Owens lost their son Jimmy in March, 1995. He was 29, and he was on the mission field. Twice, Mary warned him that he would not "fulfil the length of his days" if he didn't change his eating habits. Cholesterol is no respecter of persons. He died before his 30th birthday, weighing almost 300 pounds. Yes, he's at home with the Lord, and so is my dad who died at age 44, and my pastor friend who just died at 60; but was it necessary? Sherman told me, "God didn't take my son—ham and eggs did!" In his book, *Ladder to the Top*, he writes, "Your waistline is a collection of decisions, and those decisions can either lengthen or shorten your life."

**I WANT YOU TO FULFIL THE LENGTH OF YOUR DAYS AND COMPLETE YOUR ASSIGNMENT FOR GOD, SO MAYBE THIS WILL MAKE YOU THINK.**

**Power belongeth unto God. Also unto thee, O Lord, belongeth mercy. (Psalms 62:11-12)**

We have the right to preach divine healing, but never to say we understand it! When Jamie Buckingham died, I lost one of my dearest friends. He'd just written his book, *Summer of Miracles*, and he was standing on the Word, totally confident that God had healed him of cancer. Pastor Jack Lord said that while he was with Jamie at his home in Florida in 1992, a Christian leader called who had been diagnosed with melanoma. Jamie prayed, and the man was healed, and he's still healed today! Yet Jamie died a month later, believing God, and surrounded by the prayers of thousands. Elijah raised the dead, yet he died of sickness. (See 2 Kings 13:14, NIV.)

In this devotion we strongly encourage you to believe God for your healing, but not everyone gets healed! Is that because God is sovereign, and you have no say in it? No! It takes the hand of faith to receive what divine sovereignty has provided! When God doesn't, it's never because He can't, and it's never because He doesn't love us. Listen: "You, O God, are strong … You, O Lord, are loving" (Psalm 2:11-12, NIV ). He is loving enough to care and strong enough to intervene. He says in His Word, "You are chosen" (Ephesians 1:4); "You are indwelt by His power" (Colossians 1:27). The answer is, seek God for "a definitive word." A lot of men and women in the Bible did, and they got it!

UNTIL THAT WORD COMES . . . STAND CONFIDENTLY IN THE CIRCUMSTANCES AND BELIEVE THE ONE WHO HAS NEVER FAILED YOU.

# Shake It Off

**But Paul shook the snake off into the fire and suffered no ill effects. (Acts 28:5, NIV)**

On his way to Rome, Paul was shipwrecked on an island. As he was gathering firewood, a snake attached itself to his arm. Note what he did: the Bible simply says he "shook it off." What a picture! You can either dwell on the past, or "shake it off" and move into the future with God. Listen to what he says: "I've got my eye on the goal. I am off and running, and I am not turning back" (Philippians 3:13, TM). The only place the past can live now is in your mind!

Paul didn't forget the past, he just shook it off and kept going! You will never get to the top of the ladder if you keep trying to pull yesterday's disappointments with you. It was lies that sent Joseph to prison, and it was his own brothers who sold him into slavery. Yet when he reached the palace you didn't find a word of revenge or resentment. He had no time for it!

Maybe you're thinking, "I'll be glad when these attacks are over and I can settle down." Dream on! If you do anything significant for God you'll attract attack like a magnet! You're too valuable to the Kingdom. Satan knows your potential, and his greatest fear is that you'll discover who you really are, what you're really worth, and where you're really headed.

COME ON, CHILD OF GOD, SHAKE IF OFF AND GET MOVING FOR GOD!

# Elder—Not Old!

**They will still bear fruit in old age, they will stay fresh and green. (Psalms 92:14, NIV)**

Have you noticed that no matter how old some people get, they never lose their attractiveness? It just moves from their faces to their hearts. In our youth-oriented society, it wouldn't be hard to get the impression that your usefulness ends at age 65 or sooner. What rubbish! Picasso produced some of his greatest works at age 90. Arthur Rubenstein gave one of his greatest recitals at 89 years old. Marjorie Stoneham Douglas, who is credited with saving the Everglades, was still fighting for the cause at age 100.

I wish you could meet Dr. Victor Pearce, who serves on our board. Either nobody told him about "retirement age," or he wasn't listening. He just returned from India where he preached twice a day to 45,000 people. In one service 30,000 committed their lives to Christ, and that afternoon a multitude paraded through the streets on their way to the river, where thousands were baptized. Now here's the good part—he's 84, and he's planning to go back again to hold more crusades! Just because you retired from work, doesn't mean you've retired from life. Isaiah says, "Even to your old age and gray hairs … I will sustain you!" (Isaiah 46:4, NIV). Older Christian, we need your wisdom, your example, your prayers, and the wealth of your experience!

**LIVE WITH ALL YOUR MIGHT UNTIL THE FLAME GOES OUT!**

# Let Your Hair Down

**Then Mary took ... expensive perfume; she poured it on Jesus' feet and wiped his feet with her hair. And the house was filled with the fragrance. (John 12:3, NIV)**

Don't you like the way Mary worshiped? She let her hair down! She disregarded the critics and the customs and filled the house with the fragrance of her praise. Child of God, put aside your preconceived notions, your self-consciousness, and your concern over what others think, and pour out your love to the One who is worthy. Listen: "Because Your loving-kindness is better than life, my lips shall praise Thee ... I will bless Thee while I live. I will lift up my hands in Thy name" (Psalms 63:3-4). That's the way to do it!

Religious folks will always try to intimidate and silence you. Don't let them! When they tried it with Jesus, He rebuked them and said, "If they keep quiet the stones will cry out" (Luke 19:40, NIV). You can never worship God too exuberantly, for God knows, it's either us or the rocks! John says the house was filled with the fragrance. Go ahead, fill the place with His praise!

Nothing builds intimacy between people like words of love and appreciation. Judas will always say, "What a waste!" When you take time to stand and "bathe" your soul in the presence of God, some will say, "What a waste of time; what a waste of effort."

YOU SEE, THEY DON'T UNDERSTAND THAT
WORSHIP IS HOW YOU ENTER, HOW YOU ENJOY, AND
HOW YOU LIVE IN THE PRESENCE OF GOD.

**Live in peace. And the God of love and peace will
be with you. (2 Corinthians 13:11, NIV)**

Unless you plan to live on an island or take a vow of silence, you're going to have to learn how to get along with people. Right? Here are ten suggestions that will help:

1. Guard your tongue. Always say less than you think.

2. Make promises sparingly. Keep them faithfully.

3. Never let an opportunity pass to say a kind word.

4. Be genuinely interested in others; show it by listening and expressing your appreciation.

5. Be cheerful; don't dwell on your aches and pains. There are a dozen people in the nearest cemetery who would gladly exchange places with you.

6. Keep an open mind; discuss, but don't argue. Learn to disagree without being disagreeable. Give other people the benefit of the doubt.

7. Discourage gossip. It's destructive!

8. Be sensitive to the feelings of others. If you do, people will consider you to be wise.

9. Pay no attention to ill-natured remarks about you. Live so that nobody will believe them.

10. Don't worry about getting credit. Just keep giving your best, and be patient! God keeps records!

—∿—

**TAKE A MOMENT TODAY AND READ THESE
TEN SUGGESTIONS OVER AGAIN, ASKING GOD
TO MAKE THEM A REALITY IN YOUR LIFE.**

# Forgive!

**Forgive whatever grievances you may have against one another.
Forgive as the Lord forgave you. (Colossians 3:13, NIV)**

Be willing to forgive yourself—for God is! If you refuse to, you are making yourself better than Him! Perhaps you have never thought of it that way before. No matter how bad your sin is or the sin of the one who hurt you, if God is willing to forgive, yet you won't, you're saying, "I have a higher standard than God!" That's pride in the extreme, and you need to deal with it! There's only one way the past can be changed—forgive it! That's the one thing you can do for yourself that will change all your tomorrows. Do it—for the future is where you are going to spend the rest of your life!

Why don't you pray this prayer with me? "Father I forgive and let go of all the mistakes and failures in my life. The lessons have been well-learned. Unconditionally, I forgive _____(name those who have hurt you, including yourself). Starting today, I choose to walk in love, and I thank you for the strength and grace to do it. Amen."

There are some people you may have to pray this prayer over many times. You'll remove their name from your "resentment list," then it'll show up again. Don't be discouraged, we all go through that. Remember, Jesus said we must forgive our brother "seventy times seven" (Matthew 18:22). In other words, keep forgiving until the memory has lost its power to hurt you.

AND DON'T FORGET, FORGIVENESS IS NOT FOR
THEIR BENEFIT—IT IS FOR YOURS!

# *Warts*

**He hath made us accepted in the beloved.**
**(Ephesians 1:6)**

Let these words sink into your spirit today! With full knowledge of all your faults and failings, God says you're accepted! How wonderful! God's kindness and His favor have been poured out on you, because you belong to Christ. Here is how it works: His life covers your sins of omission, His death covers your sins of commission, and His perfect love covers your sins of disposition. Are you getting this? You're completely covered! You are justified, which means "just-as-if-I'd" never sinned. You are accepted because of Who you belong to. Then you have the right Name, all the doors open! (See Isaiah 43:1.)

Now, that sets you free to accept yourself with all your imperfections—to be comfortable being you, and once you can do that you can begin to accept others as they are, without needing to change them. Listen: "It is God [not you] Who works in you to will and to act according to His good purpose" (Philippians 2:13, NIV). When you begin to see "God at work" in others it relieves you of the enormous responsibility of playing God in their lives. All of us are insecure in certain areas. All of us struggle with different things, but when you can accept yourself, then you can begin to accept others, and that's the first step toward loving them. Jesus said, "My command is this: love each other as I have loved you" (John 15:12, NIV).

—∿∿—

**NOW FOR THE FIRST TIME,
YOU CAN BEGIN TO DO JUST THAT!**

**A generous man will himself be blessed, for he
shares his food with the poor. (Proverbs 22:9, NIV)**

When you obey God today, you position yourself to receive something you'll really need tomorrow! In 1 Kings 17, a widow gave the prophet Elijah a meal. She had no idea how that simple act of kindness would affect her future. Elijah didn't force her to give anything, and God won't force you either. His way is "not reluctantly or under compulsion, for God loves a cheerful giver" (2 Corinthians 9:7, NIV). That verse speaks about money, but it's not limited to money. A lot of us give God our money easier than we give Him our time, our stubborn wills, or our old resentments.

God will give you an opportunity to obey Him in something that may look insignificant, but the truth is, that seed will begin a harvest in your own life. It may simply be taking a few moments to share a word of encouragement with someone or to pray for them. With one small act of kindness, this woman started a harvest that lasted seven years. When her son died, it was the prophet she fed who brought him back to life. Are you getting the idea? Solomon says, "A generous man will prosper; he who refreshes others will himself be refreshed" (Proverbs 11:25, NIV). If you think you'll ever need a helping hand, then give one today. Dwarfed, shriveled, and miserable are the souls of the Ebenezer Scrooges of this world, who think, "I earned it, I'm keeping it, and I owe nothing to anybody!"

READ THE LAST THING JESUS SAID IN THE PARABLE OF
THE GOOD SAMARITAN: "GO AND DO THOU LIKEWISE"
(LUKE 10:36). THAT'S YOU HE'S TALKING TO!

# *Your Nest*

**Like an eagle that stirs up its nest and hovers over its young, that spreads its wings to catch them … The LORD alone led him. (Deuteronomy 32:11-12, NIV)**

In David McNally's magnificent book, *Even Eagles Need a Push*, we read these words, "The eagle gently coaxed her offspring toward the edge of the nest. Her heart quivered with conflicting emotions as she felt their resistance to her persistent nudging. 'Why does the thrill of soaring have to begin with the fear of falling?' she thought. The ageless question was still unanswered for her. Her nest was located high on a shelf of sheer rockface. Below there was nothing but air to support the wings of each child. 'Is it possible that this time it will not work?' she thought. Despite her fears, the eagle knew it was time. Her parental mission was all but complete. There remained one final task—the push.

"The eagle drew courage from an innate wisdom. Until her children discovered their wings, there was no purpose for their lives. Until they learned how to soar, they would fail to understand the privilege it was to have been born an eagle. The push was the greatest gift she had to offer. It was her supreme act of love. And so, one by one, she pushed them, and they flew!"

Is God stirring up your nest today? Is He pushing you out of your comfort zone?

—m—

**IF HE IS, HAVE NO FEAR; BEFORE HE'S THROUGH YOU'LL BE GLAD, YOU'LL UNDERSTAND, AND YOU'LL "MOUNT UP WITH WINGS LIKE EAGLES" (ISAIAH 40:31).**

# *Desire*

**Wilt thou be made whole?**
**(John 5:6)**

It's your desire that determines your destiny. Jesus said to this paralyzed man, "Take up thy bed and walk!" (John 5:8). What a scene! Medical science says you can't! Experience confirms it. Your friends agree because they've never seen a miracle before. The future can begin right here, or it can die right here in the court of reason. Will you dare to believe God that, despite the limitations which you were born with and the situation which you're living in, because He has spoken to you, you can get up and walk out of these circumstances? That was his choice, and it's yours, too!

Here are your options: You can be a victim and have the sympathy your problems bring. Or you can believe that we only get what we deserve. Not true! I help to support hundreds of wonderful children in Romania who live in circumstances that no child deserves. You may have come from ten generations of alcoholics, and the experts are saying that you are "genetically pre-disposed" to be one. Does that make it so? No! It simply means that the past ends right here and right now with you! The Word says that if you delight in the Lord, He'll give you the desire of your heart (see Psalms 37:4). This man took the option Jesus offered him and walked out of a 38-year prison of sickness. He said "Yes" to the question, "Wilt thou be made whole?"

—m—

**WHAT WILL YOU SAY?**

# Sam Smith

**In all these things we are more than conquerors …
through him. (Romans 8:37)**

S am Smith has built one of New England's greatest churches.
He's a big, lovable Texan, who has become "a spiritual father"
to a few thousand people who have been saved or nurtured under
his ministry. Miracles? You should hear some of them! Alcoholics
delivered, cancers withered, and crooked limbs straightened out.
Yet when it comes to his own health, few have fought a greater
battle. He has back trouble so severe he often sleeps sitting up in
a reclining chair. He's had triple bypass surgery, diabetes, and the
temporary loss of sight in one eye.

In 1982, Sam and his wife Donna lost one of their three sons.
He died mysteriously in his sleep; he was in his early 20s. One of
Sam's favorite verses is, "Fight the good fight of faith" (1 Timothy
6:12), and he has fought his way through it all. Has he ever been
tempted to give up? Oh yes. Especially during the long months of
separation from the pulpit and the people he loves. But he never
did! There are three things I've learned watching Sam:

1. What you've been taught must be tested, or it has no value.

2. Faith is not really faith until it's all you're holding on to.

3. Your assignment does not exempt you from attack, but you're
anointing will sustain you in it, and grace will bring you through
it!

—∞—

**REMEMBER, TODAY YOU ARE MORE THAN A CONQUEROR!**

**Beware of dogs.**
**(Philippians 3:2)**

Mandy was the dog who lived next door, and she loved Fridays—the day we put our garbage out. No sooner had I left our driveway than she'd go to work ripping open all the plastic sacks that held our "family secrets." But it gets worse; her favorite thing was "spreading it" the length of the street, till everyone knew what the Gass family had for breakfast, dinner, and supper. At the time, I happened to be on television every Saturday night, so my neighbors knew me; but they never knew what I was really thinking on those bitterly cold January nights in eastern Maine as I walked the length of the street picking up garbage. Only the grace of God and the fact that I didn't have a gun saved Mandy! When I moved to Georgia I discovered they have "Mandys," too. Beware of dogs that spread garbage!

And don't *be* one! Satan is called "the accuser of the brethren" (Revelation 12:10). Jesus is called "the Advocate." Listen: "But if you sin, there is Someone to plead for you before the Father" (1 John 3:3, TLB). When a member of God's family falls, that's what Jesus does. What do you do? Solomon says, "A tale bearer is a revealer of secrets; but he that is of a faithful spirit concealeth a matter" (Proverbs 11:13). Peter says, "Love covers a multitude of sins" (1 Peter 4:8). To cover does not mean to "cover up," it means to confront, to correct, and above all, provide a place of healing and restoration.

—m—

IF SOME OF US STARTED PRACTICING THIS IN OUR
RELATIONSHIPS WITH EACH OTHER, MAYBE IT WOULD
CATCH ON. IT'S AT LEAST WORTH TRYING.

SEPTEMBER 13

## Stink or Storm

**By faith Noah ... prepared an ark to the saving of his house.
(Hebrews 11:7)**

Noah didn't sail on the Queen Mary. Can you imagine spending one year in that ark with all those animals and only one window? But there were only two options—the stink on the inside, or the storm on the outside! The point is, there are no perfect churches. If you could find one, don't join it—you'll ruin it! Everybody loves to talk about the power of the New Testament Church. What about the problems? They had hypocrites! Remember Ananias and Sapphira? (Acts 5) They had a serious financial scandal. (See Acts 6.) They had a "big stink" over doctrine in Acts 15 that almost split the church down the middle. Moral problems? They had a guy sleeping with his step-mother in the Corinthian church! (See 1 Corinthians 5.) That one really stank!

So, what do you do when you have a situation that smells bad in church? First, don't talk! Love covers! (See 1 Peter 4:8.) Second, work for reconciliation. "If someone falls into sin, forgivingly restore him, saving your critical comments for yourself" (Galatians 6:1, TM). Third, burn incense! When the lamps in the tabernacle were snuffed out each evening, they left a foul smell, so God told Moses to "burn incense" (see Exodus 37:8). Don't be "thrown" when "flesh acts like flesh." Don't be part of the problem by being immature—be a part of the solution. David said, "Let my prayer be set forth before Thee as incense" (Psalms 141:2).

LET YOUR PRAYERS RISE AS INCENSE UNTO GOD
AND WATCH HIM INTERVENE TO CHANGE THE
CIRCUMSTANCES. THIS IS GOD'S WAY.

# His First Prayer

**I pray for them. (John 17:9)**

Can you imagine Jesus praying a prayer for us that the Father wouldn't answer? In John 17 He asked the Father to do five things for us. I believe we'll live to see them all fulfilled.

First, He prayed that we would see His glory! Listen, "The glory which Thou gavest me, I have given them" (John 17:22). Have you ever encountered the glory of God? When Moses had been in it, his face shone. (See Exodus 34:29.) When Isaiah saw it, he cried, "Woe is me, for I am undone … for mine eyes have seen the King, the Lord of hosts" (Isaiah 6:5). Once you've experienced His glory, it becomes the standard by which all other experiences are measured.

It's worshipers who bring the glory of God into the midst of His people! In the Psalms we learn that God inhabits the praises of His people. (See Psalms 22:3.) The Japanese have a unique interpretation of this verse. Because they carried their Emperor on a great throne, they translate the verse like this, "When we praise God, we create a seat, and God comes down and sits in it." How wonderful! Any time you make a seat of praise for Him, He always comes and sits in it. He will ride to work with you in the car. He'll fill any room in your house, for He sits in the seat of your praise, and it's there that He reveals to you His glory!

―☽―

TOO MANY OF US ARRIVE IN CHURCH PREOCCUPIED
WITH WHAT WE CAN GET, INSTEAD OF WHAT WE CAN GIVE.
THAT'S GOT TO CHANGE IF WE'RE TO EXPERIENCE
THE GLORY OF GOD.

# His Second Prayer

**I pray for them.
(John 17:9)**

Next, Jesus prayed that we would know the Word. Listen: "I have given them your Word" (John 17:14). Have you heard about the lady and the promise box? One morning she pulled out a verse which read, "And Judas went out and hanged himself." Quickly, she pulled out another; it read, "Go and do likewise." In despair, she pulled out another, and it read, "What thou doest, do quickly." You may smile, but how much time do you spend in the Word?

Samuel's mother brought him a new coat to the temple each year. Was that because the old one was out of style? No! It was because he was growing. (See 1 Samuel 2:26.) Are you still wearing that same old threadbare coat? If you are, you're not growing! John said, "I write unto you young men, because the Word of God lives in you, and you have overcome the evil one" (1 John 2:14, NIV). Peter wrote, "Desire the sincere milk of the Word, that ye may grow thereby" (1 Peter 2:2). Paul said, "Brothers, your faith is growing more and more, and the love every one of you has for each other is increasing" (2 Thessalonians 1-3). What a testimony! D. L. Moody said, "A little learning will take a man away from God, but 'full knowledge' will bring him back."

**IF YOU WANT TO FIND GOD, YOU'LL FIND HIM
IN THE PAGES OF HIS WORD TODAY.
PICK IT UP AND START READING!**

# His Third Prayer

**I pray for them.**
**(John 17:9)**

Next, Jesus prayed that we would be united in love. Listen: "That they may be one, as we are one" (John 17:11). When the Red River overflowed its banks in North Dakota, you couldn't tell one farm from another. All the fences disappeared! What a picture! When God pours out His Spirit in the last days, all the fences will disappear! Many in leadership today will be used of God, but no man will be able to control it or contain it. David said, "Behold how good, and how pleasant it is for brethren to dwell together in unity. It is like the precious ointment upon the head, that ran down ... to the skirts of his garments" (Psalms 133:1-2). Unity must start at the head, then on down to the rest of the body! That will mean an end to "turf-guarding" and "personal agendas."

Years ago in the wheat fields of western Canada, a couple was walking with their little boy. Mom thought Dad had him, and Dad thought Mom had him. Neither of them did. When they couldn't find him they gathered a search party, because it was getting bitterly cold! But after hours of looking, there was no trace of him. Then someone said, "Let's join hands; we'll begin at one end, and together we'll cover the fields." Soon a cry went up, "I found him!" But sadly he'd frozen to death. As they gathered around his lifeless form, they were heard to utter the saddest of words, "If only we'd joined hands before it was too late."

---

JESUS PRAYED FOR UNITY BECAUSE
THE JOB WILL NOT GET DONE UNTIL WE GET TOGETHER!
TODAY ASK GOD TO LET IT BEGIN IN YOUR HEART.

# His Fourth Prayer

**I pray for them.**
**(John 17:9)**

Next, Jesus prayed that we would reach the whole world with the Gospel. Listen: "As You have sent me into the world, I have sent them" (John 17:18).

An old Methodist missionary couple in China were ordered to leave when the communists took power. When they refused, they were marched, with members of their tiny congregation, to a nearby hillside. The wife was commanded to dig a grave while her husband watched. They were told, "Renounce your faith in Jesus, and we will let you go home." They replied, "Fifty years we have served Him, and never once has He failed us. We will never renounce Him!" Suddenly, the butt of a rifle came crashing down on her skull, and she collapsed into the grave. Her husband was told to bury her. When he protested, the commandant ordered that his tongue be cut out. First, the old man asked to say something. As they watched in amazement, standing there in a shallow grave in China, the old Methodist missionary began to sing, "I'd rather have Jesus than silver or gold. I'd rather be His than have riches untold, I'd rather have Jesus than anything this world affords today." Sadly, he buried his wife and returned to spend his last years in Canada. When he shared this testimony at a northeastern Bible collee, 300 young people vollunteered for missionary service!

GOD MAY BURY HIS WORKMEN—BUT HIS WORK GOES ON!
WE HAVE A JOB TO DO, AND YOU HAVE A PART IN IT.
ASK GOD TO HELP YOU FIND IT, AND DO IT TODAY!

# His Fifth Prayer

**I pray for them.**
**(John 17:9)**

Finally, Jesus prayed that we would experience His joy. Listen: "That they may have a full measure of My joy within them" (John 17:13, NIV). Listen again: "With joy shall ye draw water out of the wells of salvation" (Isaiah 12:3). Your joy comes from within. Paul was often in jail, but jail was never in Paul, so he wrote, "Rejoice in the Lord always" (Philippians 4:4). You say, "How's that possible?" Because threats are not facts to those who are informed! He said, "For I am persuaded, that neither death, nor life, nor angels, nor principalities, nor powers, nor things present, nor things to come, nor height, nor depth, nor any other creature, shall be able to separate us from the love of God which is in Christ Jesus our Lord" (Romans 8:38-39).

The other day I tried to recall the Christians I knew when I was growing up. Some of them were wonderful, but others were anti-social, censorious, brooding, pickled, withdrawn, intense, and "mule-like" of countenance. I'm sure their experience with God was real, but it did nothing for me. David said, "They looked unto Him and were radiant" (Psalms 34:5). Adoniram Judson, the 19th Century missionary to Burma, was known for his great joy. When he arrived there in 1812, he didn't know the language, but that didn't stop him. He approached a Burmese man and gave him a big hug! The man went home and reported to his family that he had seen an angel. The joy of Christ was so radiant on Judson's countenance that the people of Burma called him "Mr. Glory-Face."

**NOW THAT'S THE KIND OF JOY JESUS WANTS YOU TO HAVE—AND TO EXHIBIT TO OTHERS!**

**I called upon the LORD in distress: the LORD answered me, and set me in a large place. (Psalms 118:5)**

Pastor Clinton White told me of a black surgeon in New York City, a remarkable man, who once said to him, "I used to suffer from ghetto-head! That's the oldest disease in my race. I was born in a ghetto! Despair was my constant companion; every day it told me, 'The system is stacked against you.'

"I'm one of thirteen children who lived on the fifth floor of a run-down tenement. The street I played in was full of pushers, pimps, and prostitutes. But something happened to me. One Saturday morning I was alone in our apartment listening to the Top 20 on the radio. Suddenly a minister came on and read the words of Psalms 118:5: 'I called on the Lord in distress, and the Lord answered me.'

"I couldn't stop listening! That day I discovered two things—God was bigger than any problem I had, and I was not a prisoner of my circumstances. I was a prisoner of my *attitude*. When he gave the invitation, I knelt in that dingy apartment and committed my life to Christ. I was only fourteen years old, but that's the day my life began."

He graduated from medical school at the top of his class, and today is one of the most respected surgeons in the Northeast. He told Clinton, "Every day, before making my hospital rounds, I fill my mind with God's Word. Therefore, I never approach my patients feeling hopeless, for I know what God can do for them!"

---

HE DARED TO OPEN HIS HEART AND SEE GOD'S POSSIBILITIES FOR HIM! WHY DON'T YOU TRY IT, TOO?

# Bad Hair Days

**Love is patient, love is kind.
(1 Corinthians 13:4, NIV)**

Sometimes my wife has "bad hair days," and I have a hard time understanding her. However, having a good relationship depends on our willingness to at least try. It's a pity you don't get lessons on this in school. Imagine studying Afghanistan or the Equator, places you'll probably never visit, yet not so much as a word on insight or preparation for bad hair days!

Fortunately, God's Word has some good advice here. Listen: "As God's chosen people ... clothe yourselves with compassion ... kindness ... humility ... gentleness and patience" (Colossians 3:12). Paul is talking here about using tact. Tact is kindness with brains. It's a way of putting your best foot forward without actually putting your foot in your mouth or stepping on anyone's toes. It stems from the Latin word *tactus* which means "touch." It's a delicate, sensitive touch that works with human nature, not against it. It's just what you need on "bad hair days!" Peter says, "Add to your faith ... brotherly kindness and love" (2 Peter 1:5-7, NIV). The tact you learn at home will also serve you well at work, in church, and anywhere else you go.

One of the greatest illustrations of tact that I ever read was about a minister who had been given a pie by a member of his congregation. It was so bad that he had to throw it in the garbage. The next Sunday when his parishioner asked him what he thought of it, he replied, "A pie like that never lasts long around our house."

---

**THANK GOD FOR THE GIFT OF TACT!**

## Help Us Listen

**Ears that hear and eyes that see—the LORD has
made them both. (Proverbs 20:12)**

Charles Swindoll tells of a day when he was so busy and so tense that he found himself "snapping" at his wife and children and getting irritated at unexpected interruptions throughout the day. Before long, things at his home started reflecting the stress and strain of his attitude. He says, "I distinctly remember after supper that evening, the words of my youngest daughter, Colleen. She wanted to tell me something important that had happened to her at school. So she began hurriedly, 'Daddy, I wanna tell you something, and I'll tell you really fast.'"

By this point he could see her frustration, so he answered, "Honey, you can tell me, and you don't have to tell me really fast. Say it slowly." Swindoll says he will never forget her answer. She said "Then listen slowly!"

When you take time to listen, you're telling that person that they are really worth listening to. Everybody deserves that! Sometimes when we get successful and busy, we forget the despair we felt in those early days. Remember? If someone you admired stopped to talk to you and to listen, you'd have run on the strength of it for the next forty days! Today we even have preachers with "bodyguards," who escort them in and out of conferences so they can speak to the people without ever having to *listen* to them.

—◊◊◊—

JESUS STOPPED FOR CHILDREN, HE LISTENED TO
HURTING PEOPLE, AND HE WENT OUT OF HIS WAY
TO SHOW HE CARED.

# Commitment

**Blessed is the man who perseveres under trial,
because when he has stood the test, he will receive the crown.
(James 1:12, NIV)**

Terry Fox ran from one end of Canada to the other and raised $24 million to fight cancer, the disease that finally took his life. What's amazing is he did it with one leg—cancer had taken the other. He planned to run twenty-six miles each day, but because of severe headaches, heavy rain, snow, and icy roads, after a month he had only managed to struggle an average of eight miles a day. So why did he keep going? Because the purpose in his heart was greater than the pain in his body! They can amputate your leg, but they can't amputate your spirit!

Commitment is the willingness to do whatever it takes; it is a heartfelt promise to yourself from which you refuse to back down. There's a difference between interest and commitment. When you are interested in doing something, you do it only when it is convenient. When you're committed, you accept no excuses—only results. Only you can decide whether the rewards are worth the effort, for the truth is that there are "trade-offs." You can't have a healthy body and live on junk food. The security of a guaranteed salary is non-existent when you step out to start your own business. Television and straight A's are a rare combination. Commitment means "paying your dues." Listen to these words: "If anyone would come after Me, he must deny himself and take up his cross and follow Me" (Matthew 16:24, NIV).

**TODAY ASK YOURSELF, "TO WHAT AM I REALLY COMMITTED?"**

# *You Can Make It*

**Through acts of faith they toppled kingdoms,
made justice work, and took the promises for themselves.
(Hebrew 11:43, TM)**

Courage is all you can do—miracles are God doing the rest! What have you done about your situation? Have you persevered in prayer? On what Scriptures are you standing? Who have you talked to? You can have comfort or you can have conflict—but you can't have both! Life isn't easy, and it's not fair. Mary Tyler Moore said. "Pain nourishes courage; you can't be brave if you have only wonderful things happen to you." She's right!

In the worst storm of his life, Paul said to the captain, "Keep your courage—for I have faith in God that it will happen just as He told me" (Acts 27:25, NIV). Paul made it to his destination, and by God's grace, you will, too. When Jehoshaphat was outnumbered a hundred to one by the enemy—he changed his focus. "We know not what to do, but our eyes are upon Thee" (2 Chronicles 20:12). There's your key today. Stop looking at what's against you, and start looking at what you have going for you. Listen: "Be strong and courageous. Do not be afraid or discouraged because of the King of Assyria and the vast army with him, for there is greater power with us than with him. With him is only the arm of flesh, but with us is the Lord our God to help us to fight our battles" (2 Chronicles 32:7-8, NIV).

---

**YOU MAY TAKE A FEW HITS AND SUSTAIN A WOUND OR TWO, BUT GOD SAYS YOU ARE COMING OUT OF THIS STRONGER THAN YOU WERE WHEN YOU WENT IN!**

# Habits

**As his custom was, he went into the synagogue.
(Luke 4:16)**

If you want to be like Jesus, study His habits and make them yours! Your talent doesn't determine your future. The brilliant young actor, River Phoenix, died in a drug-induced convulsion on Hollywood Boulevard, because he couldn't "kick" his habit. If you want to know what your future holds, keep a diary of your daily habits for a month, and then you can write your own obituary. Do you want to be like Jesus? He rose before any of His disciples to pray. He wouldn't have thought of facing the day without it! Imagine, He did, but we don't! David said, "Morning, noon, and evening I will pray ... and He shall hear my voice" (Psalms 55:7). That sounds like a habit!

Do you pray even five minutes a day? That's less than one-half percent of your waking hours. During Prohibition, Congress ruled that anything that contained less than one-half percent alcohol was "non-intoxicating." That means you can't feel the effects; it doesn't change your perceptions; it doesn't change the way you walk and talk! You say, "How long should I pray?" The answer is, "Until you feel the effect—until it changes your perception—until you walk and talk differently."

---

**TODAY, TAKE A LOOK AT YOUR HABITS.
THEY'RE A PROPHECY OF YOUR FUTURE.**

# Finishing Strong

**Moses was an hundred and twenty years old when he died: his eye was not dim, nor his natural force abated.**
**(Deuteronomy 34:7)**

During his last years, Dr. Norman Vincent Peale wrote: "The longer I live, the more convinced I become that neither age nor circumstances need deprive us of energy or vitality. Although I have retired from my church, I occupy my working hours with *Guideposts Magazine*, speaking, and writing books. I go to bed as early as possible, and rise early. I try to eat sensibly, exercise regularly, and avoid bad habits of all kinds. I mentally repudiate physical, mental or spiritual decline and disability. I trust in the living God, and I recommend the same to anyone who desires a long and healthy life."

The Bible says, "The Lord blessed the latter end of Job more than the beginning" (Job 42:12). Your age is not a problem to God so long as your faith is strong. Noah didn't start building the ark until he was 500, went into it at 621, came out of it at 622, and helped to start the world all over again! So there's hope for you!

When someone told the 89-year-old poet Dorothy Duncan that she had lived a "full life," she replied sharply, "Don't you dare to 'past tense' me!" If you're not too old to learn, and if you haven't outlived your enthusiasm, then you can still "bring forth fruit in old age" (Psalms 92:14). It is up to you. If you can breathe—pray! If you can speak—encourage others! If you can recall—tell us where the "potholes" are and save us from paying twice for the same wisdom  Remember creation?

---

**IT'S WONDERFUL WHAT GOD CAN DO IN JUST ONE DAY—**
**SO GIVE HIM ALL THE DAYS YOU HAVE LEFT.**

# Perspective

**Teach us to number our days, that we may apply our hearts unto wisdom. (Psalms 90:12)**

Of all the sad words of tongue or pen, the saddest of all—"It might have been!" (John Greenleaf Whittier). My obsession is to discover and develop the gifts God has given me and to fulfil his purpose for my life. How about you? What difference does it really make if you wear a Versace suit, drive a Rolls Royce down Rodeo Drive, or live in a penthouse at the top of Trump Tower. If you don't find and fulfill the will of God for your life, what does it all mean? You may be a rich failure, or a famous failure, or a failure with more degrees than a thermometer—but you're still a failure! Paul says, "My life is worth nothing unless I use it for doing the work assigned to me by the Lord" (Acts 20:24, TLB). What has God told you to do? Are you doing it? Listen to these sobering Scriptures: "Lest by any means I should run … in vain" (Galatians 2:2). "Lest at any time we should let them slip" (Hebrews 2:1). "Lest by any means I myself should be a castaway"(1 Corinthians 9:27). That's the great apostle Paul talking! He's considering the possibility of being "disqualified"before he gets to finish the race. He's talking about "losing his grip" on what is really important.

**IF PAUL IS CONCERNED, SHOULDN'T WE BE ALSO?**

# Christopher Nolan

**I quit focusing on the handicap and began appreciating the gift. (2 Corinthians 12:9-10, TM)**

At twenty-two, Christopher Nolan was already hailed as a literary genius. With Britain's coveted Whitbread Prize for his autobiography, *Under the Eye of the Clock*, his work has been compared to that of James Joyce and W.B. Yeats. Yet it takes Christopher Nolan a quarter of an hour to write one word. Born with severe cerebral palsy, he spends much of his life strapped in a wheelchair, his face and limbs subject to uncontrollable spasms. He can't speak, but he can type. As a child he cried bitterly that he was not like other children until one day his mother, said to him, "Listen here, you can see, you can hear, you can understand, and you're loved by me and your dad just as you are." Gradually he looked at his limbs and decided that he liked himself! What a decision! He began to shift his attention away from his limitations and focus on what was possible—what he could do with his life.

He says, "My mind is like a spin-dryer at full speed; millions of beautiful words cascade down into my lap. Images gunfire across my consciousness, and while trying to discipline them, I jump in awe at the soul-filled beauty of the mind's expanse." Don't you wish you could write like that? Let go of the if only's, the comparisons and the judgments.

LISTEN TO PAUL'S WORDS: "THANKS BE UNTO GOD WHICH ALWAYS CAUSES US TO TRIUMPH IN CHRIST" (2 CORINTHIANS 2:14). WHAT A WAY TO LIVE!

## Acceptance

**This is my prayer: that your love may abound more and more.
(Philippians 1:9, NIV)**

When you can forgive yourself and others, you've finally come to terms with your own humanity and learned to be at peace with your own imperfections. It's what you've been through, plus the grace of God, that's made you what you are today! Recently I came across these wonderful words by Veronica Shoffstall, and I think you'll want to read them more than once!

"After a while you learn the difference between holding a hand and chaining a soul;  you learn that life does not mean leaning, and company does not always mean security; you begin to learn that kisses are not contracts, and presents are not promises; and you begin to accept your defeats with your head high and your eyes ahead, with the grace of an adult, not the grief of a child. You learn to build all your roads on today, because tomorrow's ground is too uncertain for plans, and futures have a way of falling down in mid-flight. After a while you learn that even sunshine burns if you get too much. You learn to plant your own garden and decorate your own soul instead of waiting for someone to bring you flowers; and you learn that (by God's sustaining grace) you can really endure, that you really are strong, and that you really do have worth!"

NOW YOU UNDERSTAND WHAT JESUS MEANT WHEN HE SAID, "I AM COME THAT YOU MIGHT HAVE LIFE AND THAT YOU MIGHT HAVE IT MORE ABUNDANTLY" (JOHN 10:10).

*Why Not?*

**When you ask, you do not receive, because you ask
with wrong motives. (James 4:3, NIV)**

If that's the question you're asking, here are some things you need to look at. Disobedience destroys your confidence before God! Listen: "If our hearts condemn us not, then [and then only] have we confidence toward God, and whatever we ask we receive" (1 John 3:21-22). You can only be bold when you know you've been obedient! Are you asking in faith? Jesus said when you pray,"believe that you receive, and you'll have it" (Mark 11:24). Until you wrap your request in faith and expectation, you'll get nowhere. God doesn't respond to your situation—He responds to your faith!

Furthermore, God is not interested in anything that stops with you. When He multiplied the loaves, He told His disciples to give it to the hungry crowd. The only blessings you can keep are the ones you are willing to give away. One man told me,"Money can make you backslide." He's right! But I asked him, "If money can make you backslide, why hasn't Satan overdosed you with it?" His comment was a "cop-out" for his lack of faith and compassion toward the needs of those around him. Here's the key: "Delight thyself also in the Lord, and He shall give thee the desires of thine heart" (Psalms 37:4).

—◦◦◦—

WHEN YOU DELIGHT IN THE LORD, HIS DESIRES BECOME
YOUR DESIRES. THEN HE CAN TRUST YOU
WITH ANYTHING.

# Dr. Joe McKelvey

**"There is hope for your future," declares the LORD.
(Jeremiah 31:17, NIV)**

Never give up on yourself; not on that one for whom you are praying, and certainly not on the prodigal! My friend, Dr. Joe McKelvey, was thrown out of Evangel Bible School for using and selling drugs. One night, driving home in the rain with a bottle of liquor and a stash of marijuana, he heard a voice say to him, "Throw it out the window, now!" The words were so strong that he just did it. A moment later, he lost control of his car and crashed, totaling two other cars and demolishing 150 feet of guardrail. He walked away without a scratch! In those days, he thought this was God punishing him. Today he knows, it was the enemy trying to destroy him. Remember, the battle is always over your future.

In May, 1982, Joe and Lynn McKelvey went to Middletown, New York, and started their church in a Holiday Inn with forty people they'd won to Christ in a crusade. Giving birth is never easy, but if it's "born of God" it is destined to grow and make a difference. A few months ago I had the privilege of speaking at their fifteenth anniversary celebration. They now have over 1,000 people, and they're getting ready to build a new church and "a Christian nightclub," because Joe remembers what it is like "to be out there."

---

NEVER GIVE UP ON YOUR PRODIGAL—FOR THE FATHER
DOESN'T. JUST KEEP HIM A SEAT AT THE TABLE,
FOR GOD HAS PROMISED THAT HE'LL COME BACK!
(SEE JEREMIAH 31:16.)

# Should or Shouldn't Go

**Train up a child in the way he should go: and when he is old, he will not depart from it.**
**(Proverbs 22:6)**

There are two sides to this familiar verse. Lynn McKelvey points out that if you continuously expose your children to negative words that tear down their self-esteem, they'll grow up and "not depart from it." Why does a little girl with an angry alcoholic dad she could never please, grow up and pick a husband just like him, and spend the rest of her life trying to please him? And worse, expose her children to it also! How come a boy with an "absentee father" who only showed up to "straighten him out," grows up, has children of his own, and discovers he can correct them, but he doesn't have a clue how to compliment them or say, "I love you"? Have you ever read the words, "Visiting the iniquity of the fathers upon the children unto the third and fourth generation" (Exodus 20:5)? Our children can only work with the tools we give them! Parent, draw a line in the sand and announce, "This destructive family system ends right here with me!"

Never say to your child, "Why can't you be like your brother or your sister?" They're not supposed to be! "Train up a child in the way that he should go." Stop trying to pour them into the mold of your lost ambitions or make them like somebody else. Celebrate their uniqueness and help them to develop it. Let's stop producing kids who feel like they never measure up.

IF THEY DO NOT HEAR WORDS OF LOVE AND PRAISE FROM
YOU, HOW WILL THEY EVER LEARN TO SAY THEM?

# Life-Changing Prayer

**Show me your ways, O LORD, teach me your paths;
guide me in your truth.
(Psalms 25:4-5, NIV)**

When David prayed, "Show me ... teach me ... guide me," he was describing the process that prayer takes us through. When God shows you His standards and His will for your life, it requires you to grow and change. Once you accept what God wants to show you, He is able to teach you. And when you are teachable, He's finally able to guide you into His plan and purpose. When God shows you, He has your heart. When He teaches you, He has your mind. When He guides you, He has your hand. When you pray, you grow to meet the very challenges about which you are praying!

In 1924, a group of climbers tried twice to get to the top of the world's tallest mountain, but failed. In fact, two of their party were killed in that endeavor. They met in London a few weeks later to talk and give a report to a crowd of interested supporters. On the stage was a large picture of Mount Everest. One of the men stood up to speak. As he addressed the crowd, he turned to the picture of Mount Everest and said, "You have conquered us once, you have conquered us twice, but Mount Everest, you will not conquer us next time." Then he turned to the audience and with determination said, "You see, Mount Everest can grow no larger—but we can!"

—m—

**PRAYER MAY NOT CHANGE YOUR CIRCUMSTANCES, BUT YOU CAN BE ASSURED, IT WILL CHANGE YOU!
(READ JOHN 16:23-24)**

# The Privilege

**He will call upon me, and I will answer him.**
**(Psalms 91:15, NIV)**

Have you stopped believing in the power of prayer? Your answer to that question is not what you say, it is what you do! Psychologists tell us that people are more apt to do what rewards them. Is that why you have been spending so little time in prayer recently? William Ward says, "We stamp and address an envelope and send it on it's way with complete confidence that it will reach it's destination; yet we wonder and even doubt if our prayers will be heard by an ever-present, ever-loving God." David said, "He shall call upon Me and I will answer him" (Psalms 91:15).

If you want to know God and have influence with God, you have to spend time with Him! Change your attitude toward prayer! Get rid of the idea that prayer has to be repetitious and boring. I do some of my best praying when I am out driving by myself. Often, I return home with solutions and new direction for my life. Sometimes I don't get beyond praise and worship, but that is okay. Love expressed draws people together.

Be spontaneous! Tell God your troubles and let Him comfort you. Tell Him your longings and let Him purify them; tell Him your temptations and let Him strengthen you! Tell Him your resentments and let Him forgive you and empower you to forgive others!

---

**OF ALL THE BENEFITS GOD HAS GIVEN YOU TODAY, NONE IS GREATER THAN THE PRIVILEGE OF PRAYER. SO USE IT!**

# Be Specific

**When ye pray, use not vain repetitions.
(Matthew 6:7)**

Have you heard the lawyers' version of, "Give us this day our daily bread"? Listen: "We respectfully petition, request, and entreat that a due and adequate provision be made, this day and date first above and inscribed, for the satisfying of petitioners' nutritional requirements, and for the organizing of such methods of allocation and distribution as may be deemed necessary and proper, to assure the reception by and for said petitioners, of such quantity of cereal products (hereinafter and herein called "bread"), as shall in the judgement of the aforesaid petitioners, constitute a sufficient amount."

That's seventy words! The entire Lord's Prayer only requires fifty-six words! Are you getting the idea? The most effective form of communication is brief and to the point. Jesus simply said, "You will be given whatever you ask for in My Name" (John 16:23). The great thing about being specific is when God gives you an answer you know it! The loved one you prayed for got saved! The sickness you lifted up was healed! When you pray about a specific area, it gives God an opportunity to tell you what needs to be changed in that area! The more specific you are in your request, the more alert you will be to the answers, and the more specific you can be with your thanks to God.

**IT'S NOT YOUR WORDS THAT MOVE GOD—IT'S YOUR
FAITH! HAVE YOU TALKED WITH HIM TODAY?**

# Get It Right

**Ask, and it shall be given you; seek, and ye shall find; knock, and it shall be opened unto you. (Matthew 7:7)**

Part of any good relationship is a sensitivity to the other persons needs and desires! God already knows what *you* need, but how well do you know what He needs? Many times God mercifully withholds His answers until you come to Him at last, with the right request. Billy Graham's wife, Ruth, says, "God hasn't always answered my prayers. If He had, I would have married the wrong man—several times!" James says, "When you ask, you do not receive, because you ask with wrong motives" (James 4:3, NIV). Jesus said, "Ask and it will be given you; seek, and you will find; knock, and the door will open to you." That's the order: "Ask, seek, and knock!"

Before you ask God, ask yourself, "Is my request fair to everyone concerned? Is it in harmony with the Word? Will it blend with my gifts? Will it draw me closer to God? What's my part in answering it? Have I obeyed God?" "Seek," means to "ask with effort." When you pray "give us this day our daily bread," God won't "rain" down groceries on you. Jesus meant, "Give us the opportunity to earn our bread." The word knock means to be "persistent!" If you stay in the presence of God long enough He will either answer your prayer or change your request!

—m—

GOD IS ASKING YOU TO BE PERSISTENT, BECAUSE HE
WANTS YOU TO GROW IN YOUR RELATIONSHIP WITH HIM.

# Get Into It

**When you pray, go into your room, close the door.
(Matthew 6:6, NIV)**

Have you ever tried to maintain a conversation with a toddler? Just when you're in the middle of a sentence, they figure it's a good time to play with one of their toys, or chase the dog. Isn't that how we treat God? We give Him a few minutes or a few thoughts, but we never set aside a time and a place to give Him our full attention. Remember, the place of prayer, is also the place of answered prayer! Our problem is "the war of wandering thoughts." Sound familiar? Things you've forgotten suddenly "parade" into your consciousness when you try to pray. To make matters worse, if you're "double minded" you get nowhere with God. (See James 1:8.) So what do you do?

Here are a few suggestions that have worked for me. *Pray aloud!* That actually makes it difficult for your mind to wander. You may feel awkward at first, but you'll soon get used to it. *Write down the distractions!* Make the devil your secretary. Keep paper and a pen close by, and when the parade starts, simply write each thing down, and then forget it until later. If you still can't help thinking about it, take it to God in prayer. *Keep a journal!* Sometimes I don't know what I want, or how I feel until I put it in writing. Like a mirror, there are my deepest needs and longings, my very subconscious on paper in front of me—and God! From that point on I can give God my full attention.

—◦◦◦—

GET INTO PRAYER TODAY.
THAT'S WHERE YOUR ANSWERS CAN BE FOUND.

# Bag Lunch or Banquet

**Seek the LORD and his strength; seek his face continually.
(1 Chronicles 16:11)**

The difference between "catching a few moments" with the Lord, or having "quality time" with Him, is like the difference between driving through McDonald's or spending the evening at a fine restaurant. At McDonald's you drive up, shout into a microphone, and drive around to a window where they hand you a bag of food. But in a fine restaurant, you sit down, spend time in fellowship, enjoy every bite, and leave satisfied and nourished. Too many of us live on spiritual "fast food" and never experience the "banquet" God has for us. Have you learned how to stay in His presence?

There are two problems, one is lack of desire. You're as close to God as you really want to be! We may complain about lack of time, but the truth is, we make time for what we truly care about. If you really want to spend time praying, give up something else! Just do it! If you ask God for the desire, He will give it to you! The second problem is, we don't know how. First, find a place with no distractions. Take your Bible, a notepad, and a pencil with you. Use a tape recorder with worship music if that helps. Just do what works for you. It will take you weeks, and sometimes months, before you have developed your pattern, but stick with it—the rewards are awesome!

AND REMEMBER, THE GOAL IS NOT SEEING
HOW MUCH YOU CAN TELL GOD—IT'S LEARNING TO
HEAR FROM HIM, TOO!

## Your Prayer Life

**If ye abide in me, and my words abide in you, ye shall ask what ye will, and it shall be done unto you. (John 15:7)**

Jesus gives us a simple plan for building a prayer life. First, He says, "Abide in Me." Center your life around Him! John leaned his head on Jesus' breast—but Peter followed afar off. How close do you want to be? It's up to you!

Next, He says, "Let my words abide in you." *Soak yourself in the Scriptures!* Learn to pray the Word! If you do, your prayer life will be transformed. Some mornings I "personalize" Psalm 34: "I will bless You Lord at all times, Your praise shall continually be in my mouth. My soul shall make her boast in You, Lord." Or when I have a need, I pray, "Lord, You are my Shepherd, therefore I shall not want" (Psalms 23:1). When you pray the Word, your Father is pleased, your faith is activated, and your enemy will flee from you as he did from Jesus. Go ahead—try it!

*Next, before you look up—look in!* David said, "If I regard iniquity in my heart the Lord will not hear me" (Psalms 66:18). Achan's secret sin had to be dealt with before Israel could go forward into the Promised Land. (See Joshua 7.) So does yours! The moment you're conscious of sin, confess it, and when you have, be confident He has forgiven you, and move on rejoicing! (See 1 John 1:9.)

**USE THIS SIMPLE PLAN TO BUILD A PRAYER LIFE!**

## Prayer of Faith

**The prayer of faith shall save the sick,
and the Lord shall raise him up. (James 5:15)**

Why do we trust others so easily, yet God longs for us to trust Him? Think about it! You go to a doctor whose name you can't pronounce, receive a prescription you can't read, take it to a pharmacist you don't know, get medicine you don't understand, and take it with confidence! That's faith! Why is it so much easier to trust these "unknowns" than it is to trust a God who is faithful and loving in every way? The answer lies in where you *place* your trust! Trust comes from knowing someone, listening to them, and spending time with them!

Ed Lucas, who lives in Atlanta, just sent me this written testimony: "Last year, I noticed that I was discharging blood. The doctors discovered a malignant tumor on my bladder, and immediately scheduled surgery. I knew Jesus was the best doctor in the world, so I prayed for Him to touch me, and I believed that I was healed. When I told the doctors, they looked at me and said nothing lest it would discourage me. On Sunday night in church, my Bishop and Bob Gass laid hands on me and prayed. Suddenly the Bishop said to me, "You're healed—go home and don't worry about it!" Sure enough, when the doctors performed the surgery, they discovered there wasn't a trace of cancer—I was completely whole!" Today Ed is perfectly healthy, he's working full time, serving in the church, and rejoicing in the Lord!

**CHILD OF GOD, YOUR PROBLEM IS NOT TOO BIG FOR GOD! START PRAYING AND BELIEVING HIM TODAY!**

# A Little Farther

**And he went a little farther, and fell on his face, and prayed, . . . not as I will, but as thou wilt. (Matthew 26:39)**

He left the crowd; He left the twelve disciples; He even left the three who were closest to Him, and He went "a little farther." It was here, face to face with the Father, that He found the strength to embrace the will of God for His life. Today, God is saying to you, "The strength to handle this crisis, and the wisdom to know which way to go will be yours, if you'll just go a little farther, rise a little earlier, stay in My presence a little longer, dig a little deeper. If you only knew how close you were to the answer." Jesus was only a few hours away from the cross, and a few days away from the resurrection, and a few months away from the birthing of a church that would change the world. Are you in Gethsemane? Surrendering your will is hard! Before heaven accepted the sacrifice of a broken body, it demanded the sacrifice of a broken will. David cried, "Teach me to do Your will" (Psalms 143:10, NIV). There's no getting around this!

Florence Chadwick failed in her first attempt to swim the English Channel because of fog. She couldn't see, yet she was less than half-a-mile from the shore. When they told her how close she had been, she broke down and wept. But she went back again and broke the world record, because she understood that everything she had lived and worked for could be hers if she would "only go a little farther."

**IS GOD SAYING SOMETHING TO YOU IN THIS TODAY?**

**I will personally deal with anyone ... who worships idols ... and then comes to me for help. (Ezekiel 14:4, TLB)**

Is there anything you're putting ahead of God? Sometimes it's hard to tell. One of the ways to know is to ask yourself, "Would I be willing to give this thing up if God asked me to?" When God asked Abraham to sacrifice his son Isaac, He wasn't asking for a "human sacrifice" from Abraham, especially when he condemned it in the surrounding heathen nations. No, He just wanted to know, "Is there anything you love so much, that you would put it before Me? Is there anything I could ever ask that you wouldn't give?"

My experience has taught me that anything—absolutely anything—that I put before God I inevitably lose. Sports can be an idol if it keeps you away from God's house. Money and success can be idols if they absorb so much of your time, that there's no time left for God. A relationship can be an idol if that person has caused our heart to grow cold. Jesus said, "Seek ye first the Kingdom of God and His righteousness, and all these things shall be added unto you" (Matthew 6:33). He wants first place in your life and your affections. When He gets it, His Word says, "No good thing will He withhold from them that walk uprightly" (Psalms 84:11). The songwriter said, "The dearest idol I have known, what e'er that idol be, I gladly tear it from my heart, and worship only Thee!"

CHILD OF GOD, IS HE NUMBER ONE IN YOUR LIFE TODAY?

# Surrender!

**My son, give me your heart and let your eyes keep to my ways.**
**(Proverbs 23:26, NIV)**

Have you heard about the old Scottish lady who earned her living by peddling her wares along country roads? Each day she'd go out, and when she came to an intersection, she'd toss a stick into the air. Whichever way the stick pointed when it landed was the way she went. One day a man saw her tossing the stick into the air, once, twice, three times. He asked, "Why are you throwing your stick like that?" She said, "I am letting God show me which way to go by using this stick." "But why did you throw it three times?" he inquired. She replied, "Because the first two times He was pointing me in the wrong direction!" When you pray, if you don't like what He tells you, do you pray again, hoping He'll say what you want to hear? If so, you've never exchanged your will for His!

Jesus said, "I am the vine; you are the branches. If a man remains in me and I in him, he will bear much fruit; apart from me you can do nothing" (John 15:5). When you stay "connected," you bear fruit spontaneously and naturally. There's no striving and straining; it's just an outgrowth of your intimacy with Him. Just as the life flows from the vine into the branches, so power flows from the one who dwells within you and begins to affect every area of your life.

MARTHA SPENT TIME WORKING FOR HIM, BUT MARY SPENT TIME LISTENING TO HIM, AND JESUS SAID, "SHE HATH CHOSEN THAT BETTER PART"(LUKE 10:42).

# Sowing and Reaping

**He that ministereth seed to the sower both minister bread for your food, and multiply your seed sown.**
**(2 Corinthians 9:10)**

God speaks about "sowing and reaping" for two reasons. First, when you believe God, you honor God! Listen again, "If you sow bountifully, you will reap bountifully" (2 Corinthians 9:6). That's God's Word!

The Word says, "Pray ye therefore the Lord of the harvest, that He would send forth laborers into His harvest" (Luke 10:2). Laborers cost! It takes money to support missionaries, build hospitals, and print Christian literature. When communism fell, Iran immediately sent $1 billion to build powerful radio stations on the Russian border and flood the eastern block with the message of Islam. What about us? We must succeed in our businesses, and prosper on our jobs, if we're going to win the battle for a lost world! Anything less is selfish!

Next, when you plant seed, you release your faith and raise your expectation. The moment a farmer puts his seed into the ground he starts looking and preparing for a harvest! If you don't "expect" a harvest you can miss it, because it comes in so many forms: a new relationship, the sale of a property, a promotion on your job, a reduction in your taxes, or protection from danger and disease. Remember this: God only multiplies the seed you "sow."

**HE MAKES PROMISES TO "SOWERS" THAT HE DOESN'T MAKE TO ANYONE ELSE. (READ 2 CORINTHIANS 9:6-11.)**

# The Trumpet

**For the trumpet shall sound, and the dead shall be raised incorruptible, and we shall be changed.**
**(1 Corinthians 15:52)**

Minnie Jones was present that night, and she never got tired of telling the story: A little English pastor with a "flair for the dramatic," announced that he would be preaching on Sunday night on "the second coming of the Lord." He told the trumpeter from the church orchestra to hide behind a curtain, and when he shouted, "The trump of God shall sound," he was to hit a loud blast on his trumpet. Well, Sunday night came, the trumpet sounded, and what happened next was a sensation!

The first group of people fainted; the next group screamed and ran for the door. But the funniest group of all was the one who jumped up on the pews, flapped their arms frantically, and tried to "fly!"

I cannot guarantee that this story was not embellished a little, but I can tell you with certainty that when Jesus comes again all three groups will be present: "the fainters," "the runners," and "the flappers!" Some of us are living like Jesus has changed His mind. He hasn't! It's only His mercy that has extended time to give us an opportunity to gather in the harvest before "the Lord of the harvest returns." Make no mistake about it —Jesus is coming again!

LISTEN: "BUT OUR CITIZENSHIP IS IN HEAVEN. AND WE EAGERLY AWAIT A SAVIOR FROM THERE, THE LORD JESUS CHRIST" (PHILIPPIANS 3:20).

# God's Time Clock

**When these things begin to take place, stand up and lift up your heads, because your redemption is drawing near.
(Luke 21:28, NIV)**

Dr. C. M. Ward tells of flying on a plane with a 7' 4" basketball star. Ward, an avid sports fan, asked him, "When you're told to 'block' a player, what do you look at? His eyes, to see which way he is looking? His feet, to give you an indication as to which way he might run?" The young man replied, "No, Reverend, I look at his belly button—until that moves, he ain't goin' nowhere!"

Point well taken! Jerusalem is the political and spiritual "navel" of the world, and until things begin to move there—we ain't goin' nowhere! Jesus said, "Jerusalem will be trampled on by the Gentiles until the times of the Gentiles are fulfilled" (Luke 21:24). The "last days" began in May 1948 when the Jews miraculously came home from the four corners of the world, to establish Jerusalem as the capitol of their new nation. In spite of death camps, and assimilation into the nations of the world, God preserved their identity and fulfilled His Word. Why? To prove to a skeptical, doubting world that, "The Most High ruleth in the affairs of men" (Daniel 4:17).

Now if He kept that promise (see Amos 9:14-15), He'll keep this one too: "At that time they shall see the Son of Man coming in a cloud with power and great glory" (Luke 21:27).

———

**REJOICE, CHILD OF GOD—JESUS IS COMING AGAIN;
YOU CAN ABSOLUTELY COUNT ON IT!**

# What's Your Name?

**And he said unto him, What is thy name? And he said, Jacob.
(Genesis 32:27)**

Don't be surprised if God asks you the same question He asked Jacob. God forced Jacob to look at his identity! He wrestled him into a revelation of who he was—not who others said he was. His answer was pitiful! "I'm Jacob" (which means "Deceiver"). His parents gave it to him, others called him by it, so he believed that's who he was, and that's who he'd always be. Child of God don't buy it! You're not who others say you are! Why should they name you? Determine who you are before God; let Him set the limits of your success!

Why should others be allowed to live at their highest potential—but not you? If you can hear me behind that protective shell, then listen: You're more than your childhood! More than your past! More than the color of your skin! More than your bank account! More than your circumstances! Tell them "You're confusing me with somebody else. God says my name is "Israel," a prince with God. If I'm a prince, then I have the right to be treated like one!" The Word says, "You're a royal priesthood" (1 Peter 2:9). "You're an overcomer"(1 John 2:13-14). "You're the head and not the tail; you're above and not beneath" (Deuteronomy 28:13,14).

LIFT YOUR HEAD, SQUARE YOUR SHOULDERS, DRY YOUR TEARS; GOD SAYS YOU ARE "SOMEBODY SPECIAL," AND IT'S TIME YOU STARTED BELIEVING AND ACTING ON IT!

# Holding a Grudge?

**Be kind and compassionate to one another, forgiving each other, just as in Christ God forgave you.**
**(Ephesians 4:32, NIV)**

No one had more justification to hold a grudge than Joseph. You have a right to expect more from your own family. Disloyalty is not just a mistake, it's a character flaw. Joseph's brothers were jealous and vindictive. They "lied through their eye teeth" about him, and he finished up in prison for 13 years. Now he's the Prime Minister of Egypt, and here come his brothers looking for help! What would you have done? You'll be able to answer that by looking at how you've treated people who've done much less to you. Have you ever heard the words, "Hell hath no fury like a woman scorned"? We laugh, as though that's the way we're supposed to act. (Read Matthew 7:1-2.)

It is tough when God tells the one who's been hurt to be the first to extend mercy and forgiveness! Yet Joseph did! And Jesus did too! And He is telling you to do the same thing today! Listen to these words: "Bear with each other and forgive whatever grievances you may have against one another. Forgive as the Lord forgave you" (Colossians 3:13).

Sure it's hard—but the moment you do it, all your questions will subside, and the first person to be set free will be you.

—◆—

**DON'T WAIT, DO IT TODAY!**

# *True Values*

**The integrity of the upright guides them,
but the unfaithful are destroyed by their duplicity.
(Proverbs 11:3, NIV)**

One night in New York City, two boys broke into a department store and switched all the price tags. The next morning an umbrella was selling for $4,000, and a full length mink coat for $11.95! Suddenly, everything had lost its value!

So, what are your values? Joseph told Potiphar's wife, "I cannot … sin against the Lord" (Genesis 39:9). Nothing will "put the brakes on" faster than knowing your sin is against the Lord. When the apostles were threatened, they said, "We cannot but speak the things which we have seen and heard!" (Acts 4:20). Some of them would die for their stand, but their allegiance to Jesus was total. The values you give children today, are the foundations on which they'll build their lives tomorrow, so don't waffle!

Before God destroyed Sodom, He gave Lot a chance to get his children out. Listen: "And Lot … said, 'Get out of this place; for the Lord will destroy the city.' But he seemed as one that mocked" (Genesis 19:14). He had lost respect with his own family! Why did they mock? Questionable business deals? Broken promises? Did he preach one thing, but live another? He switched the price tags, and it cost him dearly! Honesty is a character trait! Pastors with fine churches often inflate the numbers. In their circles, size is success, so they don't count heads—they count fingers and toes!

**HONESTY! LOYALTY! HARD WORK! FAITHFULNESS!
MERCY! KINDNESS! THOSE ARE GOD'S VALUES.
WHAT ARE YOURS?**

# Sour Grapes

## What more could I have been?
### (Isaiah 5:3, TLB)

Listen to this parable: "My well-beloved hath a vineyard. He fenced it, gathered out the stones, planted it with the choicest vine, built a tower in the midst of it, and also made a wine press; and he looked that it should bring forth grapes, and it brought forth wild grapes" (Isaiah 5:2). Next, God asks the question, "What more could I have done?"

You say, "What does it all mean?" The vineyard is a picture of the church.(See John 15:5.) We read, "He fenced it"—divine protection! David said, "He that dwelleth in the secret place of the Most High, shall abide under the shadow of the Almighty" (Psalms 91:1-2). Then He "gathered out the stones." He's opened the way! The last stone was removed on Easter morning. Next, He "made a winepress"—that's a picture of the Holy Spirit. Jesus said, "Ye shall receive power after the Holy Ghost is come upon you" (Acts 1:8). Finally we read, "He planted it with the choicest vine." What a picture of Jesus—your source, your strength, and your Savior.

Now after He did all this, what did He get back? Sour grapes! Have you met them? They're smart enough to graduate, but foolish enough to say "no" to eternal life. They're smart enough to split the atom, but foolish enough to reject the Sermon on the Mount. Have you accepted God's gift of eternal life?

—◆—

YOU MAY DIE UNSAVED, BUT YOU'LL NEVER DIE UNLOVED. TODAY GOD IS ASKING YOU, "WHAT MORE COULD I DO?" WHY DON'T YOU GIVE HIM YOUR LIFE?

# Sow What You Need

**A man reaps what he sows.
(Galatians 6:7, NIV)**

You don't always reap *where* you sow; you don't reap *when* you sow; but you'll always reap *what* you sow; so start sowing what you need. You can give from your heart to any cause God tells you, and expect nothing back from them. Think of the problem that solves; others cannot disappoint you or control you, for they're not your source. If they were, you'd end up manipulating them or resenting them. But the Bible says that God will "multiply your seed sown" so that you will be "enriched in everything" (2 Corinthians 9:10,11). Did you notice the word "everything"? Your health, your marriage, your career, your family—everything! All you have to do is "sow," and God will be your multiplier.

Note again, you don't reap *when* you sow! This is hard if you're impatient or your need is urgent. God's Kingdom works in seasons, and if you respect them you'll be blessed. Imagine a farmer sowing a field of grain in the morning, and sitting up all night watching it. When you ask him "why," he says, "I am waiting for the harvest." You say, "Ludicrous!" Yes, but are you doing the same thing? The Word says, "Cast thy bread upon the water; for thou shalt find it after many days" (Ecclesiastes 11:1). Another version says, "Give generously, for your gifts will return to you later."

YOUR HARVEST IS CONNECTED TO A SEASON,
THAT SEASON IS SCHEDULED BY GOD. IN A WORLD OF
UNCERTAINTY, YOU CAN COUNT ON ONE THING;
WHAT YOU SOW YOU WILL REAP!

# Mature Love

**When I was a child, I spake as a child, I understood as a child, I thought as a child: but when I became a man, I put away childish things. (1 Corinthians 13:11)**

We seem to forget that today's verse is found in the love chapter, 1 Corinthians 13. There are two kinds of love, childish love and mature love. Which one is yours? A child demands his own way; he has to be the center of attention; he needs continuous excitement; he throws a tantrum when things don't go his way!

Now listen, "But when I became a man I put away childish things." That's mature love! Paul says, "Husbands love your wives as Christ loved the Church and gave Himself for it" (Ephesians 5:25). It's one thing to fall in love, it is entirely another to grow in it. Mature love doesn't demand things—it earns them, and then they mean something. Mature love accepts responsibility and refuses to live like a victim. Until you stop fixing the blame, you can't even start fixing the problem. Benjamin Franklin said, "Keep your eyes wide open before marriage, and half shut afterwards." That's mature love! Marnie Crowel says, "To keep a fire burning brightly there's one rule: Keep the logs together—near enough to keep them warm, and far enough apart for breathing room. Good fire! Good marriage! Same rule!"

**TODAY YOU WILL HAVE A CHANCE TO PRACTICE MATURE LOVE. ASK GOD TO HELP YOU DO IT!**

# Inner Environment

**Renew a right spirit within me.
(Psalm 51:10)**

Sherman Owens says, "Don't let the environment you grew up in grow up in you!" What insight! You'll naturally seek out the same environment that's within you! Why? Because you're comfortable there; nothing more is required of you. You're with "your own kind," and that demands no growth, no stretching, and no "paying the price" to change. But there's a power that can change the environment inside you—the Word of God. Jesus said, "Now are ye clean through the Word which I have spoken unto you" (John 15:3). The key is finding the right thoughts and the right words. Listen: "Keep my message in view at all times. Concentrate! Learn it by heart! Those who discover these words live—really live; body and soul, they're bursting with health" (Proverbs 4:21, TM).

Get rid of the false teachers inside you. Jabez cried, " 'Oh that you would bless me and enlarge my territory. Let Your hand be with me and keep me from harm' … and God granted his request." (1 Chronicles 4:10, NIV).

Make this your prayer today,"God, enlarge me. Set me free from the environment inside; tear down the strongholds!

**" Connect me to Your plan, Your power,
and Your purpose for my life."**

# The Power of Purpose

**And do not forget to do good and to share with others, for with such sacrifices God is pleased.**
**(Hebrews 13:16, NIV)**

You probably don 't know Bob Doss. He began the "Upward Bound Academy" in Bridgeport, Connecticut, after his daughter told him how many kids were getting messed up on drugs and dropping out of school. Remembering his own struggles as a teenager, he felt a tremendous desire to do something besides "just talk about it."

Somebody had to give these "going-no-where" kids a chance in life. So in 1986, with $25,000 of his own money and a clear purpose, he founded his academy to help get inner city kids into college. Using a creative blend of academics and athletics, the school earned a national reputation as a basketball powerhouse and a place of hope that got many kids off the streets and into college—kids who would not ordinarily have made it. If you haven't heard of Bob Doss, it doesn't matter. You see, he has the power of purpose! Anybody who ever made a difference in this world does.

A life without purpose continually needs to be filled up from the outside. When Ernest Hemingway couldn't find anything more outside, he blew his brains out. Fill your mind with God's purpose for your life.

---

**DWELL ON IT! TALK ABOUT IT! PRAY OVER IT!**
**SEEK TO EXCEL IN IT!**

# How Goes the Battle?

**I delight in God's law; but I see another law at work ... waging war against the law of my mind and making me a prisoner. (Romans 7:22-23, NIV)**

You are never defeated until you are defeated on the inside! That's where the attack will come! If you're not expecting it, you won't be prepared. It was while Samson slept that Delilah stripped him of his power. It was while the servants slept that an enemy sowed "tares among the wheat." Peter says, "Be watchful ... for your enemy ... goeth about like a roaring lion, seeking whom he may devour" (1 Peter 5:8). You don't have to be "flaky" and look for "demons" under every bush, but for your own sake—be alert!

Paul wrote to the Thessalonian church and said, "We would have come unto you ... but Satan hindered us!" (1 Thessalonians 2:18). If Satan could do that to Paul, imagine what he could do to you! Satan loves it when you downplay his power, for he does his best work in the dark! Anybody who could delay the answer to Daniel's prayers for twenty-one days is a force with which to be reckoned (see Daniel 10:13). One of his strategies is to use "old programming." There are "weeds" that were planted in you as a child that need to be uprooted, because they are sabotaging your future. For example, if you believe that somehow God is against success, you won't even put your foot on the ladder, much less climb to the top. If you believe that you are "not good enough," then you'll never "come boldly to the throne of grace," and get what's available to you (see Hebrews 4:16).

PULL UP THOSE WEEDS! DECLARE WITH DAVID,
"THIS I KNOW, GOD IS FOR ME" (PSALMS 1:3).
HE REALLY IS!

# The God of Supply

**My God shall supply all your need.**
**(Philippians 4:19)**

God is not poor! Listen, "The silver is Mine, and the gold is Mine, saith the Lord" (Haggai 2:8). Jesus told Peter where to find the money to pay their taxes. He took a boy's lunch and turned it into a feast for 5,000. This is your God we're talking about!

Are you thinking about moving? God knows where you'll succeed, and He'll direct you if you'll get close enough to Him to listen. In the middle of the biggest depression ever to hit the nation, God told Elijah, "Turn thee eastward, and hide thyself by the brook … I have commanded the ravens to feed thee there" (1 Kings 17:3-4). The will of God for your life is tied to people and places. If God has told you He wants to bless you there, and you decide to stay here—you'll be disconnected from your source.

Have you noticed that God commanded everything He created to multiply"? Listen: "Let the earth bring forth grass, the herb yielding seed" (Genesis 1:11). Why seed? Because anybody can count the seeds in an apple, but only God can count the apples in a seed. One apple can feed one person, but the five seeds in that apple could produce five trees, each generating many bushels, and feed scores of people. Are you getting the idea? The Kingdom of God is all about "sowing and reaping." The Bible says God only gives seed to "sowers"—not hoarders (see 2 Corinthians 9:10).

WHEN YOU WITHHOLD, YOU VIOLATE GOD'S LAW, AND YOUR SOURCE DRIES UP. IT'S CONSECUTIVE SOWING THAT GUARANTEES CONSECUTIVE REAPING.

# George McKim

**Has the Lord redeemed you? Then speak out!
(Psalm 107:2, TLB)**

At age seventeen, George McKim joined the "para-militaries" in Northern Ireland, and he served time in the famous Maze Prison. There he found Jesus. When he got out, he began attending church and was called to the ministry under Dr. James McConnell. Today he's building a great church in Falkirk, Scotland. The interesting thing about George is, he has "the gift of comfort" at a hospital bed, and "the gift of boldness" when he walks into a bar and tells men about the God he knows personally. What can they say? Their arguments melt like ice before the fire and force of his experience of God.

Jesus was branded "a Friend of sinners" because He mixed with them. Do you? A lot of Christians don't even know how to talk to them! I've been with Charles and Francis Hunter (The Happy Hunters) in restaurants, and without fail, they witness to the staff, and ask each of them if they would like to "receive Christ." I don't know if all those waiters really prayed out of conviction or just to escape from the Hunter's, but some of them were truly saved, and all of them heard the Word. I felt like a wimp, for I'd been in those restaurants many times and hadn't even left a tract. When your cup is full—it will overflow!

———

TODAY ASK GOD TO GIVE YOU LOVE AND BOLDNESS, AND THEN GO OUT AND SHARE THAT LOVE WITH SOMEONE WHO IS HURTING. HAS THE LORD REDEEMED YOU? THEN SPEAK OUT!

# The Director

**And thine ears shall hear a word behind thee, saying,
This is the way, walk ye in it, when ye turn to the right hand,
and when ye turn to the left. (Isaiah 30:21)**

Pastor Sarah Utterbach says, "God doesn't necessarily give you a word of direction before you move; He comes behind you with a word of confirmation. Listen: "Thine ears shall hear a Word behind thee saying, 'this is the way.' It matters not whether you are turning to the right or left, for your steps are already ordered by the Lord."(Psalms 37:23). If you've "acknowledged Him, then He's already "directing your paths. (See Proverbs 3:6.) Think about that a moment!

Wherever your path leads, move with confidence, knowing the Good Shepherd is right behind you, letting you know everything's okay. If you don't hear His Words—stop! It's time for a mid-course correction! So often we become immobilized and fearful, waiting for clear direction. Is that where you are today? If it is, listen: "I will instruct thee and teach thee in the way which thou shalt go. I will guide thee with Mine eye" (Psalms 32:8). Take hold of this truth. He will teach you, and He will instruct you how to walk in His will, so that it becomes natural for you. He'll guide you with His eye and confirm it with His mouth. His eye sees what yours can't; every bend in the road, every mountain, and every valley. He's concerned about the very things about which you're concerned. Don't stop every few miles and question Him. If you get "off track," He'll let you know.

BUT UNTIL THEN, WALK WITH CONFIDENCE AND
FAITH IN HIM. IT IS THE ONLY WAY TO GO, AND
IT'S THE WAY FOR YOU TODAY.

**Bless the LORD, O my soul, and forget not all his benefits.
(Psalms 103:2)**

Listen to these words: "Who forgiveth all thine iniquities; Who healeth all thy diseases; Who redeemeth thy life from destruction; Who crowneth thee with lovingkindness and tender mercies; Who satisfieth thy mouth with good things" (Psalms 103:2-5).

Look what you brought to the table; iniquity, disease and destruction! Now look what He brought; healing, for all your diseases. The Bible says, "He healed them all" (Matthew 8:7). Rejoice, child of God, what He was, He still is, and what He did, He still does! Forgiveness, for all your iniquities. Love without measure; grace without limit! What an arrangement! Redemption. Deliverance from all your destructive ways and habits. Sometimes He delivers you instantly, other times He does it "day by day!" Lovingkindness and tender mercy; He's above—watching over you, beneath—upholding you, around—embracing you, and inside—filling the emptiness in your life. Satisfaction that doesn't depend on what you wear, what you drive, what you have in the bank, or on which side of the tracks you live. (See Psalms 16:11.) He saves! He keeps! He satisfies!

Notice, everything He brings to the table is for your benefit. You don't have to earn it, and you can't deserve it!

—⚋—

NOW WHY IN THE WORLD WOULD YOU WANT TO FOCUS ON WHAT YOU BROUGHT WHEN YOU CAN FOCUS ON WHAT HE BROUGHT?

# Deal With Your Sin

**If we confess our sins, he is faithful and just to
forgive us our sins, and to cleanse us from all unrighteousness.
(1 John 1:9)**

One day a minister walking down the street spotted a small boy jumping up and down in front of an old fashioned doorbell that he was too short to reach. Feeling sorry for him, the minister went over and rang the bell. Next, he smiled at the boy and said, "Now what?" "Now," exclaimed the boy, "we run like crazy!" You may smile, but sin made Adam run and hide, and it will make you a fugitive from God, too, until you deal with it!

No matter who you are, what you do, or what your position is in the church, you're never above the need to confess your sin and pray for forgiveness. If you think you are, you're in big trouble! God is never surprised by what we do! You can't keep anything from Him, and you can't hurt His feelings by telling Him, so you might as well be honest. When you're not, you're only fooling yourself and hurting your relationship with Him.

You never have to worry about unknown sin in your life. If you have a real desire to walk with God, He'll tell you when things aren't right. The Holy Spirit's job is to "convict us of sin" (John 16:8), and there's a reason why. When sin is tolerated, it increases! Sin left unchecked will eventually consume you.

TODAY, COME TO GOD, CONFESS YOUR SIN AND CLEAR
THE AIR. IT WILL ALLOW YOU TO COMMUNICATE WITH HIM
WITHOUT ANY HINDRANCES OR ROADBLOCKS.
TAKE CARE OF THIS TODAY!

# Intercessors Needed

**My intercessor is my friend.**
**(Job 16:20, NIV)**

Many of us want to live in the spotlight, but God is looking for intercessors! Listen: "So Joshua fought the Amalekites ... and Moses, Aaron, and Hur went to the top of the hill. As long as Moses held up his hands, the Israelites were winning, but whenever He lowered His hands, the Amalekites were winning. When Moses' hands grew tired ... Aaron and Hur held his hands up ... And Joshua overcame the Amalekite army with the sword" (Exodus 17:10-16, NIV). What a picture of the power of intercessory prayer! Far from the crowd, but seen by the eye of God, are precious Christians who "hold up the hands" of great ministries in ceaseless prayer—and God's looking for more of them!

Charles Finney had an intercessor called Abel Clary, who traveled with him wherever he went. Finney wrote, "Mr. Clary continued as long as I did, and did not leave until after I had left. He never appeared in public, but gave himself wholly to prayer." Finney may have shaken the nation for God, but he didn't do it alone. That's the ministry of intercession, and God could be calling you to it today. It's a ministry of identification in which you "stand" with others. It's a ministry of sacrifice which calls you away from the pleasures and comforts of life. And it is a ministry of authority, for God will hear your prayers on their behalf!

---

**ASK GOD ABOUT THIS TODAY!**

*Intercession*

**And I sought for a man among them, that should make up the hedge, and stand in the gap before me for the land.**
**(Ezekiel 22:30)**

Do you remember Dunkirk? Thousands of allied troops were trapped on the beaches, about to be slaughtered like cattle. But Britain cried out to God, and He heard her. He draped a protective curtain of fog around the troops, and spoke "peace" to the wind and the waves. An armada of vessels—anything that could float—made it through that day; it lifted our boys from the jaws of death and defeat, and brought them home to fight again—and win!

Today, our nation is obsessed with the pursuit of material things, and has grown comfortable without God—but only until the next crisis! The challenge of this hour is for "intercessors," who will "stand in the gap" before God.

When you become an intercessor, two things automatically happen. Instead of receiving, your concern becomes giving. Instead of your own injuries, your focus is now to bring healing to others. David said, "Pour out your hearts to Him, for God is our refuge" (Psalms 62:8).

IS GOD CALLING YOU TO INTERCEDE?
TAKE SOME TIME OUT TODAY AND THINK ABOUT THIS!

# The Perfect Pastor

**Respect those who work hard among you, who are over you in the Lord. Hold them in the highest regard in love because of their work. (1 Thessalonians 5:12-14, NIV)**

He preaches exactly twenty minutes and then sits down. He condemns sin, but never steps on anyone's toes. He works from eight in the morning until ten at night, doing everything from preaching sermons to vacuuming the church. He makes $400 a week, gives $100 of it back to the church, drives a late-model car, buys lots of books, wears fine clothes, and has a nice family. He stands ready to contribute to every good cause and to help panhandlers who drop by the church on their way to somewhere.

He's thirty-six and has been preaching for fifty years. He's tall, on the short side, heavy set, in a thin sort of way, and handsome. He has eyes of blue or brown, as the occasion demands, and wears his hair parted in the middle—left side dark and straight, right side brown and wavy. He has a burning desire to work with youth, and spends all his time with the senior citizens. He smiles all the time while keeping his face straight, because he has a keen sense of humor that finds him seriously dedicated. He makes fifteen calls a day on church members, spends all his time evangelizing non-members, and is always found in his study if he is needed. *Unfortunately he burned himself out and died at the age of thirty-two.*

—⟩⟩⟩—

**TODAY, WHEN YOU PRAY,
LIFT UP YOUR PASTOR BEFORE THE LORD!**

# Paul's Prayers

**We have not stopped praying for you and asking God
to fill you with the knowledge of his will.
(Colossians 1:9, NIV)**

Here's a wonderful plan for you to follow when you pray. First Paul prayed that, "They would know, and do the will of God"(Colossians 1:9). Can you think of anything more important? What a testimony the Christians in Rome had. Listen: "Everyone has heard about your obedience" (Romans 16:19, NIV). Your obedience is the badge of your character, and when your name is mentioned, no one should even dare to suspect you of compromise.

Next, Paul prayed for *success in their lives.* Listen: "… bearing fruit in every good work"(Colossians 1:10). I've seen what a few businessmen with a heart for God can do. Now I'm praying for an army of them to prosper and catch the vision of going into all the world preaching the Gospel! (See Matthew 28:19.) Why shouldn't you be one of them?

Next, he prayed for *power in their lives.* Listen: "… strengthened with all power according to His glorious might"(Colossians 1:11). Think of your vacuum cleaner; if it's not plugged in, it's useless! It depends on another source to make it effective. If you pull the plug, it's worthless! We're like that! Without God's power, we're no good!

Finally, Paul prayed for them to *have a right attitude.* Listen again: "… giving thanks to the Father" (Colossians 1: 11-12). Joy is an attitude, and it affects every other area of your life and the life of everyone you come into contact with, too!

---

**SO THERE ARE SOME THINGS FOR YOU TO
PRAY FOR TODAY!**

# The United Way

**The burden is too heavy for me.**
**(Number 11:14, NIV)**

You can't do it by yourself—and that's the way God planned it! Moses had to find that out the hard way! Finally God told him to take seventy men, and He would, "Take of the spirit that is on you and put the spirit on them. They will help you carry the burden … so that you will not have to carry it alone" (Numbers 11:16-17). Burn-out victims, God is talking to you! You're not John Wayne, and you're not Rambo! Big battles are won by armies who march in step together.

Paul Harvey says, "We revere the airplane pilot who did it alone and the country doctor who never left the bedside. That spirit of independence served us well and caused us to grow tall. But we'd never have made it to the moon with that spirit; we'd never have eradicated typhoid, small pox, or polio without a cooperative effort. No person alone could fetch oil from beneath the ocean, or keep the city lights burning all night—that takes inter-dependence. We are all becoming increasingly inter-dependent! That spirit will not cost more than it's worth. On the steep slope ahead, holding hands is necessary, and it just might be that we can learn to enjoy it."

Now there's a word to the Church! Jesus said, "Where two or three come together in My Name, there am I with them" (Matthew 18:19-20, NIV). Alone we're vulnerable, but together we can win the day!

---

CHILD OF GOD, REACH OUT FOR THE HELP THAT'S
AVAILABLE TO YOU TODAY!

# Change Your Church

**But prayer was made without ceasing of the church
unto God for him. (Acts 12:5)**

After Wilbur Chapman's first sermon at Wannamakers Church in Philadelphia, a man met him and said, "You're pretty young to be pastor of this great church; we've always had older men. I'm afraid you won't succeed, but since you preach the Gospel, I'm going to help you all I can." Chapman thought, "What a crank!" But the gentleman continued, "I'm going to pray for you, and a few others have covenanted to join me."

Later, Dr. Chapman wrote, "I didn't feel so bad when I learned that they were going to pray for me. Soon the three became fifty, the fifty became two hundred, who met before every service to pray for me. In another room, eighteen elders knelt so closely around me that I could put out my hand and touch them. I always went into my pulpit confident that I would have God's anointing in answer to the prayers of those people. It was easy to preach—a real joy! And what was the result? Eleven hundred people were saved and joined the church in the next three years; six hundred of them were men. It was the fruit of the Holy Spirit in answer to prayer. Church members have much more to do than go to church as curious, idle spectators to be amused and entertained. It is their business to pray mightily that the Holy Spirit will clothe the preacher with power and make his words like dynamite."

THE PROPHET SAID, "IT IS TIME TO SEEK THE LORD TILL HE COMES AND RAINS RIGHTEOUSNESS UPON YOU" (HOSEA 10:12). YOU CAN CHANGE YOUR CHURCH THROUGH PRAYER!

# Learning to "Wait Well"

**My future is in your hands.
(Psalms 31:15, NLT)**

In her great book, *When God, When?*, Joyce Meyer says, "God has taught me to keep living the life I now have, while I am waiting for the things that are in my heart to come to pass. We can become so intent on trying to birth the next thing, that we neither enjoy nor take care of things at hand. I had a vision from God ten years before I began to see it fulfilled. During those years, I believe I missed a lot of joy trying to give birth outside of God's timing. Learn to enjoy where you are, while you're waiting to get to where you want to be."

You'll spend more time in life waiting than you will receiving. And when you receive what you're waiting for, you'll begin waiting for something else. That's life! If you don't learn to "wait well," you'll live with endless frustraton. Waiting well is what will deliver your dream. Listen: " ... in due season we shall reap, if we faint not" (Galatians 6:9). Due season is when God knows you're ready, not when you think you are. He has set appointments to accomplish certain things in your life, so you might as well settle down and wait patiently, because that's when it will happen—and not before. God knows what you need; He knows when you need it; and He knows how to get it to you. All He asks you to do is trust Him.

**ANYTHING LESS, AND WE ARE A TOTAL FLOP!**

# Revival

**If my people, who are called by my name, will humble themselves and pray and seek my face and turn from their wicked ways, then will I hear from heaven and will forgive their sin and will heal their land. (2 Chronicles 7:13, NIV)**

What will it take to turn the heart of this nation back to God? The answer is revival! But what is revival? Dr. Armin Gesswein says, "The revival we need is simply a return to normal New Testament Christianity; where the churches are full of prayer, full of power, full of people, full of praise, and full of divine happenings all the time. We want something normal, not just 'special.' God's normal that is." God's "normal" is greater than all of our "specials" put together! Revival is not a process we can use to manipulate God. You can't plan revival, you must seek it!

God gives us the pattern in 2 Chronicles 7:14. Here's how it works:

1. The people pray.

2. God comes.

3. The people repent.

4. God revives the people.

5. The people begin to minister and pour out their lives into others.

6. God equips and empowers them, making up the difference.

Anytime God is going to do something wonderful, He begins with a *difficulty*. When He is going to do something *very* wonderful, He begins with an *impossibility*. If you look around today, I think you will agree that this nation is in an impossible situation.

ONLY GOD CAN SAVE OUR CHURCHES, OUR FAMILIES, AND OUR NATION. AND HE WILL IF WE PRAY! COME ON, CHILD OF GOD, IT'S TIME TO START!

# Open-Face Relationship

**He ... blotted out the charges proved against you, ... He took this list and destroyed it, by nailing it to Christ's Cross ... He took away Satan's power to accuse you. (Colossians 2:14, TLB)**

You say, "What about my sin?" The answer is, Jesus "nailed it" once and for all!" And my accuser?" Jesus made "a public spectacle of him!" "So where does that leave me?" Listen, "But we all, with open face, beholding as in a glass, the glory of the Lord, are changed into the same image" (2 Corinthians 3:18). No more hiding! Now you have "an open-face" relationship with the God, who sees your deepest yearnings and knows your darkest cravings.

Adam was so humiliated by his sin that he hid! And we've all been hiding ever since! We hide our weaknesses, our proclivities, and our curiosities. We hide our fears, and we even hide our love. T.D. Jakes says, "Our 'trench coat mentality' has left us—collars up, hats down—draped in pretended secrecy and cringing in false obscurity before the eyes of God." Listen: "I heard thy voice ... I was afraid ... I was naked ... I hid myself" (Genesis 3:10). That was our story—but not any more. Now we have an "open face" relationship with the Lord. How wonderful! He has chosen to love you beyond your failures and lift you beyond your despair. The blood of Jesus has purchased a righteousness you couldn't earn in a million years, so why don't you take time out today to come away and refresh yourself in His presence. Come to Him and let Him heal your wounds and give you a safe place to lay your head.

**I PROMISE YOU IF YOU COME, YOU WON'T BE DISAPPOINTED!**

**The LORD is on my side; I will not fear.**
**(Psalms 118:6)**

Here are eight fear-fighting Scriptures that will unlock your faith and destroy the giants of fear that rise within you. Memorize them! Repeat them! Stand on them!

1. "Fear thou not, for I am with thee: be not dismayed; for I am thy God: I will strengthen thee, yea, I will help thee, yea, I will uphold thee with the right hand of My righteousness" (Isaiah 41:10).

2. "For the Lord your God is He that goeth with you, to fight for you against your enemies, to save you" (Deuteronomy 20:4).

3. "Be strong and of good courage and do it: fear not, nor be dismayed: for the Lord God … will be with thee" (1 Chronicles 28:20).

4. "The fear of man bringeth a snare: but whoso putteth his trust in the Lord shall be safe" (Proverbs 29:25).

5. "Fear not: for I have redeemed thee, I have called thee by thy name: thou art Mine" (Isaiah 43:1).

6. "The Lord is my light and my salvation; whom shall I fear? The Lord is the strength of my life; of whom shall I be afraid?" (Psalms 27:1).

7. "He hath said, I will never leave thee nor forsake thee. So that we may boldly say, the Lord is my helper, I will not fear what man shall do unto me" (Hebrews 13:5-6).

8. "For God hath not given us the spirit of fear, but of power, and of love, and of a sound mind" (2 Timothy 1:7).

—m—

THE WORDS OF GOD ARE POWERFUL.
READ THEM ALOUD EVERY DAY FOR THE NEXT THIRTY DAYS, AND YOU'LL SEE CHANGES BEGIN, DOORS OPEN, AND A RIVER OF JOY FLOW INTO YOUR LIFE!

# Blessing by Association

**He that walketh with wise men shall be wise.**
**(Proverbs 13:20)**

Here's a principle you need to learn if you want God's best. Blessing comes by association! You have a choice—you can walk with Joshua and Caleb and fulfill your destiny, or you can hang around with the other ten spies who believed "it can't be done" and die in the wilderness. When Joseph entered Potiphar's house, he brought the favor of God with him. When he went to Pharaoh's palace, he preserved and prospered the entire nation. Listen to what Laban said to Jacob: "I have learned by experience that the LORD hath blessed me for thy sake." Blessing and increase by association!

The Philippians had a thirty-year partnership in the Gospel with Paul. They supported him, and he ministered to them. Listen: "When I pray for you, my heart is full of joy because of all your wonderful help in making known the good news about Christ from the time you first heard it until now" (Philippians 1:7, TLB). And what was their reward? Paul says, "You are partakers of my grace" (Philippians 1:7). Paul got it from Jesus, and the Philippians got it from Paul. Look for those who walk in the blessing of God and get as close to them as you can.

**AND DON'T LET IT STOP WITH YOU—BECOME A "CARRIER!"**

# You've Got to Deal With It

**"Nevertheless what saith the Scripture? Cast out the bondwoman and her son ..."**
**(Galatians 4:30)**

Ishmael was Abraham's attempt to hurry up the plan of God, and fulfill it by his own fleshly efforts. You've probably tried something similar yourself. We all have our Ishmael's—good ideas that weren't God's ideas—and they can really complicate our lives. When God said to Abraham, "Cast out the bondwoman and her son," He was saying, "It's time to deal with your past and to clean out your closet!"

Sometimes your miracle and your mistake can grow together under the same roof. Things can be so bad in one area, yet so good in another. But God is saying, "Because of the blessing and the destiny I have for you, you've got to put this thing out of your life."

It's painful putting away something your flesh loves and craves, but you have no choice. Here are your options: you can be moved by their cry and miss God's best, or you can say, "As much as I love you, I love the Lord more." When you can walk away from something you thought you had to have, because you love God—that's the sacrifice of praise. When you offer it up to Him, you position yourself to receive a new level of His blessing in your life.

IS GOD SPEAKING TO YOU TODAY THROUGH THIS? IF HE
IS, DEAL WITH IT—FOR THAT'S THE WORD FOR YOU TODAY.

# God's Favor

**They did not conquer by their own strength ... but by your
mighty power because you ... favored them.
(Psalms 44:3, TLB)**

Before you leave the house each morning, declare the favor of
God over your life! Favor that opens doors; favor that protects
from all harm; favor that goes before you to arrange things for
your benefit. God has promised you favor. When the boss calls to
say, "You've been promoted," shout, "Favor!" When the agent calls
to say, "You're qualified for the loan," or, "We've found a buyer for
your house," tell someone, "That's favor from God."

God promised that when you find yourself in battle, you won't
have to lift a finger to protect yourself, for He will go before
you and fight your battle. It was favor that took David from a
sheepfold to a palace. (See 1 Samuel 16:22.) It was favor that
caused Esther to win the first beauty pageant, and save her nation
from destruction. (See Esther 2:17.) It doesn't matter where
you are or what you are going through—mistreatment, abuse,
lies, and even imprisonment cannot keep the favor of God from
operating in your life.

OPEN YOUR HEART TO IT.

## On the Offensive

**Now unto him that is able to do exceeding abundantly above all that we ask or think, according to the power that worketh in us. (Ephesians 3:20)**

It's time for us to move from a survival mentality into a position of "ruling and reigning"! From just getting by to having more than enough! Recently I asked someone, "How are you?" They replied, "Okay, under the circumstances." I thought, what are you doing there? Paul said, "We are more than conquerors" (Romans 8:37). A conqueror wins, but "more than a conqueror" rules and reigns—they're in control!

We're not told to cope with the devil, we're told to resist him and he will flee (see James 4:7). The Greek word for flee means "to run in terror." Imagine living in such a way that when you wake up, the devil trembles and shouts, "Help—he's up again!" Paul said, "Don't give place to the devil" (Ephesians 4:27). Satan has no place unless you give it to him! You see, his goal is to separate you from your faith; for it's by faith that you overcome every circumstance, and it's by faith that you receive every benefit God has promised you. (See Hebrews 11:6.)

THREE TIMES IN THE BIBLE WE ARE TOLD, "THE JUST SHALL LIVE BY FAITH." IT IS A LIFESTYLE! SO ASK GOD TO HELP YOU LIVE BY FAITH 24 HOURS A DAY.

# The Colonel and Christ

**While we were still sinners, Christ died for us.
(Romans 5:8, NIV)**

Bill Bakkeby was a colonel in the U.S. Army, and he was going places. But his wife, Elaine, and most of his friends didn't know that Bill had become a closet alcoholic and his life was spinning out of control. Sometimes he'd come out of a blackout and find himself driving down the highway at seventy miles an hour and have no idea how he got there. Next the voices of suicide started speaking in his head.

By this point his marriage was in trouble. So he agreed to go to a marriage encounter group with Elaine. When the instructor asked them to write a letter to each other sharing something they had never shared before, Elaine found this easy. But Bill was terrified and wrote nothing. When Elaine pressed him, he wanted to leave. But suddenly God gave Bill the grace to tell her about his drinking problem. Relieved, she said, "Oh, is that all it is!" At this point the colonel dissolved into tears, and the only prayer he could get out was, "God, help me." That's all God required. That moment, God heard Bill Bakkeby and saved him.

Today, Bill and Elaine pastor a fine church in Washington, D.C., and God is using them greatly.

**YOU NEVER KNOW WHAT YOUR LIFE CAN BE—
UNTIL YOU GIVE IT TO JESUS.**

# The Jonah Spirit

**But Jonah was greatly displeased and became angry.
(Jonah 4:1, NIV)**

Have you ever heard of the Jonah spirit? When God told him he was going to save the city of Nineveh, Jonah was angry. He had already judged them, and if God had called for a vote, he was voting against them. These people meant nothing to Jonah. Could it be that you have become so wrapped up in yourself that you don't care about those around you anymore? Has your holiness become hardness and made you exclusive? Are you like the priest and the Levite whom Jesus said, "passed by on the other side"? (See Luke 10:30.)

Listen to Paul: "For I could wish myself accursed from Christ for my brethren, my kinsmen according to the flesh" (Romans 9:3). And what about Moses, who stood between God and the condemned people of Israel and put his life on the line saying, "Yet now, if thou wilt forgive their sin—and if not, blot me, I pray thee, out of thy book" (Exodus 32:32)? These words should bring us to our knees.

God told Isaiah, "Behold, I will do a new thing" (Isaiah 43:19). If the way we have done things in our churches for years isn't working like it used to, don't you think it is time for a new approach? People only do what rewards them. They go where their needs are met. Could it be that God is trying to change us before He changes them?

BREAK OUT OF YOUR DENOMINATIONAL SHELL AND START GIVING THE BREAD OF LIFE TO THOSE WHO ARE DYING, REGARDLESS OF HOW THEY ACT, OR LOOK, OR WHERE THEY LIVE.

# Danger of Not Knowing

**My people are destroyed for lack of knowledge.
(Hosea 4:6)**

I used to think that blessings were all spiritual. I resented folks who were well off and told myself they were probably miserable. I knew it would take money to reach the world with the Gospel, but I had no idea, and even less concern, where it would come from.

Then one day I read, "They ... searched the Scriptures daily to see whether these things were so" (Acts 17:11). I knew God used the word "prosperity" many times, but I'd seen it abused and couldn't get comfortable with it until I heard it defined as *having enough to do the will of God.* Surely if God has a will for me, then He intends me to have enough to carry it out! Your purpose determines your prosperity.

So here's what I can tell you for certain: The whole world will hear the Gospel (see Revelation 14:6); God will use His people to do it (see Matthew 28:19); they can't do it if they're broke. It's time to claim God's provision so that we can carry out God's purposes (see Deuteronomy 8:18). God says clearly, "Whoever sows sparingly will also reap sparingly, and whoever sows generously will also reap generously. And God is able to make all grace abound to you, so that in all things at all times, having all that you need, you will abound in every good work" (2 Corinthians 9, NIV).

**NOW ASK GOD TO MAKE THAT REAL IN YOUR LIFE.**

# Ever Increasing Faith

**The just shall live by faith.
(Romans 1:17)**

Satan's goal is to separate you from your faith, because faith pleases God. (See Hebrews 11:6.) Faith makes you an overcomer. (See 1 John 5:4.) Faith gets answers to your prayers. (See Mark 11:24.) Jesus said, "When you pray ... believe that you receive ... and you shall have it" (Mark 11:24). Do you really believe that? If you do, you'll act on it! Listen: "Fight the good fight of faith" (1 Timothy 6:12), so there must be enemies of faith. One of the biggest is ignorance of God's Word. Listen: My people are destroyed for lack of knowledge; because thou hast rejected knowledge, I will also reject thee" (Hosea 4:6). It is one thing to know, it is entirely another to reject what God shows you.

You can be exposed to a disease but not get it because you've been inoculated against it. Religion can inoculate you against receiving all that God has for you! Negative people can do that, too. Just keep listening until you hear. Faith comes continually by hearing the Word of God (see Romans 10:17). When you really know, you'll do. And you'll really know that you know, because you're still acting on it.

**THIS IS NOT SOMETHING YOU COMMUTE IN AND OUT OF.
IT MUST BECOME A WAY OF LIFE FOR YOU.**

**Husbands, be considerate as you live with your wives.**
**(1 Peter 3:7)**
**Wives are to be women worthy of respect.**
**(1 Timothy 3:11, NIV)**

An old couple was asked on their fiftieth wedding anniversary what their secret was. He replied, "The day we were married we agreed that if a problem arose, I'd go out and stand on the porch until I cooled off. It worked! Fifty years of good old outdoor living was just what this relationship needed!" Now that you are smiling let me share a few words you need to consider:

1. Commitment—*"You're first."* That's easy to say on special occasions, but hard to do seven days a week. Recently, a famous movie star who'd been married seven times said, "I'd given up trying to find the right person. Now I'm working on *being* the right person!"

2. Compatibility—*"Are we a good fit?"* Marriage is all about friendship, and that requires time—time spent together. Love will make two people sit in the middle of the bench when there's room at both ends.

3. Coping—*"We can work it out."* You'll have problems—lots of them. But together you can work them out. You can't avoid conflict, so make it work for you. Use it as a chance to conquer the problem, not each other.

—◊—

**LOVE IS AN UNUSUAL GAME. THERE ARE EITHER**
**TWO WINNERS OR NONE AT ALL.**

*Righteousness*

**The righteousness of God which is by faith … upon all them that believe. (Romans 3:22)**

Righteousness simply means "right-standing." It gives you the right to stand in the presence of God without fear or condemnation. Once you have an attitude of confidence before God, you will be able to believe Him for victory in every area of your life. But you say, "How do I become righteous?" It comes by faith! You receive it the same way you received salvation.

Developing a "righteousness consciousness" will create in you a "victory consciousness." First there are some things you need to know.

1. He has blotted out all record of your sins. (See Colossians 2:14.) You are no longer under the curse of the law, but under grace. (See Romans 6:14.)

2. Jesus has set you free from "the curse of the law, which is sickness, lack, fear, defeat, and death" (Romans 8:2). Stop saying you're unworthy! That's what you were when He found you—but not anymore. You're a new creation. (See 2 Corinthians 5:17.) Have you ever seen anything that God created that was unworthy or no good? No!

YOU'RE HIS WORKMANSHIP (SEE EPHESIANS 2:10), AND YOU CAN STAND IN HIS PRESENCE WITH CONFIDENCE.

# Go After It!

**When ye see the ark … then ye shall remove from your place, and go after it. (Joshua 3:3)**

Sherman Owens says, "You will never arrive if you don't set out. The tragedy of life is not that it ends to soon, but that we wait too long to begin it." It's your job to discern when God is moving and be willing to leave and follow Him—and you may have to go alone.

Elisha was willing to leave everything and follow Elijah for twenty years to get a "double portion." You can't get it in one church service, one book, or one tape set. It has got to be the passion of your life. It will keep you turning the pages of God's Word to see what He has to say next. It will make you take down the walls of your tradition and cry like David, "So panteth my soul after thee, O LORD" (Psalms 42:1).

A lot of us see the Ark moving, but because of fear we never set out and go after it. When we first meet Abraham he has nothing but his family, his dream, and his God. But that's OK! You don't have to know where you're going, you just have to know you're following God! Before it's all over God is calling him His friend, he's the father of nations, and he's one of the richest men on earth.

**IF YOUR LIFE HAS BEEN ON HOLD, THE MESSAGE FOR YOU TODAY IS "GO AFTER IT!"**

# The Strategy

**And immediately all the doors were opened.**
**(Acts 16:26)**

All Paul and Silas did was to heal a poor demon-possessed girl, and they landed in prison. But Satan overplayed his hand! God had set the stage for a miracle! Is that where you are today? Confined by circumstances? Mistreated by people? Why don't you try what they did? You won't feel like it, but do it anyway! Listen: "At midnight Paul and Silas prayed and sang praises unto God ... and suddenly there was a great earthquake ... and immediately all the doors were opened" (Acts 16:26). The is the "prayer and praise" strategy.

Have you prayed about it? God says, "Call upon me, and I will answer you" (Psalms 91:5). I know you've worried, but have you prayed? Have you declared His Word over your situation? Listen again: "The Lord working with them, confirming His Word with signs following" (Mark 16:20). The only thing God will confirm is His Word, so use it!

E. V. Hill says, "When Paul and Silas began to sing, God began to tap his foot, and that caused an earthquake to hit that Philippian jail, and all the doors were opened!"

—m—

COME ON, CHILD OF GOD, YOU'VE TRIED EVERYTHING
ELSE, NOW TRY "THE PRAYER AND PRAISE" STRATEGY—
IT'S GOD'S WAY FOR YOU.

# Intents of Our Hearts

**For the word of God is ... a discerner of the thoughts and intents of the heart. (Hebrews 4:12)**

The question God asks of you today is not "what did you say, or do?" but "what did you intend?" David didn't personally kill Bathsheba's husband, he just arranged it! Jesus warned of doing things to be seen. (See Matthew 6:1.) When you do, you're doing a good thing for a bad reason, and you'll get no reward! Hannah said, "The Lord God who knows, and by Him deeds are weighed" (1 Samuel 2:3).

After four decades of Christian living, I'm still amazed at the deceit, manipulation, and pride that surfaces in my heart at times. That's why David prayed, "Create in me a pure heart, O God" (Psalms 51:10, NIV). The other day I heard about a lady in a prayer group who said, "Let's all pray for sister Hones. I just heard she is having an affair!" Clearly her intent was not to pray, but to expose, and she put herself in a very dangerous place before God. Listen: "The same way that you judge, you will be judged" (Matthew 7:1, NIV). Perhaps you personally would never do that, but would you share something damaging with someone who would?

Speaking of the Day of Judgment, John said, "The books were opened" (Revelation 20:12). I've often wondered if one of them will be "the book of motives." That book would ruin the value of many a noble deed, for it wouldn't ask *what* you did, but *why* you did it.

—◊—

**TAKE A LITTLE TIME TODAY, GET INTO GOD'S PRESENCE, AND EXAMINE YOUR HEART.**

# Thinking About Lydia

**In all their distress he too was distressed,... In his love and mercy he redeemed them; he lifted them up and carried them all the days of old. (Isaiah 63:9, NIV)**

Bill and Lydia had been married only one year when he collapsed in their bathroom with a massive heart attack and died at age 51. They were so happy together! When I talked to Lydia a week later, she said, "I just can't believe it. I keep looking for him to come through the door at any time." I've stopped saying to people, "I know how you feel," because I don't. But there's One who does! He is touched by the feeling of our infirmities. (See Hebrews 4:15.) Jesus didn't weep at the grave of Lazarus because He was powerless. He wept because He was touched.

You're not alone in your heartache, for He feels it, too. When you can't seem to take another step, He'll pick you up and carry you, day by day! David said, "Yea, though I walk through the valley of the shadow of death I will fear no evil, for Thou art with me" (Psalms 23:4). Child of God, you're going to come through this valley, because, "He is with you." That's a promise! When I hung up the phone after talking with Lydia, I thought of my loved ones and I prayed, "Father, help me to enjoy this day and every day and live each one to the fullest."

—m—

**MAYBE THAT'S A PRAYER YOU WOULD LIKE TO PRAY, TOO?**

# Grace and Peace

**Grace and peace be multiplied unto you through the knowledge of God, and of Jesus our Lord.**
**(2 Peter 1:2)**

This verse is not just a greeting, it's a promise! One of the best definitions of grace is "all of God you'll ever need for anything you'll ever face." God told Paul, "My grace is sufficient for thee" (2 Corinthians 12:9). When you have Him, you have it all! And what about His peace? It's a state of "being" where you are not anxious or afraid anymore. You stop striving because God has everything under control. You may be surrounded by circumstances, but you are not controlled by them. David said, "Great peace have they which love Thy Law; and nothing shall offend them" (Psalms 119:165).

You'll notice God didn't say He will *add* these things to you, He said he would *multiply* them. God doesn't add—He multiplies! You may ask, "How do grace and peace come?" Through the knowledge of God and Jesus Christ our Lord. There's the key: getting to know Him better. You may say, "I need to find myself!" I can assure you, there's no peace in that. Jesus said, "The flesh profiteth nothing; the words that I speak unto you, they are spirit and they are life" (John 6:63). He told the woman at the well, "Whosoever drinketh of the water that I shall give him, shall never thirst" (John 4:13).

**THE WAY TO KNOW SOMEONE IS TO SPEND TIME WITH THEM! HAVE YOU SPENT TIME WITH HIM TODAY!**

# Katy's Testimony

**Despise not one of these little ones; for I say unto you, That in heaven their angels do always behold the face of my Father which is in heaven. (Matthew 18:10)**

When three-year-old Katy Reardon fell into the pool in her back yard, she was fully clothed and couldn't swim. Her dad was at work, her mom was in the kitchen, and there was no one to help her. They had warned her not to go near the deep end of the pool, but on that sunny day in May 1996, she reached over to get her doll, and fell in head first. No one knows how long she was in the pool.

When her mother, Barbara, heard the scream, she froze in terror and then ran toward the back door. She saw Katy crying, moving toward her in dripping wet clothes with her arms extended. When Barbara asked her what happened she said, "I was playing, and I fell into the deep end, and I couldn't swim, so I asked Jesus to help me, and a hand came down out of the clouds and pulled me out of the water." When her mother asked her again, she repeated the story several times without missing a word. Finally, her mother asked her, "What did the hand look like?" Katy simply replied, "You know, Mom—like a cloud."

Today I talked with Katy's dad on the phone, and he told me that every time there's a baby dedication in church, he sits in tears of joy as he remembers what God did for his little girl. Jesus said that our children have angels assigned to watch over them. Perhaps you think I am a simple soul, but I believe it with all my heart.

—⁂—

I CLAIM IT FOR MY CHILDREN AND MY GRANDCHILDREN, AND I THANK GOD FOR IT. FURTHERMORE, I THINK YOU SHOULD TOO.

# The Right Place

**You have circled this mountain long enough.
(Deuteronomy 2:3)**

I've seen very gifted people struggle because they were in the wrong place, and I've seen less-talented people thrive because they were in the right place! Jesus knew that geography matters. "And he must have needs go through Samaria" (John 4:4). Why? Because there was a woman there who needed Him, and an entire city that would be reached. Abraham was instructed to leave his father's house and set out for a new land. Five hundred were instructed to go to the Upper Room. Only 120 obeyed, but they got the promised blessing. Are you getting the idea? You can't work on the wrong job, for the wrong boss, doing the wrong things forty hours a week, and wonder why two hours in church doesn't sort you out! God will not bless you just anywhere, He'll bless you if you're where He wants you to be.

Have you noticed that when you're with certain people you laugh at certain jokes, and the topic of your conversation changes? In other words, where you are determines what grows within you—weeds or flowers, strengths or weaknesses. God has promised you favor, but sometimes He has to change your address to get it to you! It was when Ruth moved to Bethlehem that she met Boaz, and her life was filled with blessing. Blind Bartimaeus went to where Jesus was—and he got his miracle. Where you are matters. It controls the flow of favor in your life.

**NEVER FORGET, "ONE DAY OF FAVOR WILL DO MORE THAN A THOUSAND DAYS OF HARD LABOR."**

# God's Economy

**I will accept nothing belonging to you, not even a thread …
so that you will never be able to say,
"I made Abram rich." (Genesis 14:23, NIV)**

Tithing is not about money, it is about obedience. Will you obey His Word, and will you trust Him to take care of you? (See Malachi 3:10; Proverbs 3:9.) The first man in the Bible to tithe was Abraham. When the King of Sodom tried to give him riches for helping him in battle, Abraham replied, "I will accept nothing belonging to you, so that you will never be able to say, 'I made Abraham rich'" (Genesis 14:22-23). Instead, Abraham tithed and trusted God with his future. My friend John Tonelli says, "Abraham hooked up to God's economy!"

God may use other people to bless you and meet your needs, but He will always be your source! The Bible says, "The just shall live by faith" (Romans 1:17)—not by their bank account, or the stock market, or their real estate holdings, or their government pension. God is your source! James says, "Every good and perfect gift is from above, coming down from the Father" (James 1:17, NIV). God told His people, "Carefully follow the terms of this covenant, so that you may prosper in everything you do" (Deuteronomy 29:9, NIV). Paul says, "God gives us richly all things to be enjoyed" (2 Timothy 6:17). Solomon says, "Every man to whom God hath given riches and wealth, and hath given him power to eat thereof, and to take his portion, and to rejoice in his labor; this is the gift of God" (Ecclesiastes 5:19).

—⚬⚬⚬—

CHILD OF GOD, YOUR FATHER WANTS ONLY
THE BEST FOR YOU!

# Two Natures

**Why am I thus?**
**(Genesis 25:22)**

Has your "flesh" been acting up lately? If so, welcome to the Kingdom of God! We all deal with it. Walking in the Spirit is a choice you'll have to make every day, and some days will be harder than others! We see an illustration of this at the birth of Jacob and Esau. Listen: "And Rebecca his wife conceived. And the children struggled together within her, and she said, 'Why am I thus?'"

Have you been asking that? If so, read on: "And the Lord said unto her, 'Two nations are in thy womb ... and the one ... shall be stronger than the other'" (Genesis 25:22-23). The battleground will always be between the flesh and the Spirit. What you feed will grow; what you neglect will die—it's that simple! Take another look at your greatest areas of defeat, and nine times out of ten you'll find an unopened Bible and an empty prayer closet.

Even Paul said, "My new life tells me to do it right—but the old sin nature ... still loves to sin. Oh, what a terrible predicament I am in! Who will free me from my slavery to this deadly lower nature? Thank God! It has been done by Jesus Christ our Lord. He has set me free!" (Romans 8:23-25, TLB). There it is in black and white—the secret of victory: Jesus Christ!

—m—

SPEND TIME WITH HIM! DRAW CLOSER TO HIM!
FEED ON HIS WORD, AND "WHATSOEVER HE
SAITH UNTO YOU, DO IT!" (JOHN 2:5).

# Get Into the Word

**Study to show thyself approved unto God, a workman that needeth not to be ashamed, rightly dividing the word of truth. (2 Timothy 2:15)**

Don't "surf the net" of God's Word, study it! Always come to it like you are coming to it for the first time. Meditate on it! Memorize it! Discuss it! Ask yourself, "What is God saying to me in this?" If there is a promise, what are the conditions? Have I obeyed them? Do the words I speak agree with what God has said? Don't read words of life and then speak words of death. Remember, faith cometh by "hearing," not "having heard," or you'd have to hear it only once. (See Romans 10:17.) If there's no faith present, it is usually because there's no Word proclaimed. Many of us cannot believe that God will heal us or meet our needs, because we have not heard enough of the Word!

Jesus said, "Take heed what you hear" (Mark 4:24). No matter how good they may be, the people in your life can't give you faith if they don't have any of their own. In Ephesians 6, Paul says, "Take the sword of the Spirit, which is the Word of God." If you're going to win this battle, you'd better know your weapon, its range, its penetrating power, and how to use and maintain it. The devil came at Jesus three different ways, and each time He answered, "It is written." He had the Word in His Spirit! When you're sick, you can't say, "He took my sickness and bore my infirmities" (Matthew 8:17) if you don't have it in your spirit!

—✺—

**SO TODAY GET INTO THE WORD, AND GET THE WORD INTO YOU!**

## Invest It!

**Live—making the most of every opportunity.**
**(Ephesians 5:16, NIV)**

Here are some keys to help you make your time count. Try to plan your day, for if you don't, somebody else will! Make each hour productive by deciding what's really important in your life. Look again at the life of Jesus; there's not one wasted hour in it! Schedule time for learning and growing in God's Word, for the level of your faith will be determined by the time you spend there. Schedule time for fellowshipping with the Lord, and be aware that the devil will do everything in his power to keep you from it.

Schedule time for exercise and good health. God gave you a body—maintain it properly! Schedule a time for your family; don't sacrifice them on the altar of your ambition. There are some opportunities you won't get a second time, so sow lots of love on this end, and you will reap it on the other. Schedule some time for restoration and relaxation; take a nap, a walk in the park, or watch a video. Don't be a workaholic—even God took one day a week off. Unclutter your life; eliminate the things that God didn't tell you to do.

—∞—

WHEN YOU LEARN TO HAVE ONE GOOD DAY, PRACTICE
UNTIL YOU ARE ABLE TO HAVE ONE GOOD WEEK, AND
BEFORE YOU KNOW IT YOU'LL HAVE ONE GOOD LIFE!

# Lies and False Impressions

**And there shall in no wise enter into it anything that ...
maketh a lie ... (Revelation 21:27)**

When you create an impression you know is not true, the Bible calls it "making a lie." That's a tough verdict, expecially if all you had in mind was making an extra dollar, or sparing somebody's feelings. No human being would have set such a standard, but God did. Is He serious? Check out Ananias and Sapphira. When they tried to create false impressions about their giving, God slew them—right in the middle of a church service. Then we read, "No one else dared join them ..." (Acts 5:13 NIV). Would you have? Peter said, "... thou hast not lied unto men, but unto God ..."(Acts 5:4). Now that puts a whole new slant on things—wouldn't you say?

The other day I heard about a guy who went fishing and caught nothing, so he stopped by a market on his way home and bought three big fish. Then he said to the shop assistant, "Throw them to me, then when I get home I'll be able to tell my wife I caught them." I smiled as I recalled how often I've rewritten the rules of golf, inflated the numbers in my audience, and done other things I won't mention. The worst lies are the ones we tell ourselves and end up believing. You see, a liar's biggest problem is that he can't believe anybody else, for as you live your life, you judge your neighbor. Today I read again that, "The Lord detests lying lips, but He delights in men who are truthful" (Proverbs 12:22, NIV).

**I THINK GOD'S TRYING TO SAY SOMETHING TO ME.
HOW ABOUT YOU?**

*Failing*

**Even though on the outside it often looks like things are
falling apart ... on the inside ... not a day goes by without his
unfolding grace. (2 Corinthians 4:9, TM)**

Successful Christian people recognize that defeats can lead
to even greater victories! Trying is more important than not
failing! When I make mistakes I ask, "What did I do wrong, and
how can I do it better next time?" Failure affects some of us so
negatively that it stops us permanently. Don't let that happen to
you! Edison tried thousands of experiments before he was able to
produce an acceptable light bulb. Look at your failure as a fresh
opportunity—not a final defeat. When Paul was shipwrecked, he
used it to preach the Gospel. When he was thrown into prison,
he wrote books that are still being read 2,000 years later. He said
to those who were so concerned about him, "Now I want you to
know, brothers, that what has happened to me has really served
to advance the Gospel" (Philippians 1:12, NIV).

Failing to try is the greatest failure anyone can experience, for if
you don't make the attempt, you've failed already! This can be seen
in the life of baseball player Ty Cobb. In 1915, he set the record for
stolen bases in a season—96 steals. Seven years later, Max Carey set
the second-best record with 51 stolen bases. What is remarkable
is that while Carey failed only twice in 53 attempts. Cobb failed
38 times in his 134 attempts. If Carey had tried more times, he
may have set a record that would still be unbeaten today!

ATTEMPT GREAT THINGS WITHOUT WORRYING ABOUT
THE POSSIBILITY OF FAILURE. IF YOU PERSEVERE,
WITH GOD'S HELP YOU'LL SUCCEED.

# On the Way to Carmel

**Now bring all the people ... to Mount Carmel.
(I Kings 18:19, TLB)**

Elijah's destiny was to stand on Mount Carmel and call down fire out of heaven. But he could only get there progressively—for that's how God works. First, God sent him to a brook at Cherith, which means "covenants." At some point in your spiritual journey, you've got to learn that your God is a covenant-making, covenant-keeping God. To do it, He'll dry up rivers, make axe heads swim, and order fish into a net, but He'll keep His promise to you, come what may. Note, God told Elijah, "... I have commanded the ravens to feed thee there" (ll Kings 17:4). Had he gone anywhere else, God wouldn't have met his need, for a covenant is two-sided. You must fulfill your part! Take a moment and ask yourself honestly, "Have I? Am I where God wants me to be?"

Next God sent Elijah to Azrephath saying, "... I have commanded a widow woman there to sustain thee" (1 Kings 17:9). God uses ravens and widows and whatever He likes—so stop trying to second-guess Him. One day, Sarah Utterbach said to me, "Bob, since your steps are already ordered of the Lord, why are you trying to figure it out?" (See Psalm 37:23.) Good question! Zarepath means "the meltjng pot." It's where metal was refined. If you're "going through the fire" today, rejoice. God's just separating the gold from the impurities in your character.

**HANG IN THERE! WHEN YOU'VE PASSED THE TESTS AT CHERITH AND ZARLPHATH, THEN YOU'LL BE READY TO GO TO MOUNT CARMEL.**

336

# Knowing What You Believe

**But speak thou the things which become sound.
(Titus 2:1)**

You may not think doctrine is important, but it is. Pilots fly by the laws of aerodynamics, and surgeons operate by the doctrines of medical science. Aren't you glad they think doctrine is important?

Let me illustrate what I mean. A psychology student in the army was given kitchen duty, so he decided to test the response of the different groups of soldiers to apricots. First he took the negative approach: "You don't want apricots, do you?" Ninety percent of then said, "No!" Then he tried the positive approach: "You do want apricots, don't you?" Over half said, "Yes." With the third group he tried the either/or technique: "Would you like one dish of apricots or two?" In spite of the fact that most of them didn't like apricots, 40% took two dishes, and 50% took one. The point is, if you have no doctrine of your own, you are at the mercy of everybody else's.

Now listen to Paul's challenge to Timothy—and you: "Preach the Word; be prepared in season and out of season; correct, rebuke, and encourage with great patience and careful instruction. For the time will come when men will not put up with sound doctrine…" (2 Timothy 4:2-3, NIV). When your feelings won't sustain you, your beliefs will, for one is built on emotion, and the other is founded on the eternal Word of God.

—⚍—

**GET INTO THE BOOK.**

# Learning From Pain

**Before I was afflicted I went astray:
but now have I kept thy word.
(Psalms 119:67)**

Never think that God will ignore small acts of disobedience. Discipline always comes! Achan kept only a tiny portion of the treasures of Jericho, but everybody paid the price. (See Joshua 7:1.) The Israelites lost their confidence with God, and they lost their respect in the eyes of the world. One person's disobedience can create pain and judgment for so many. One person out of the will of God can cause many problems for everybody else around them. When you get the wrong people out of your life, the wrong things will stop happening!

If you are walking in contradiction to God's laws, expect painful experiences on the road ahead. Pain is corrective! Your affliction can turn out for your good if you are willing to learn from it.

Pain forces you to look to God for answers. Pain also forces you to lean on Him instead of other people. Pain forces you to learn where you went astray. Pain forces you to long for His presence and His healing touch. And pain forces you to listen for God's instructions and to be sensitive to the changes He wants to bring in your life.

TURN YOUR PAIN INTO PROFIT; LET GOD TAKE YOUR
LOSSES AND TURN THEM INTO LESSONS THAT WILL MAKE
YOU BETTER AND STRONGER IN THE DAYS AHEAD.

# Your New Body

**How will the dead be raised?**
**What kind of bodies will they have?**
**(1 Corinthians 15:35, NLT)**

There's a bulletin board in the Mayo Clinic which reads, "Cancer is limited; it cannot cripple love. It cannot shatter hope. It cannot corrode faith. It cannot eat away peace. It cannot destroy confidence. It cannot kill friendship. It cannot shut out memories. It cannot silence courage. It cannot invade the soul. It cannot reduce eternal life. It cannot quench the spirit, and it cannot lessen the power of the resurrection."

The Bible gives us three answers to the question "… what kind of bodies will they have?" (1 Corinthians 15:35). First it speaks of anatomy: "There are different kinds of flesh—whether of humans, animals, birds, or fish" (1 Corinthians 15:39). Just as fish are designed to handle the pressures of the deep, and birds are designed to fly, your new resurrection body will have "no limitations." (Imagine travelling at the speed of thought!) Next, it speaks of astronomy: "For one star differeth from another star in glory, so also is the resurrection of the dead" (1 Colnthian 15:41-42). There will be degrees of honor and differences of reward when we all get home. Your service now is what determines your status. (See Romans 2:6.) Finally, it speaks of agriculture: "… it is sown in weakness; it is raised in power" (1 Corinthians 15:43). The sexton's word for "cemetery" means "God's acre." How wonderfull! Christians don't get buried; they get planted.

**GO AHEAD, LIVE TODAY AND EVERY DAY IN THE LIGHT OF THAT MOMENT.**

# Been With Jesus

**When they saw ... that they were unschooled, ordinary men, they were astonished, and they took note that these men had been with Jesus. (Acts 4:13, NKJV)**

To these New Testament Christians it wasn't a language, it was their lifestyle! They were ordinary, and they were unschooled, but they all had their B.W.J.—*Been With Jesus!* They acted like Him, they talked like Him, and they did the works He did. (See John 14:12.) Daniel said, "The people who know their God shall be strong, and carry out great exploits." What does it mean to know God? It means to know His Word and what He has to say on the subject. It means to know His character, because that never changes. It means to know your authority as a believer, because you are living in fellowship with the One who gave it to you.

Jesus said, "I have given you authority ... to overcome all the power of the enemy; nothing will harm you" (Luke 10:19, NIV). Paul said we should reign in life through Jesus Christ. (See Romans 5:17.) These disciples were not waiting to reign, they were demonstrating the Kingdom everywhere they went. A man who had been paralyzed for 38 years was dancing in the Temple. 5,000 men had been won to Christ in a single day. The religious authorities feared them, the people loved them, and everywhere they went they brought the presence of God. What was their secret? B.W.J! They'd *Been With Jesus!*

—m—

**TODAY, MAKE THAT THE PRAYER AND THE PASSION OF YOUR LIFE.**

# It's Time

**It is time to seek the LORD.**
**(Hosea 10:12)**

For Muslims the call to prayer goes out five times a day—the first call comes at dawn. Try calling a dawn prayer meeting in your church, and see what happens. The prophet said, "It is time to seek the Lord."

If you're spending hours in front of your TV, but you don't have a few minutes to spend with God, it's time to seek the Lord. If you're living comfortably with habits that once troubled you—it's time to seek the Lord! If you're still speaking words of bitterness toward someone who has hurt you—it's time to seek the Lord! If having money and things consumes so much of your time that there's none left for God and your family—it's time to seek the Lord!

The New Testament Church grew so fast that the apostles found themselves with no time to pray; but they did something about it. They said, "This is not right" (Acts 6:2). That's where we all have to start. If you've forsaken the place of prayer then something is not right; it will show up sooner or later. Listen to what they decided: "We will give ourselves continually to prayer" (Acts 6:4). Look what happened: "The Word of God increased, and the number of the disciples multiplied."

THINK; IF YOU'VE GOTTEN THIS FAR WITHOUT PRAYER,
HOW MUCH MORE YOU'LL ACCOMPLISH WHEN YOU PRAY!

*Jehovah-Jireh*

**You open your hand and satisfy the desires of every living thing. The LORD is righteous in all his ways and loving toward all he has made. (Psalms 145:16-17)**

When God introduced himself to Abraham, He went by the name of *El Shaddai*, which means "the Provider of all." God is saying, "I'll be everything you need!" Now we all agree that He is *able*, but so few of us dare to confess that He is *willing*! Just a revelation of God's ability alone is not sufficient to secure His blessings; you must also know that He *will* in order to build a solid foundation.

One day, a leper said to Jesus, "If You will, You can make me clean." Jesus said to him, "I will" (Mark 1:40-42). The leper knew Jesus *could*; he just wasn't sure that He *would*. But Jesus revealed His heart by saying, "I will."

When God's compassion becomes a revelation to you, your faith will be released. Don't allow Satan to convince you that God may or may not meet your need. Paul says, "My God shall supply all your need" (Philippians 4:19). The Bible does not say, "God is power," it says, "God is love." The Word magnifies God's willingness to use His power, rather than the power itself. Because He is love, He will use His power to meet and fulfill your needs. Micah says, "He delighteth in mercy" (Micah 7:18). God actually gets great pleasure out of meeting your needs and being compassionate toward you.

COME TO HIM TODAY WITH COMPLETE ASSURANCE.

# Fishing for Souls

**I will make you fishers of men.
(Matthew 4:19)**

If you want to catch fish, you've got to go where they are, for they're not going to come and jump into your boat. One pastor I know sent his church members downtown to the bars and ,the nightclubs and told them to say, "We've come to apologize. Two thousand years ago Jesus told us to go into all the world and preach the Gospel (see Matthew 28:19), but instead we've been waiting for you to come to us." Someone said to me, "The problem is, the government has taken prayer out of schools." I replied, "That's no problem, they haven't taken you out, and if you're there, prayer is there, hope is there, and God is there!" Wherever you are, turn on the light!

Any smart fisherman will tell you if your bait isn't working—change it. For God's sake, and the world's sake, be honest enough to say, "What we're doing is not working." When I pastored, I learned how to build my Sunday School from a Baptist, how to win souls from a Presbyterian, and how to develop home groups from a Pentecostal. If you don't know, ask somebody who does. Don't just sit there and say, "We're the chosen few" Jesus said, "… compel them to come in that my house may be filled" (Luke 14:23). It's time you went fishing! Remember, the net will drag in everything, so be patient. You can't clean a fish until you first catch it. Some people will require "intensive care"—give it to them.

**YOU MAY BE THE ONLY CHRISTIAN THEY'LL EVER MEET,
SO DON'T LET THEM DOWN.**

# Bond Servants

**Paul, a (bondservant) of Christ Jesus, called as an Apostle.
(Romans 1:1, NAS)**

Paul knew what he was called to be. Do you know what your calling is? When he called himself a "bondservant," he was referring to one who served his master faithfully for six years. But in the seventh year the Law said he had to be set free. But if, when he was released, he turned back and said, "Master, I'm not serving you because I have to; I'm serving you because I want to," then the master took him before a judge and pierced his ear, signifying that he belonged to him forever (Exodus 21:6). Sometimes we just need to look up and say, "Lord, I'm not serving You because I have to; I'm serving You because I love You. Pierce my ear, Lord. Mark me as Yours. Bond me together with You so I can never belong to another." When ministry loses its passion, it becomes an empty profession.

The very word "minister" is a verb, not a noun—it's what you do, not what you claim to be. The word "servant" also referred to a third-level galley slave chained to the oar of a Roman ship. Day and night he rowed to the beat of another, and whether he was in battle or in merchant service, he expected to die chained to that oar, What a picture! Listen: "And so, dear brothers and sisters, I plead with you to give your bodies to God, Let them be a living and holy sacrifice—the kind he will accept."

**WHEN YOU THINK OF WHAT HE HAS DONE FOR YOU,
IS IT TOO MUCH TO ASK?**

# Worry Coupons

**So do not worry, saying, "What shall we eat?" or "What shall we drink?" or "What shall we wear?" For the pagans run after all these things. (Matthew 6:31-32, NIV)**

The other day I was really stressed out over something when I heard a minister say, "Worry is a lack of trust in God." Then I started worrying over the fact that I was worrying! Someone else said, "Just don't worry about it." Sounds simple enough, but I come from a line of descendants who speak faith but show fear. Maybe you've met them!

Then a friend came up with this novel idea: "Why don't you try this 'worry coupon?' It entitles you to worry as much as you like, but only if: a) it will feed and clothe you; b) it will add to your life instead of taking from it; c) it will make tomorrow better; and d) you don't mind acting like the pagans do." *Point taken.*

Then he said, "If that doesn't work, make a list of all the things that you're worried about, put it in a box, and then put it up on a shelf somewhere. If God is either *unable* or *unwilling* to take care of you, you can always go get the box back and start worrying again—but at least give Him a chance to work on your behalf! While you're waiting, pray, stand on the Word, and don't give your worries a voice."

YOUR WORDS HAVE THE POWER OF LIFE AND DEATH,
SO SPEAK LIFE!

**Go! I am sending you out like lambs among wolves.
Do not take a purse or bag or sandals; and do not greet
anyone on the road. (Luke 10:3-4, NIV)**

Dr. James McConnell points out that what Jesus said to His disciples was, "Carry no purse"—no hoarding! "No bag"—no involvements! "Greet no man"—no wasting time!

*No hoarding!* God will bless the man or woman who'll say, "Every penny you give me above my needs, I'll use to tell the story to those who've never heard." Imagine standing at the Judgment Seat of Christ with a pile of money invested, while multitudes starve and the world is unreached with the Gospel! What could you possibly say? (See 2 Corinthians 5:10.)

*No excess baggage.* "Let us strip off everything that slows us down … and let us run" (Hebrews 12:1, TLB). Whatever can get your attention can influence you; whatever can keep your attention can master you! Satan dreads the completion of your assignment. Fight to keep your focus!

*Don't waste time!* Question any relationship that doesn't contribute to your destiny! Paul said, "And if any man obey not our word by this epistle, note that man and have no company with him, that he may be ashamed" (2 Thessalonians 3:14). The hour is too late, and the assignment is too urgent! When I lived in Maine, they closed down the schools for a three-week period, and everybody would go into the potato fields to gather the harvest. To wait is to be too late!

---

IT'S THE SAME IN YOUR LIFE, TOO!

## Take Responsibility

**So then, each of us will give an account of himself
to God. (Romans 14:12, NIV)**

If God's will is ever accomplished in your life, it will be because you decided to pay the price! Stop blaming others for your circumstances and your decisions! All of us have had people in our lives we thought would be a blessing, but they became a burden. Reversals and roadblocks are all part of the journey. Change usually takes place only when the pain is so great that you can't stand it another minute. Your present can only continue with your permission.

Paul said, "I have fought a good fight, I have finished my course, I have kept the faith" (2 Timothy 4:7). You've got to fight; you've got to finish; you've got to keep the faith! Have you learned the lessons of your present circumstances? Look at your schedule. What does it say about priorities, your values, your future? Your future is a reward, not a guarantee!

Have you spent time seeking God? If not, how could you possibly make the right decisions? Have you done what He has already told you to? You'll have no peace until you do. Are you willing to do what it takes in terms of patience and preparation? There are no overnight successes in the Bible.

—❦—

**IF YOU ARE GOING TO MAKE A DIFFERENCE,
YOU'VE GOT TO BE WILLING TO WAIT AND WORK AT IT!**

*Grace*

**And if by grace, then is it no more of works:
otherwise grace is no more grace. (Romans 11:6)**

Dr. Gerald Mann tells the story of how he got his doctorate in Greek. There were only six students in his class. The professor had never given anyone an "A." On the first day, he held up a Greek textbook and to their amazement he announced, "I have already written your grades, and no matter how much you study or what you score—I have given every one of you an 'A!'" Dr. Mann said, "Out of six students, five of us learned more Greek in that class than we ever thought possible. The other fellow just got by and never really applied himself." Here's the point: Grace is the power to excel or the license to just get by, but either way you're accepted!

Why would God do things in such a way? Because He's a Father! The love He gives us is unconditional, and only our unconditional love can satisfy Him. Amazing! Our God makes himself vulnerable to the rejection of His children. Maybe you are wondering, "How can I know if I truly love Him?" That's easy: You'll love your brother and sister (see 1 John 4:21); you'll keep His commandments—all of them (see John 15:10); you'll spend time with Him. David said, "My soul longs for thee" (Psalms 42:2).

WHY DON'T YOU TAKE TIME TODAY AND JUST
TELL HIM HOW MUCH YOU LOVE HIM?

# God's Presence

**They shall mount up with wings like eagles; They shall run and not be weary; They shall walk and not faint.**
**(Isaiah 40:31, NKJV)**

Have you been exhausted lately? Have problems made you feel like quitting and walking away? Before you do, try one more thing—get into God's presence. As you stay there, you'll discover that He can cause you to "mount up with wings" as eagles. It's called "miraculous intervention" and God did it over and over again for His children in the Bible. He can lift you above it, too! (See Psalms 91:15.)

Or, He can cause you to "run and not to be weary." When you're emotionally drained and you've nothing left to give, listen: "He gives power to the tired and worn out, and strength to the weak" (Isaiah 40:29, TLB). He wants to put you back in the race! He wants to give you a new direction! Listen: "He will be ... a source of strength to those who turn back the battle at the gate" (Isaiah 28:6, NIV).

Or, He can help you to "walk and not faint." When you can't see any way out, just put one foot in front of the other and start walking. As long as you're in motion, you're a winner.

WITH GOD, WINNING IS BEGINNING—WHICHEVER WAY
HE DOES IT, HE'S PROMISED TO BRING YOU THROUGH!

**First the blade then the ear, after that the full corn in the ear.**
**(Mark 4:28)**

If you're having a problem with impatience, listen: "And he said, so is the Kingdom of God, as if a man should cast seed into the ground; and should sleep, and rise night and day, and the seed should spring and grow up, he knoweth not how. For the earth bringeth forth fruit of herself; first the blade, then the ear, after that the full corn in the ear ... immediatly he putteth in the sickle because the harvest is come" (Mark 4:26-29).

Before you receive what God's promised you, you'll often go through certain stages—this is called "The Law of Progression." First, there's the "I don't know" season. Your seed is in the ground, and you're "in the dark." How and when your harvest will come is entirely up to God. All you know is that it will! Next comes "the blade" season. It's only a tiny blade blowing in the breeze, but it's enough to encourage you and let you know the answer is on the way. Next comes "the ear"season. Now it's starting to look like what you prayed for. So you begin to water it with prayer, fertilize it with the Word, and protect it from those who would try to uproot it. Finally you enter "the full corn" season. That's when you hear the words,"... put in the sickle because the harvest is come." Note, you've got to recognize it and reach for it!

**WHATEVER SEASON YOU'RE IN TODAY, STAND FAST AND KEEP TRUSTING, FOR YOUR HARVEST IS ON THE WAY!**

# Dealing with Prejudice

**He must needs go through Samaria.**
**(John 4:4)**

Jesus had to go through Samaria—and so must we! Listen to what the woman at the well told Him: "The Jews have no dealings with the Samaritans" (John 4:9). This may be touchy, but the God who sees our hearts won't put up with racism—He's color blind! One of the worst offenders was Peter, but God dealt with him in a vision and then sent him to preach the first sermon ever heard by Gentiles. Listen to what Peter told those Italians, "It is against the Jewish laws for me to come into a Gentile home like this. But God has shown me . . . that I should never think of anyone as inferior" (Acts 10:28, TLB). Paul said, "Jews and Gentiles are the same" (Romans 10:12).

I was raised in a divided Belfast and grew up among "my own kind." We went to school together, played together, and believed we should avoid "the other kind"—for God wanted it that way! Christians in America are amazed when I tell them about it; but you should see their reaction when I ask why black children had to ride in the back of the bus? We've all got to go through Samaria, because we're all going to live together in an "undivided city," with a "a great multitude ... from every nation, tribe, people and language, standing before the throne" (Revelation 7:9).

—◊◊◊—

**TODAY TAKE A LOOK INTO YOUR HEART.**

351

# Discipline

**Run in such a way as to get the prize.**
**1 Corinthians 9:24, NIV**

John Wesley was ordained at 24, preached for the next 64 years, and died at 88. He preached 42,000 sermons and rode over 250,000 miles, mostly on horseback. He attributed his good health to rising at 4 a.m. and preaching at 5 a.m. every day for 60 years. Now that's discipline!

Here's what you can learn from his life. First, you have to start! That might seem obvious, but so many of us are still stuck in the starting blocks waiting for someone or something to get us going. Next, you've got to give it all you've got! Divers in the Olympics have more than one try before the judges, but the winners don't save all their effort for the final dive. Instead, they concentrate on nailing every single one, thus increasing their chances for a gold medal. Don't settle for mediocrity at any stage in your journey!

And don't quit! In the 1992 Olympics, Derrick Redmond of Britain was competing in the 400-meter race when he suffered a torn hamstring and fell. As the other runners breezed past him, he began to struggle to his feet and his father, whose face was covered with tears, ran down from the stands to help him up. Slowly, agonizingly, they made their way around the rest of the track and crossed the finish line, as the stadium in Seoul burst into thunderous applause. Derrick didn't win a medal, but he won something more important—he won the respect of the world!

---

**RUN TO WIN!**

# Resentment List

**You must make allowance for each others faults and
forgive the person who offends you ...
(Colossians 3:13, NLT)**

There I was the other morning, alone in my kitchen making coffee—talking to myself. I was telling somebody off, and it wasn't the first time either. Such rage and resentment—I wanted to kill them! Ashamed, I thought, "I'm not supposed to have these thoughts; I'm a man of God; I write a daily devotional, telling others how to live." Immediately I prayed, "Father, I choose to forgive them, and I ask you to forgive me." I can't remember how many times I've prayed that particular prayer, but it's been a lot—at least "seventy times seven" (Matthew 18:22).

Some of the people on my resentment list don't stay there for long; after one or two good prayers, they're gone. But some keep showing up regularly. (How about you?) Then I heard God whisper to me, "If it's in your heart, you've got to deal with it" (Psalms 66:18). Now if anyone else had told me I was harboring resentment, I'd have argued them into a corner. But there I was, talking to somebody who wasn't even listening because they'd moved on, and my thoughts weren't fit to print. So I added another line to my prayer: "And, Father, whatever I ask for myself in blessing, I ask for them, too; and make it a double portion." Suddenly I had a sense of peace, and I started feeling like I'd taken back some ground.

**DO YOU NEED TO DEAL WITH RESENTMENT TODAY?**

**And Joseph dreamed a dream, and he told it his brethren:
and they hated him ...
(Genesis 37:5)**

To fulfill your dream you're going to have to make some trade-offs. You'll trade off popularity for excellence and short-term pleasure for long-term fulfillment. Accepting the security men offer in exchange for the significance that doing God's will brings is a lousy deal!

Learn from Joseph! He discovered that it's a mistake to share your dream with false brethren, for it only reminds them of the dream they never had or the one they've abandoned. When somebody tries to talk you out of your dream, they're usually just trying to talk themselves back into their own comfort zone. To do it, they'll give you any rational lie they ever gave themselves. Don't buy it! Love them, help them if you can, but don't be influenced by those who have "given up."

Dreamers are survivors. It was Joseph's dream that caused him to overcome temptation, betrayal, imprisonment, and a lot of things that cause us to quit. Remember, God's purpose alone should be the stuff of which your dreams are made. To discover your dream—get to know yourself, your strengths, and your weaknesses. Look at your opportunities. Examine where God has put you, then seek His counsel.

**IF YOU DO, HE'LL GIVE YOU A DREAM FOR YOUR LIFE.**

354

# Bless Your Children

**Joseph said unto his father, they are my sons ... and he said,
bring them ... and I will bless them.
(Genesis 48:9)**

My grandson Alexis at the "testing" stage. First he'll give me a big grin, then he'll try something he knows he's not supposed to do. He's pushing the limits today and practicing for the future when the issues will be much bigger. (Welcome to the terrible twos!) Seriously, a child who understands how far he can go is relieved of a great burden. When he knows your authority will stand, it gives him security. Also, if he learns today that "no" really means "no," then he'll be able to say it one day to his peer group—and to his impulses.

Parents in the Old Testament laid their hands on each generation because they believed that blessings were transferable. If nobody did that in your life, then start a new tradition. For with God's blessing comes health, peace, long life, and prosperity (see Deutoronomy 28). That's why the enemy has attacked you so often. He's trying to break the link through which the blessings flow. Don't let him!

The other day, I held Alex in my arms and prayed, "God, if you ever made a man, make me one now. May he grow up to think that Abraham Lincoln was a horse thief and George Washington was one of the Jessie James boys by comparison to his grandfather. Let my life, my example, and my prayers mold him into a man you can use, and, Lord, take me out of this world 24 hours before I ever say or do anything that would cause him to stumble. Amen.

**MAYBE THAT'S A PRAYER YOU'D LIKE TO PRAY TOO.**

# Don't Be a Phony!

**And the Lord called unto Adam ... "Where art thou?"
(Genesis 3:9)**

The most important question you can ask yourself today is, "Where am I—really?" You could be in trouble if you don't know the answer, or if you do, but you just don't deal with it. When God asked Adam, "Where art thou?" he replied, "... I heard ... I was afraid ... I was naked ... I hid ..." (Genesis 3:10). It's amazing the lengths we'll go to in order to hide. We'll bury ourselves in work, or get involved in an affair, or put up a brick wall around our hearts—anything but face the truth. God wasn't trying to find Adam, for He already knew where Adam was—He just wanted Adam to find himself. Until you do that, you're truly lost!

The problem is when you hide, you become a phony. Have you any idea how much emotional energy it requires to keep up a charade for others? Only two things are worse: being a phony with yourself, and being a phony with God. Furthermore, you'll find it difficult to "open up" to others, give them a hug, pay them a compliment, or look them in the eye, because you'll be afraid they'll look inside your heart and see the real you.

Is that where you are today? Afraid to look into your own heart? The good news is Adam was naked, but God clothed him; he was terrified, but God gave him peace.

—m—

IF YOU'LL COME TO HIM TODAY. HE'LL CLEANSE YOU,
CLOTHE YOU, AND CHANGE YOU!
HE'S JUST WAITING FOR A CHANCE TO DO IT.

**But let patience have her perfect work, that ye may be perfect and entire, wanting nothing. (James 1:4)**

Are you trying to get out of something that God is trying to bring you through? Have you been asking God why the waiting period is so long? If so, here are three reasons:

*Waiting brings results!* "It is good that a man should both hope and quietly wait for the salvation of the Lord" (Lamentations 3:25-26). Waiting time is learning time, and as long as you're learning, you're not losing. God will spend time training you for the battle, because He's a good general. "Blessed be the LORD my strength, which teacheth my hands to war, and my fingers to fight" (Psalms 144:1).

*Waiting will reveal those around you.* Motives are not easily discerned. Trust God, but test people! That's scriptural. "The LORD your God led you … 40 years, to humble you and to test you, in order to know what was in your heart" (Deuteronomy 8:2, NIV). The wrong people can keep their mistakes and their motives covered for a long time, but waiting forces the truth to the surface.

*Waiting gives God time to address your problem miraculously.* He's a miracle God; so don't get ahead of Him and rob Him of an opportunity to prove His power in your life.

—∞—

**THE WORD FOR YOU TODAY IS "WAIT!"**

*Getting Back Up!*

**Rejoice not against me, O mine enemy:**
**when I fall, I shall arise.**
**(Micah 7:8)**

The most natural thing to do when you fall is to get up again. Someday, maybe even the next time you try, you'll walk without stumbling. But until then, refuse to stay down. You've got to get up on the inside before you can get up on the outside. When the pressure is on and the enemy says, "You're not going to make it," tell him, "I've got you right where I want you. I may be down, but I'm not out. My wounds will heal, my tears will dry, and I'll be back tomorrow, stronger than ever."

America's 26th president, Theodore Roosevelt, said, "It is not the critic who counts, nor the man who points out how the strong man stumbled, or where the doer of deeds could have done better. The credit belongs to the man who is actually in the arena, whose face is marred by dust and sweat and blood; who strives valiantly; who errs and comes up short again and again, because there is a no effort without error or shortcoming; who spends himself in a worthy cause; who at best knows in the end the high achievement of triumph, and who at worst, if he fails while daring greatly, knows his place shall never be with those timid souls who know neither victory nor defeat."

—m—

CHILD OF GOD, RISE UP AND SAY,
"THOUGH I FALL, I SHALL ARISE!"

# The Virgin Birth

**Behold, a virgin shall be with child ... and
they shall call his name Emmanuel ...
(Matthew 1:23)**

The first group ever to question the virgin birth of Jesus was religious leaders. How interesting! The Pharisees said, "We were not born of fornication" (John 8:41). That was meant to be cruel. After all. He couldn't point to Joseph and say, "He's my father," for His father filled the universe. Jesus had to be God in order to save us, and He had to be man in order to die for us!

You were the child of an earthly father, hence you have your father's DNA—you were born in sin. But not Jesus! He was the earthly son of a heavenly Father. He broke the cycle of sin before He was born. In the Bible, the sacrificial lamb had to be without blemish (a birth defect), or without spot (something picked up along the way). Since Jesus had neither inherited sin nor practiced sin—He alone qualifies as "... the Lamb of God which taketh away the sin of the world" (John 1:29).

I believe in the virgin birth because: a) The angel of the Lord announced it (Matthew 1:20); b) Mary's husband-to-be accepted it (Matthew 1:24); c) Elizabeth, her cousin, got it by divine revelation (Luke 1:4); and d) the story was written by a respected medical doctor who'd known the character of all concerned. He wrote, "... know the certainty of those things" (Luke 1:4). God first laid His gift in a manger—then He hung it on a tree.

---

GOD FIRST LAID HIS GIFT IN A MANGER—THEN HE HUNG IT ON A TREE. TODAY RECEIVE THAT GIFT BY FAITH, AND THIS WILL TRULY BE THE GREATEST CHRISTMAS YOU'VE EVER HAD.

# The Man in the Glass

**I have finished my course. (2 Timothy 4:7)**

When you get what you want in your struggle for self
    And the world makes you king for a day,
Just go to the mirror and look at yourself
    And see what that man has to say.
For it isn't your father or mother or wife
    Whose judgment upon you must pass,
The fellow whose verdict counts most in your life
    Is the one staring back from the glass.
He's the fellow to please; never mind all the rest,
    For he's with you clear to the end,
And you've passed your most dangerous, difficult test
    If the man in the glass is your friend.
You may fool the whole world down the pathway of years
    And get pats on the back as you pass,
But your final reward will be heartache and tears
    If you've cheated the man in the glass.

—ɯ—

NOW THERE'S SOMETHING TO THINK ABOUT!

## Hard Work

**Keep your spiritual fervor. (Romans 12:11, NIV)**

He worked by day and toiled by night,
He gave up play and warm sunlight.
Dry books he read, new things to learn,
    And forged ahead success to earn.
He plotted on with faith and pluck,
    And when he won, they called it luck.

Mary I. Smith said, "The only place you will find success before work is in the dictionary." Listen: "I consider my life worth nothing to me, if only I may finish the race and complete the task the Lord Jesus has given me" (Acts 20:24, NIV). The clock meant nothing to Paul, because he was on a mission. He was not affected by the weather, the circumstances, or the opinions of others; all that mattered to him was fulfilling his destiny. Child of God, are you looking for an example or looking for an excuse? The Bible is not a book of shortcuts. It's a workbook! Listen: "Work while it is day." "Ever abounding in the work of the Lord." "The people had a mind to work." "Keep your spiritual fervor."

After a concert, a fan rushed up to the famed violinist, Fritz Kreisler, and said, "I'd give my whole life to play as beautifully as you do." Kreisler replied, *"I did!"* That's the price of success, and it costs each of us exactly the same.

**"SERVE WHOLEHEARTEDLY, AS IF YOU WERE SERVING THE LORD, NOT MEN" (EPHESIANS 6:7, NIV).**

**Thou shalt love the Lord thy God with all thy heart.
(Luke 10:27)**

When Israel was threatened by Assyria, their king went to Elijah for help. Elijah told him to pick up the remaining arrows and begin striking them on the floor. But he only did it three times and stopped. Elijah was angry with him and said, "… you should have struck the floor five or six times, for then you would have beaten Syria until they were entirely destroyed; now you will be victorious only three times" (2 Kings 13:19, TLB). It's a sad story of partial victory, of what might have been if only Joash had put more into it. It's not just the opportunity—it's the spirit that meets the opportunity that determines the outcome.

God will give you chances to win, but it's your commitment that determines the size of your victory and, ultimately, the effectiveness of your life. Stop blaming others. God has put arrows into your hand—use them! The enemy is no problem to God. Have you any idea how often God has defeated him? No, the problem lies in you. You've got to activate your faith, focus your vision, release your compassion, and do something! If the fire in your heart has become a smoldering ash, get into God's presence quickly and stay there until He rekindles in you a divine intensity and a new love for Him.

—m—

**THAT'S THE WORD FOR YOU TODAY.**

# The $6 Haircut

**Continue to live in him, rooted and built up in him,
strengthened in the faith as you were taught.
(Colossians 2:6-7, NIV)**

Just because something sells books and tapes and draws a crowd doesn't mean God is in it.

It may just be good marketing, but you couldn't support it from the Word to save your life. Once I had to recall an entire series of "prophetic" teaching tapes because the Soviet Union had unraveled and the Berlin Wall had come down. I remember thinking, "There go some of my finest insights!" All of us have a tendency to think that our revelation is not only important, but that it is the final one that will usher in the coming of the Lord. Denominational graveyards are full of wonderful people who believed that.

A small-town barber was doing well until a big company moved in across the street. They blitzed the area with signs reading, "EVERYTHING FOR $6. Six-dollar Haircuts! Six-dollar Perms! Everything for $6!" The barber lost all his customers. In despair, he hired an advertising expert. "I'm finished," he declared. "I can't compete with them!" The expert picked up the phone and called the town's only billboard company and told them to put a big sign on the top of the barber's shop. "And what do you want us to put on the sign?" they asked. He replied, "In big, bold letters put the words, 'WE FIX $6 HAIRCUTS!'"

CHILD OF GOD, MAKE SURE THAT WHEN THE
"NEW WAVES" COME IN AND GO BACK OUT THAT YOU ARE
STILL ROOTED AND GROUNDED IN THE TRUTH.

# What's It All About Anyway?

**A man's life does not consist in the abundance of his possessions. (Luke 12:15, NIV)**

In the 1920s, some of the world's most successful men met in the Edgewater Hotel in Chicago. Present were the presidents of America's largest steel company, utility company, and gas company; also the presidents of the New York Stock Exchange and the Bank of International Settlements. Together these were the faces of power and success. The ones we all want to be like!

But twenty-five years later the story was so different. The president of the largest independent steel company, Charles Schwab, lived his last years on borrowed money and died bankrupt. The president of the largest gas company, Howard Hopson, went totally insane, and the president of the New York Stock Exchange, Richard Whitney, was released from Alcatraz to go home and die. Finally, the president of the Bank of International Settlements, Leon Fraser, committed suicide.

Every one of these men knew how to make a living—but not one of them knew how to live! Jesus told us, life is not built on things; it's built on relationships, and the first relationship you need is with God.

—m—

**DO YOU HAVE ONE TODAY?**

# Do You Have a Dream?

**I am focusing all my energies on this one thing.
(Philippians 3:13, NLT)**

Before you can set out on your life's journey, you need a road map. That's called your dream. For Moses, it was leading God's children to the promised land. For Florence Nightingale, it was bringing healing and hope to dying soldiers in Crimea. For Thomas Edison, it was illuminating the world. Anyone who's ever made a difference started with a dream, and eventually it became their life's obsession. Mine is to put God's Word into the hands of every person I can, during my lifetime!

You say, "How can I know my dream is of God?" Because it will always bless and benefit others. If your dream is to live in a castle and accumulate a fortune for yourself—don't count on God to go into business with you. And, furthermore, your dream is only worth what you're willing to pay for it. Inspiration without perspiration is only a daydream.

Forty percent of the people you meet have great ideas, but all they do is talk about them. Another forty percent work hard, and they'd be willing to give their all to a great dream, but they don't have one. The remaining twenty percept have a dream and the faith to make it come true. If you are part of that remarkable twenty percent, there are no guarantees that you'll succeed—but you've got a good chance—better than eighty percent of your friends.

—꽈—

**THAT'S THE WORD FOR YOU TODAY.**

# Index

## A

anger 78, 191, 200, 205, 219, 240, 319

angry 5, 52, 57, 274, 318, 336

anointing 19, 38, 74, 137, 142, 215, 220, 254, 308, 354

## B

battle 34, 94, 101, 134, 142, 176, 186, 221, 227, 242, 254, 273, 286, 315, 330, 332, 349, 357

## C

compassion 41, 43, 49, 84, 88, 135, 160, 263, 272, 342, 354

courage 47, 141, 205, 221, 223, 252, 266, 312, 359

## D

death 15, 41, 59, 64, 91, 142, 145, 175, 213, 242, 250, 259, 261, 288, 304, 322, 326, 332, 336, 337, 345

discipline 68, 75, 90, 270, 352

discourage 1, 33, 65, 97, 101, 122, 143, 150, 167, 198, 249, 266, 282

## E

encourage 23, 49, 102, 244, 268

encouragement 144, 251

# F

fail 19, 25, 76, 84, 89, 108, 109, 142, 143, 204, 209, 214, 221, 234, 252, 299, 336

failing 108, 133, 136, 186, 204, 220, 335

failure 6, 96, 113, 121, 133, 142, 143, 150, 151, 156, 166, 204, 206, 209, 269, 335

# G

giving 14, 39, 46, 61, 79, 84, 101, 110, 150, 155, 163, 164, 183, 189, 198, 229, 239, 248,

304, 318, 354, 356, 359

grace 5, 6, 30, 33, 34, 49, 51, 56, 87, 128, 163, 186, 190, 211, 214, 222, 249, 254, 255, 266, 271, 297, 301, 313, 314, 317, 319, 322, 327, 335, 348

guilt 21

# H

happiness 82, 125, 129, 236

hate 58, 107, 112, 157, 222

health 36, 95, 138, 159, 195, 240, 254, 293, 295, 333, 344, 352

heaven 4, 25, 44, 54, 73, 107, 131, 133, 233, 283, 287, 310 328, 337

# J

joy 13, 21, 24, 30, 31, 35, 37, 61, 76, 81, 167, 171, 178, 189, 215, 226,

240, 241, 261, 308, 309, 312, 313, 328

# K

kindness 61, 80, 84, 132, 223, 250, 251, 263, 314, 355

# L

love 10, 13, 46, 49, 50, 61, 69, 70, 75, 78, 79, 80, 81, 93, 95, 100, 102, 105, 107, 112, 114, 118, 123, 132, 136, 140, 148, 151, 154, 179, 188, 196, 200, 207, 212, 214, 215, 238, 240, 241, 244, 247, 248, 249, 250, 252, 258, 259, 261, 263, 271, 274, 284, 294, 299, 305, 311, 312, 326, 327, 333, 342, 343, 348, 355, 365

# M

mercy 51, 73, 92, 118, 177, 219, 244, 287, 290, 301, 326, 336, 342, 356

money 113, 120, 138, 163, 171, 175, 179, 200, 202, 217, 251, 272, 286, 296, 298, 314, 319, 330, 341, 346, 364

# P

pity 100, 263

prosper 2, 22, 28, 87, 120, 163, 166, 202, 229, 240, 251, 286, 306, 313, 319, 330, 353

# S

salvation 14, 95, 161, 189, 194, 214, 261, 309, 312, 322, 336, 357, 364

security 36, 89, 176, 265, 271

sorrow 32

strength 3, 6, 8, 32, 34, 37, 76, 77, 87, 97, 129, 134, 139, 142, 143, 156, 158, 172, 184, 186, 206, 230, 235 237, 249, 264, 280, 283, 292, 312, 315, 349, 357

strong 12, 14, 17, 22, 39, 43, 45, 64, 89, 95, 111, 117, 124, 134, 135, 140, 141, 159, 190, 198, 204, 221, 230, 244, 266, 268, 271, 273, 295, 312, 331, 338, 340, 358, 359

success 8, 11, 12, 13, 46, 47, 48, 54, 78, 82, 96, 98, 107, 120, 121, 140, 148, 150, 166, 176, 204, 217, 230, 284, 289, 291, 297, 306, 353, 361

# U

understanding 11, 188, 197, 216, 222, 237, 263

# W

wisdom 16, 38, 72, 78, 87, 107, 128, 149, 182, 191, 198, 22
2, 228, 246, 252, 268, 269, 283, 337

wise 4, 12, 17, 23, 107, 117, 124, 149, 159, 182, 185, 195,
248, 313

worry 53, 59, 68, 69, 89, 108, 232, 248, 282, 302, 345

worth 16, 17, 22, 23, 31, 35, 78, 80, 90, 100, 111, 127,
129,130, 133, 147, 153, 161, 169, 188, 189, 196, 198,
206, 207, 210, 220, 231, 237, 245, 247, 255, 264, 265,
269, 271, 306, 307, 321, 322, 358, 361

# Y

no entries

# Z

no entries